Now is the Time for All Good Men to Come to the Aid of Their Planet

Now is the Time for All Good Men to Come to the Aid of Their Planet

A Shaman Warrior's Perspective

J. THEO OLONIA

NOW IS THE TIME FOR ALL GOOD MEN TO COME TO THE AID OF THEIR PLANET
A SHAMAN WARRIOR'S PERSPECTIVE

iUniverse books may be ordered through booksellers or by contacting:

iUniverse
1663 Liberty Drive
Bloomington, IN 47403
www.iuniverse.com
1-800-Authors (1-800-288-4677)

ISBN: 978-1-4917-4930-2 (sc)
ISBN: 978-1-4917-4929-6 (e)

Library of Congress Control Number: 2014919624

Printed in the United States of America.

iUniverse rev. date: 11/13/2014

Contents

Preface

Ever since childhood, I have always felt a strong connection with my surroundings, particularly if I was in a natural setting. I feel fortunate that I was raised in a rural town in northern New Mexico. Taos was nestled in a high plateau valley, surrounded by the Rocky Mountains, and my father was an avid fly fisherman, so that during his breaks from work he would head for the mountain streams or to the Rio Grande, the Red River or some of the small lakes in the area. I would sometimes accompany him and my uncles: companions with a common interest. I would fish for a time, but I would soon be distracted by something shining in the water, the rocks, the trees, the contours of the land and the flow of the river. I always felt a thrill at the sculpting that nature could accomplish, using the tools of wind, sun, ice, and water erosion.

This connection and fascination also extended to the firmament, especially at night where there was little light pollution and on moonless nights, the cosmos was a dazzling sight. It was at this point {around age eight} that I developed an interest in astronomy. I read as many books on the subject as I could find. From that point on I was an amateur astronomer, and went right from a provincial view straight into a cosmic view. Later in life, when I was better able to afford more, I dove into reading a couple of hundred books on the subject, and eventually acquiring a telescope. Much of the material in chapter one I already knew, and some research was done to bring some of the material up to date, since new discoveries are constantly being made and theories modified.

My father, having worked first for the U. S. Forest Service and later for the New Mexico Fish and Game Department, as a heavy equipment operator, was always being sent on jobs that were mostly in the mountain areas of New Mexico. There were many summers that we would live at these various job sites and I would spend my time hiking and exploring the country side. All this exposure to pristine areas, where the human incursion was minimal, formed the basis for my appreciation of the beauty and uniqueness of the undeveloped land.

After marriage and the birth of our three sons, we still continued to camp, hike, fish and back pack in wilderness regions in our own state, and also to some of the wild places in the western United States during extended vacations, when it was so much less costly to travel.

This book reflects my experiences as an outdoor enthusiast. However, while submerged in enjoying the outdoors during the prime of my life, I never gave much thought to the direction that our ecology was taking, until the last thirty years. My awareness of what was taking place then had not come to the fore-front of my perceptions. Now when I visit some of the places that we used to camp and fish at, the land seems dull, drier, over used, and always overcrowded; a feeling I get on the highways, as well as the cities that we visit.

The need for expansion as the population of the earth grows, will only put more and more pressure on the land, water, air and the environment in general. This is the main reason that I feel that if we don't get a handle on population growth, we will eventually find ourselves in a collapse of civilization. The instinct for survival in humans is so strong that if no civilized means is available, there is the possibility that a large portion of humanity might revert to barbarism.

In the last thirty years, through the practices that I describe in the chapter, My Path, my awareness of everything that surrounds me has grown to the boiling point, and it felt like the only release for this pressure was to write this book and try to influence people to become more present, take off the blinders and realize where this ship is heading. Perhaps this time we can steer away from the iceberg in time to save this beautiful planet and as many life forms as possible; including our own.

Acknowledgments

I thank my wife, Juanita, for her support, enthusiasm, and her help in proof reading all the content of this book. Her contributions in having introduced our whole family and many clients to the healing procedure of Reiki and therapeutic massage, were very beneficial. For her belief in Angels; may they continue to watch over all of us.

I thank my three sons; Robert Raymond, Joseph Martin, and James Lee, for the long discourses that we have engaged in, over the course of this writing, which in turn helped solidify some of the material and ideas in the book. I continue to learn much from them; for they are the next generation, and consequently the next evolutionary step.

Introduction

In chapter one I begin with the scientific view of the creation of the universe from the *Big Bang*, through the expansion of time, space and matter that led to creation of galaxies, stars, and planets. I describe the formation and evolution of our own solar system.

I then proceed to explain the evolution of our home world through four and a half billion years, including the evolution of humanity, in order to arrive at some of the factors that channeled us into what we are today. I feel that all the inhabitants of the world face some serious problems in the quality of air, water, and soil. Of course, all the inhabitants of earth have had to face challenge's in survival through out their rise and evolution, but, I feel that some of those challenge's that we face in the immediate future are of our own making, and thus, can come under our control by the choice's we now make, or should have already made.

Subsequent chapters describe how wild places are in serious decline, from human encroachment, over use, and the adverse effect it has on the indigenous wild life. I try to address how we are coerced and more importantly controlled by our social order, which directly affects the choices we make with respect to our environment.

Religion and governments have played a major role in our psychosocial orientation. The threat of damnation and the rule of law are very strong and influential in all of the world societies, and I feel are at least, partially responsible for the exponential rise in population; that and our own uncontrolled drive toward procreation, that if left unchecked will only serve to over-burden the finite resources we have available.

I feel *energy* and our reckless use, is also over-burdening our resources. Our lack of motivation in moving toward renewable forms of energy is going to have a serious impact on our way of life when we begin to run out of fossil fuels, that are also responsible for decline in the quality of the atmosphere; one of the major components of life and health.

The chapter, My Path, describes modalities that helped turn my life around, making me more aware and conscious of every aspect of living; as well as saving me from the traps of addiction and the veiled hell associated with it.

I delineate who we are from my own perspective; dealing with our paradoxical nature that has produced wonders and atrocities out of the same source, and the chapter on The Future addresses some of the possible out-comes by what our choices are in the immediate present.

The chapter In Conclusion ties all the ideas in the book together, and bring forth a new concept of how we are to relate to our Earth-Mother.

How we relate will set our historical course of being

stewards of our world, taking what we need, with awareness and gratitude, but also giving back in measure to maintain a sustainable, viable world. Or, we can stay on this head-on collision course of use and abuse, and reap the continuing decline of our environment, and possibly our own demise.

Prelude
Before The Beginning

There was consciousness, there was awareness and perception, even though, there was nothing there to be aware of. The void was complete in its true significance and the awareness was only aware of itself, suspended in an infinite nothingness that was eternal in its reach. The perception was like floating in a vast ocean that has no water in it, and gave real meaning to the term being in the middle of nowhere, since nowhere is without substance or direction; no up or down; there is no reference at all in mass, distance or time; they just don't exist yet.

Patience is non-applicable here, since patience evinces a time continuum and consciousness, awareness and perception can only be viewed as suspended; just there, and waiting as if some great crescendo was building to a climax.

As I write these lines, an automatic feeling of peace and contentment envelopes my being; for in describing this pure void, I realize there is nothing there to corrupt this peaceful feeling that has surrounded me. However, I soon look around and realize that this feeling is not going to last long. I do exist in a universe of matter and time, with all its sharp edges and noises that wakefulness brings.

I remember being suspended in this peace and contentment before, when in deep meditation, where time and space seem to dissolve into bliss. Perhaps this is where I went in deep meditation; zooming back to that place before time and matter came into being.

Back at our perfect void, our waiting consciousness, awareness and perception, suddenly, as if in the first tick of a clock, the opening of the eyes, and the sensation of the first tactile feel, a concussion occurs and a pin-point of light is perceived for only a billionth of a second before it begins its expansion to infinity. And thus, time and space are born.

The cosmic question that has been with humanity for as long as conscious thinking began to formulate is; who struck the match that ignited this wondrous fire-works we have named the Big Bang.

If one is scientifically minded, it is the point of creation. It could also be creationism that the religious minded believe in, for who is to say how long a God day is. It could be that thirteen point seven billion years equals seven God days, thus the creation explained.

Nothing has been explained, and every time we think we have an answer, it just begs ten more questions. We can accept the creationism concept that wraps it all up in a nice tidy package, and if there are any loose ends, we just say, well that's just the will of God at work. I personally don't have any problem with that, except my analytic mind and instincts tell me; there has to be more to it than the simple explanation that creationism offers. We have to realize that creationism comes from a time when scientific investigation was practically non-existent and most esoteric beliefs were accepted as a matter of faith.

We should never stop in our quest for evolution, and I believe that if we evolve far enough, eventually we will all come to the same conclusion; that many of our beliefs are just illusions: illusions that we have created ourselves in our role of co-creators. I believe that creation and evolution is the same for everyone and our difference in beliefs is regional, and accented by our paradoxical nature that give us the ability to fly-off in any direction if we are not aware and grounded.

There are not that many real truths that relate to our survival. We have to eat and breathe; we need shelter, water and food; we mate for our basic survival, and that is all our earliest ancestors had to contend with. However, since the early days of man and his rise to intelligence, we have created a plethora of ideologies and constructs that for the most part have only led us to conflict because of our inflexible stance on our beliefs, that will probably change at some future time. It sometimes seems that we use these ideologies as an excuse to bolster our war like nature, and is something I believe we are going to have to evolve out of for our own welfare and our planets survival. Let us now launch into what we scientifically consider the evolution of our universe; after this short addendum.

From the mind and heart of Juanita Olonia:

When will man stop killing man? We kill in the name of difference.

Difference in color, race and religion. We need such a small excuse.

We have forgotten that we are brothers and sisters; children of the creator.

None of us see our selves in each others eyes.

Will we ever evolve to see ourselves as one and connected?

We kill each other, we kill the animals, we kill our air, our water and our

Mother Earth, and we diminish ourselves.

Children of God, open your eyes and see what we are doing.

We have all become so intelligent, but for what?

We all become specialists, but not humane specialists, and no one teaches us

to specialize in love for all.

Leaders of all countries need to specialize in love for all mankind.

Chapter 1

In The Beginning

Around 13.7 billion years ago, according to scientific investigation, an event of truly cosmic proportions occurred with such power and magnitude that it created both time and space and eventually created all the basic elements that make up, not only our Mother Earth, but all of the universe of stars, solar systems, and galaxies that we observe today. This event goes by the term, *Big Bang*, although I think *Big Boom* would be more appropriate for an event of that magnitude.

What the composition of that singularity, or any of its characteristics may have been, scientists have not been able to come up with a working model, or even a theory, since the laws of physics seem to break down at some where before 10 to the -37 seconds after the big bang, so, there are no explanations for the initial conditions; rather the model describes the general evolution of the universe since 10 to the -37 sec after the initial condition, where the laws of physics seem to start to apply, and leads to the explanation of the abundance of light elements of hydrogen and helium in the rapidly expanding and cooling of the first few minutes of the Universe, according to the *Big Bang* model.

The *Big Bang* was followed by very high temperatures and rapid expansion, which continues to this day, with a gradual cooling as time passed. There is a postulation that space itself is expanding, and is carrying all matter along with it, and as space expands the distance between galaxies or to be more exact, between clusters of galaxies, is getting larger. Galaxies and clusters of galaxies do not follow this expansion, because galaxies revolve around a central core, and are gravitationally bound to a gravitational nexus that holds the clusters bound to each other, but the distance between clusters of galaxies continues to increase. There is movement within clusters of galaxies as they gravitationally interact with each other, and this interaction sometimes produces collisions, where galaxies will sometimes merge, and sometimes pass through each other; but in either case the structure of those galaxies involved will be altered.

After 10 to the -37 seconds the universe grew exponentially, and consisted of a quark-gluon plasma as well as other elementary particles. Temperatures were very high and particle-anti particle pairs were constantly being created and destroyed in collisions. As the expansion continued, somehow the particles won out, and the universe turned to matter instead of anti-matter, which continues to this day, and the same thing occurred for electrons and positrons, with electrons finally dominating.

After about 400,000 years the electrons and nuclei combined into atoms of mostly hydrogen, thus the homogeneous and isotropic elements that exist today, began to appear, and also radiation decoupled from matter and continued through space unimpeded, which results in the cosmic back-ground radiation that we observe today through out the entire universe. During this period, gravity was the major factor in the control of the expansion of the universe.

Astronomers in the early part of the 20th century discovered that the universe is expanding, and at first it was expected that at some point in the future, this expansion would begin to slow and eventually stop, and would then begin to slowly collapse, picking up speed as time elapsed, back to the original singularity from which it originated, and this was termed as a closed universe. However it was not long after the discovery of the expansion, that it was discovered that the expansion is in the process of accelerating, which means that our universe is not likely to stop expanding, and this is termed as an open universe. Scientists postulate that the reason for this accelerating expansion is the newly discovered dark matter and dark energy, having the gravitational effect of 70% of all matter in the universe, although it has not been observed directly, its effect is felt.

A combination of observation and theory, suggests that galaxies and quasars formed about a billion years after the Big Bang, and as billions of years passed, clusters and super clusters of galaxies were formed.

Massive blue and white stars formed from the abundance of primordial clouds of basic elements, mostly hydrogen. Some of these early stars were thousands to millions of solar masses, and pressures and temperatures at their cores was so high, that they fussed their hydrogen so fast that they were very short lived, some only lasting a couple of million years; compared to smaller stars like our sun whose active span life is expected to be 10 billion years. At the end of their lives these massive stars will supernova, thus creating all the heavier elements and dispersing it into the ether, to mix with other primordial clouds of gases, thus seeding the gaseous clouds with the heavier elements of which we find on our own planet. This indicates that our sun and its solar system are second generation systems, and are a product of previous supernova remnants. The internal pressure inside a massive star can only create elements up to iron, and all the heavier elements require the enormous pressure that occurs when a red giant star finally collapses, and a super nova occurs. The rapid implosion and rebounding explosion cause's a rapid expansion of all the newly created heavy elements that will now seed other primordial clouds to create new star systems with the heavy elements, such as our own home solar system.

Some of the oldest structures in the universe are globular star clusters, which are composed of hundreds of thousand to millions of stars, and are usually found in the halo of most spiral galaxies. Globular star clusters are mostly composed of older stars and do not contain much or any primordial matter, so that new star formation is not likely to occur. Also, not much is known about their origins.

It is theorized that galaxies began to form from massive gas clouds of hydrogen, where the density of the cloud was a little higher. At this point, gravity began to attract more matter, and a cascade of accretion would occur. As this concentration of matter grew larger, the law of conservation of angular momentum began to apply, and the whole mass would begin to rotate. It would also have the effect of flattening the whole mass, which would eventually produce an almost flat spiral structure. Scientists theorize that these structures at first were small in comparison to the large structures we observe in the present day universe, and that present day structures are a product of collisions of smaller galaxies, until they reached their present size. Galaxies to this day are still colliding in many areas of the universe. Our own galaxy and the Andromeda galaxy, who are close to the same size, are heading toward each other, and are expected to interact some time in the distant future.

Once these large disks of gas and dark matter began to form; and keep in mind that dark matter is not directly observable, but can only be detected by its gravitational influence; then star formation can begin to manifest. This occurs by the same mechanisms that formed the host galaxy, by primordial gravitational fluctuations, which attracted gas and dark matter to the denser areas of any particular region of the newly formed galactic disk. Some observations of very distant galaxies, {13 billion light years plus} indicate that galaxies were already forming 500 million years after the *Big Bang.*

Galaxies in the universe are distributed in a cosmic web of filaments, and where the filaments meet, there are dense cluster of galaxies that began as small fluctuations in the primordial matter.

There are many shapes and sizes of galaxies. There are spirals with very flat disks, irregular galaxies that do not have a cohesive shape, elliptical galaxies that are very massive and are thought to be the products of galaxy collisions. Elliptical galaxies do not display arms like spiral galaxies, and there is a minimal amount of star formation, compared to spiral galaxies that display star formation through out the arms. Irregular galaxies are usually small, but are still active in star formation, and are usually found as companions to larger galaxies; such as the large and small clouds of Magellan that accompany the Milky Way.

It is hypothesized that at the center of most galaxies, there exists a massive black hole that is fed by the gas and stars in the central bulge, and also, whose gravitational force keeps the whole spiral in tow, along with the gravitational influence of dark matter.

There are billions of galaxies in the universe, and yet there is only one that can be seen with the naked eye; and that is the Andromeda galaxy, which appears to the naked eye as an oval smudge in the constellation of Andromeda. Even in amateur telescopes, thousands of galaxies can be seen in the night sky, and can be seen in any direction we choose to look.

At a more local level, and getting closer to home, we come to the genesis of our solar system, which is thought to have begun its formation four and a half to five billion years ago, two thirds of the way out from the center, in one of the spiral arms of the Milky Way galaxy.

The nebular hypothesis is the most widely accepted, and was originally applied only to our own solar system, but is now thought to be at work in other star forming regions of our galaxy, and through out the universe as well. According to the solar nebula disk model, stars form in massive and dense clouds of molecular hydrogen that are gravitationally unstable, where matter coalesces into smaller denser clumps, which then proceeds to collapse into stars. This collapse always produces a gaseous proto planetary disk around the newly forming star, which can give birth to planetary systems if the conditions are favorable. The solar nebula is kept from collapsing into the host star by its acquired rotation. At this stage the disk of gas and dust is so opaque, that not much energy escapes until later in the evolution of the disk, which is thought to take around 100 million years to form.

As in the formation of the galaxy, the matter in the disk which continues to feed the central star, starts the proto planetary disk rotating, by the law of the conservation of angular momentum. In time the initial high temperatures cool and the disk then moves into what is known as the T tauri stage where the formation of dust and ice particles will eventually coagulate into kilometer size planetesimals; after which run away accretion begins and Moon and Mars size planets form in a span of 100 thousand to 300 thousand years. These small planetesimals begin a process of mergers that finally results in the Earth-Venus size planets. This last stage will take from 100 million to 1 billion years. The above process describes the formation of the inner planets which are the solid rocky spheres that occur below what is called the snow line, where the temperatures closer to the proto-star are high enough to keep gases and water ice from solidifying.

Further out, beyond the orbit of Mars and beyond the orbit of the asteroid belt, we come to the realm of the giant gas planets, which reside above the so called snow line, where the distance to the sun is great enough so that gases and ice remain in a solid state. The cores of these giants are composed of a combination of dust and ice and have to reach a volume of at least five to ten earth masses; the threshold value necessary to begin accretion of hydrogen-helium from the disk. This accumulation of gas is slow at first, but will finally turn into run away accretion once the proto planet reaches 30 earth masses, and will continue until the gas in the disk is exhausted. The evolution of Saturn was much the same as Jupiter's, but it is thought that Uranus and Neptune started their formation too late, when much of the material in the disk was mostly used up; in conjunction with the strong solar wind starting to blow gas and lite particles out of the solar system. The solar wind of a newly formed star can be 10 times stronger than that of an older star that has reach the main sequence; such as our own sun.

After the initial formation of the planets, there was still

an extensive amount of rock and dust that was in orbit around the sun, and would be attracted, if perturbed by outside forces, eventually colliding with the planets and their moons; a process that continues to this day.

If it were not for wind, water, atmosphere, and tectonic movement on our planet, the surface of the earth would look just like the moon. The earth being 7 times more massive than the moon, has attracted more space born matter than our moon; some of which are credited with causing the nuclear winters that led to mass extinctions at certain periods in earths history. Some of this debris comes from the asteroid belt that resides between the orbits of Mars and Jupiter. These objects range from dust to rocks that are many miles across, and are some times perturbed out of their orbits by the gravitational influence of Jupiter. Any particle no matter how large or small, will be pulled into a planet or moon, if they come within the gravitational influence of a larger body. At present, there are Earth crossing asteroids with significant mass to cause world wide devastation, if they crashed onto the surface of the Earth, and astronomers are trying to keep track of the ones whose orbits are known, and have been cataloged.

Comets from the outer reaches of the solar system; the Oort cloud, which is estimated to be a half a light year from the sun, also pose a threat to the Earth and other planets in the solar system. These comets are thought to be the remnants of the matter that was blown out of the inner solar system by the powerful solar wind that occurs when a star is in its infancy, and consist mostly of, frozen gasses, water, ice and dust. When a comet approaches the sun, such as Haley's comet, which is in a stable orbit around the sun, the frozen gasses and water ice begin to evaporate, creating what is called the coma of the comet, and can have a diameter of thousands of miles, but the coma is very tenuous, and is only vapor and dust, usually with two tails; one of vapor and one of dust. The vapor tail being straighter than the dust trail, because the dust trail is heavier, which will be more influenced by the gravitational pull of the sun, as the solar wind tries to blow all the lighter elements away from the sun. As the comet begins its transit around the sun, the tail will always point away from the sun, so that the tail will lead the comet on its outward bound journey.

There is evidence that comet showers occur every 15 million years or so, and are produced by perturbations in the Ort cloud, by large passing objects, and can cause a large number of comet bodies to be flung both out of the solar system or towards the sun. Some of the comets that are perturbed toward the sun, will find stable orbit, and will become periodic comets, which will re-appear in a timely cycle. However, some comets will not find stable orbits and do a parabolic orbit once around the sun, never to be seen again, being flung out of the solar system permanently. During a comet shower, there are so many comets, that impact is almost sure to occur, causing severe damage to the ecological system of any world; no matter what that ecological system might be. All the planets in our solar system exist in a critical balance that can be very easy to upset, and certainly, the impact of a large mass, especially on earth could cause severe changes and even extinctions, such as the ones that have occurred in the past.

So, you might say, what's the sense of trying to save this world, when some natural disaster is going to come along and wipe us out any way. And the answer to that question is: the events that I have described above are produced by nature, and we have very little control over such phenomenon, and they occur on a cosmic time scale, which could happen tomorrow or millions of years from now. However, human impact on the ecology of our home world is immediate and the consequences are not far off in the future. This is where our role as stewards of our world is going to have an immediate impact. But more on that subject later, as I continue the evolution of own home world.

Our home world was formed out of the same components of gasses and dust in the disk shaped solar nebula that was left over from the formation of our sun and star, as well as all the other planets in the solar system, which occurred around 4.6 Ga {billions of years}, making the Earth roughly one third the age of the universe. Formed from small concentrations of matter and growing into small planetesimals, which then collide by gravitational attraction to each other, and eventually growing to their present size and mass.

Initially the whole mass of the Earth was molten, but did not take long to cool enough to form a solid crust after water began to accumulate in the atmosphere, and is also the period of formation of the oldest dated rocks, around 4.2 Ga.

The super eon known as the Precambrian, runs from 4.6 Ga to 542 Ma {millions of years}, and covers ninety percent of earths geological time, also encompasses three major eons known as the Hadean, Archean and Proterozoic eons, which are broken down into many more subsections that will not be addressed here, as it would take volumes to put down all the geological data available, and the intent here is to give a brief but succinct view of the formation of the earth that led to the emergence of humans and the rise of civilization, and the ramifications of, contrasts, ethnicity, religion, and culture, that has had a significant impact on our Mother Planet, as we know it today.

The first eon of the Earths history is called the Hadean, and runs from 4.6 Ga to 3.8 Ga; of which very little is known, because not much from that period has survived, except for a limited collection of rocks and crystals. Also during this eon, the Earth was under heavy bombardment from meteorites from the solar nebula that was still rich in raw material and had not yet been sucked up by the sun and the planets, a process that continues to the present, although not at near the rate that was present then.

One of the theories for the formation of the Moon is that a planet size body the size of Mars or slightly smaller, collided with the earth at a glancing angle, and part of the mantle and crust of the earth as well as part of the colliding body were hurled into space where it eventually coalesced into what is now our Moon. In the ratio of comparative mass between planet and satellite, our Moon is much larger than any of the Moons of any of the other planets including the gas giants. Most of the inner planets do not have natural satellites: Mercury and Venus do not have satellites and it is believed that Mars two satellites are captured asteroids from the asteroid belt; they are small and irregularly shaped. It is believed that the same impact that created the Moon is also responsible for the 23.5 degree tilt of the Earth's axis, which is responsible for our seasonal changes. Conditions on this planet must have been cataclysmic during the first 500 million years, and the name of this eon [Hadean] comes from the word Hades, which depicts a Hell like environment.

The next eon in the Earths history is called the Archean, and runs from 3.8 Ga. to 2.5 Ga. During this period the Earth's crust had cooled enough that rocks and continental plates began to form. It is believed by some scientists, that because the Earth was hotter, tectonic activity was much more pronounced than it is today, which would cause the crust material to be recycled at an accelerated rate. This may have prevented the permanent formation of continents until the further cooling of the mantle, when subduction and convection had slowed down.

It was during this time that the Earths magnetic field was established, and the solar wind was 100 times the value of the solar wind at the present time. The formation of the Earths magnetic field helped prevent the planet's atmosphere from being blown away, which is probably what occurred on Mercury and Mars, although, during the Archean eon the magnetosphere was about half of what it is now, because the core of the Earth had not had time to form to its present size, the dynamo effect was not as strong.

During the first part of the Archean eon, the heavy bombardment of the inner planets was beginning to subside, although it will never completely stop. There are always some particles, varying in size from dust size to miles across that are in orbit around the sun or are perturbed inward from outside the solar system, which also includes comets.

Due to the lack of oxygen in the atmosphere, and the lack of an ozone layer, it is speculated that life was not likely to have existed on the surface of the planet, although some scientists believe that some form of primitive life could have started in hydrothermal vents below the surface of the Earth, supported by some fossil finds dating to around 3.5 Ga.

The large amounts of water on the Earth's surface probably did not originate here, but were more likely produced by frozen comets and icy planetesimals that were more prevalent in the inner solar system during the Archean eon. These impacts would have also enriched the terrestrial planets atmospheres with carbon dioxide, methane, ammonia, nitrogen and other volatile gasses. As the planet cooled and water accumulated in the atmosphere, rain would have created the oceans, and evidence suggests that by the beginning of the Archean eon, oceans already existed on the surface of the Earth. Also, at this point, volcanic activity was very intense.

Tectonic plates were much smaller and tectonic movement was more rapid, due to the inner earth being much hotter than at present, causing subduction to occur more rapidly. However an initial crust was formed and was probably basaltic like the ocean floor, but this original crust was destroyed by tectonic movement and the intense impacts of the late bombardment period from space. However, what did survive of these early crust formations, called cratons, would later form the core of the larger continental landmasses. There is evidence that there were already colonies of algae in the early Archean Eon. Some of the oldest rocks have been found in the North American craton of Canada, and date back 4 Ga.

The Proterozoic Eon embraces almost half of the geological history of the earth that lasted from 2.5 Ga to 542 Ma. During this period, the cratons began to grow into full sized continents of modern size, and plate tectonics began to move the continents around the planet sometimes scattering them and sometimes coalescing into one super continent. Another development of this eon, was an oxygen rich atmosphere, and life from prokaryotes [bacteria], into eukaryotes [larger and more complex], into multi cellular life forms, developed. During this eon, there were several severe ice ages that also set the stage for the Cambrian Explosion that accelerated the evolution of life on Earth.

Cells fed on organic material, but as this food supply began to diminish, some cells adopted a new strategy of using the Sun as an energy source, and photosynthesis was born, using plentiful carbon dioxide, water as raw materials, and the energy of sunlight, led to the production of energy rich organic molecules. Oxygen was released as a waste product into the atmosphere at first in minute amounts, but finally accumulating to its present state. Some of the oxygen was bombarded by ultraviolet radiation in the upper atmosphere to produce ozone which absorbs ultraviolet radiation, thereby protecting all organic life on Earth. Without the ozone layer, it would be impossible for more complex life forms to evolve. The increase in oxygen in the atmosphere was probably directly responsible for the initiation of the subsequent ice ages, in that methane [which is a stronger greenhouse gas] reacts with oxygen to form carbon dioxide, which in turn is turned into oxygen by photosynthesis, and would have the effect of cooling the atmosphere to the point of initiating an ice age.

By 1.1 Ga, single cells may have appeared in colonies, where a division of labor began to take place, eventually creating a co-dependent state where groups of cells would depend on each other and single cells would die off.

Between 1 Ga and 830 Ma, most of the continental mass was united in what is called the super continent of Rodinia, and then broke up again and reformed several times. Toward the end of the Proterozoic Eon, there occurred at least two super ice ages, referred to as snowball earths, where even the oceans may have been frozen. Around 250 Ma, the last super continent, called Pangaea, which is easier to depict than earlier super continents, because many of the coast lines of present individual continents match up if they were again united. Between 1 Ga and 900 Ma, multi cellular plants began to appear, and multi cellular structures had also evolved in animals, with important development in muscular and neural cells.

The Cambrian Explosion [542 to 488 Ma], saw the sudden origin of many new species, phyla, and forms, that was unprecedented before and since that time, and by the end of the Cambrian, most modern phyla were already present, with the development of hard body parts such as shells, skeletons and exoskeletons, made the fossils more readable because they are more readily preserved and more of the subject remains to be studied.

During the Cambrian, the first vertebrate animals, among them the first fishes would appear. Between the Cambrian and Ordovician period, [488 to 444 Ma] there occurred a mass extinction in which some new groups disappeared altogether. Some of these Cambrian groups appear complex but totally different to modern life.

Plants and fungi started growing at the edges of the water, and then out of it, and the oldest fossils land fungi and plants date to 480 to 460 Ma. At first they remained close to the water's edge, with mutations and variations resulting in further colonization of the new environment. Evidence suggests that the first animals to leave the water occurred around 450 million years ago, perhaps thriving and becoming better adapted due to the vast food source that the land plants provided. Descendants of these fishes that came out of the water to feed, would return to the sea to lay their eggs, giving rise to the present day amphibians.

Around 365 Ma, there was another mass extinction, perhaps due to global cooling, and shortly there after plants evolved seeds, dramatically accelerating their spread on land. 20 million years later the amniotic egg evolved, which could be laid on land, and offering a survival advantage to tetrapod embryos, and also resulting in a divergence of amniotes [internal egg development] for amphibians. Around 310 Ma, saw the diversion of synapsids [including mammals] from the sauropsids [including birds and reptiles]. Other groups of organisms continued to evolve and lines diverged in fish, insects, and bacteria, all this at the time that Pangaea, the super continent was formed.

At the beginning of the Mesozoic era [middle life] that spanned 187 million years, the most severe extinction event to date, took place at 250 Ma, when 95% of life on Earth died out, caused by a nuclear winter effect. Theories of the cause vary from severe volcanic activity to possibly a major extra terrestrial impact where the Gulf of Mexico now exists. But, life goes on, and around 230 Ma, dinosaurs split of from their reptilian ancestors. Another extinction between the Triassic and Jurassic periods [200 Ma], spared many of the dinosaurs, and they soon became the dominant species among the vertebrates. At this point, mammalian lines began to separate, but existing mammals were probably all small animals resembling shrews.

By 180 Ma, Pangaea broke up into Laurasia and Gondwana. The boundary between avian and non avian dinosaurs is not clear, but Archaeopteryx, considered one of the first birds, already existed around 150 Ma. The angiosperm evolving flowers occurred some 20 Ma later. Competition with birds drove many pterosaurs to extinction and the dinosaurs were probably already in decline when at 65 Ma, a ten kilometer meteorite struck Earth just off the Yucatan Peninsula where the Chiexulub crater is today, ejecting large quantities of matter and vapor into the air, blocking the sun light and inhibiting photosynthesis. Most large animals including the dinosaurs, became extinct, marking the end of the Cretaceous period and the Mesozoic era. This marked the beginning of the Cenozoic era [65 Ma to present] and thereafter, in the Paleocene epoch, mammals rapidly diversified, grew larger and became the dominant vertebrates. Around 63 Ma, the last common ancestors of primates lived. By the late Eocene epoch, 34 Ma, some terrestrial mammals had returned to re-inhabit the oceans, such as Basilosaurus which led to the dolphins and baleen whales.

Living around 6 Ma, a small African ape was the last animal whose descendants would include both modern humans and their closest relatives, the bonobo and chimpanzees, and only two branches of its family tree have surviving descendants. Very soon after the split, apes in one branch developed the ability to walk upright. Brain size increased rapidly, and by 2 Ma, the very first animals classified in the genus Homo had appeared. Around the same time other branches split into the ancestors of the common chimpanzees and the bonobo as evolution continued simultaneously in all life forms.

The ability to control fire probably began with Homo erectus at least 790,000 years ago, although there is controversy that fire may have been discovered as early as 1.5 Ma. Also there is a lot of controversy about when language developed, whether Homo erectus could speak or if that didn't occur until Homo sapiens came on the scene. As brain size increased, babies were born sooner, before their heads grew too large for the pelvis, and as a result, they exhibited more plasticity, and thus possessed an increased capacity to learn, but also required a longer period of dependence. Social skills became more complex, language became more advanced, and tools became more elaborate, which also contributed to brain development. Anatomically modern humans [Homo sapiens] are believed to have originated somewhere around 200,000 years ago, or earlier in Africa. Some of the oldest fossils date back to around 160,000 years ago. About 139,000 years ago modern humans [Homo sapiens] dispersed throughout Africa, the Middle East and Europe. They were characterized by a more graceful skeleton and higher domed skull than their European contemporaries, the Neanderthals. Cave paintings suggest that by 40,000 years ago they had developed a sophisticated culture, and some authors attribute this to the appearance of a complex spoken language.

The first humans to show evidence of spirituality are the Neanderthals; they buried their dead, often with food and tools. However, evidence of more sophisticated beliefs, portrayed by early Cro-Magnon cave paintings, did not appear until some 32,000 years ago. Cro-Magnons also left behind stone figurines, probably also significant of religious beliefs. By 11,000 years ago, Homo sapiens had reached the southern tip of South America, the last of the uninhabited continents. Tool use and language continued to improve, and interpersonal relationships became more complex.

Throughout more than ninety percent of its history, Homo sapiens lived in small bands as hunter-gatherers. As language became more complex the ability to remember and transmit information resulted in a new sort of replicator; the meme [culture and socialization], and ideas could be rapidly exchanged and passed down to the generations. Cultural evolution quickly outpaced biological evolution, and history proper began. Somewhere between 8500 and 7000 BC, humans in the Fertile Crescent in the Middle East began the systematic husbandry of animals and the agriculture of plants. This spread to neighboring regions, and developed independently elsewhere, until most Homo-sapiens lived sedentary lives in permanent settlements as farmers.

Not all societies abandoned their nomad ways, especially those in isolated areas of the globe poor in domestic-able plant species, such as Australia and the middle east where cultivation was only possible along large water courses that produced a rich bottom land of fertile soil. However, among those civilizations that did adopt agriculture, the relative security and increased productivity provided by farming allowed the population to expand. Agriculture had a major impact, and humans began to affect the environment as never before. Surplus food allowed a priestly or governing class to emerge, followed by an increasing division of labor. This led to the first civilization at Sumer in the Middle East, between 4000 and 3000 BC. Additional civilizations quickly arose in ancient Egypt, the Indus River valley and in China.

Starting around 3000 BC, Hinduism, one of the oldest religions still practiced today, began to take form, and others soon followed. The invention of writing enabled complex societies to arise. Record keeping and libraries served as a storehouse of knowledge and increased the cultural transmission of information. Humans no longer had to spend all their time working for survival--curiosity and education drove the pursuit of knowledge and wisdom. Various disciplines, including science, arose. New civilizations sprang up, traded with one another, and engaged in war for territory and resources, and empires began to form. By around 500 BC, there were empires in the Middle East, Iran, India, China, and Greece, approximately on equal footing. At times one empire expanded, only to decline or be driven back later.

In the rich and fertile land of Mesopotamia, some of the oldest sedentary civilizations of the ancient world arose, with Sumerians, considered by historians to be the oldest civilization, at about 5000 BC, and contributing to later societies with several crucial innovations such as writing, boats and the wheel. Over time, Mesopotamia would see the rise and fall of many great civilizations that would make the region one of the most vibrant and colorful in history, including empires like the Assyrians and trade kingdoms such as the Lydians and Phoenicians, all of which were influential to neighboring civilizations. North-west of Mesopotamia were the Hittites, who were probably the first people to use iron weapons. To the south-west was Egypt, not as old as Sumer, but one with rich resources that supported a thriving culture. Politics were always in flux, partly because of the lack of natural defenses in the region. In 538, the Achaemenidae Persians, first led by Cyrus the Great, conquered Babylon, Anatolia, and Egypt, combining almost all of Mesopotamia and southwest Asia into his empire.

Iran has had a long history, with some of its earliest states and civilizations: the Elamites, and the Medes. In 549 BC, Cyrus, the king of Ashan, created a vast empire; the biggest empire yet. Because of its physical integration and cultural diversity, this dynasty, the Achaemenians, is often considered the first true empire in the world. Alexander's conquest eventually replaced the Achaemenians with the Seleucids, who were in turn overthrown by the Parthians. The Parthians ruled Persia parallel to the times of the Han and Roman Empire. In this flourishing time and the next, Persia served as the link between Rome and China. Internal weakness caused the Parthian Empire to collapse and the Sassanid Dynasty to rise. The splendid Sassanid Dynasty brought the revival of the old Achaemenian traditions, including Zoroastrianism. However, exhausting wars with Byzantium, left the empire unready to face the Muslim armies from Arabia.

Whether in Europe, Asia, or Africa, the land around the Mediterranean has always been rich in civilization. The Ancient culture of the Minoans thrived in Crete. In the Maghrib, Phoenician settlers built the city of Carthage. There were also the Greeks, who built city-states not only in Greece, but in various other places in the Mediterranean. The Greeks, who gave many important scientific, philosophical, and political innovations and ideas, are often considered to be the root of western civilization.

Under Alexander's conquests, Classical western ideas spread eastward. Many important elements of Greek culture would later be used by the Romans, who built a significant empire that brought cultural unity to much of Europe and established a basis for future western states. Enormous economical activity also extended outside the Empire: into the East African coast, and most famously, eastward toward Persia and China on the Silk Road. The classical era ended with the fall of the Western Roman Empire in the fifth century AD.

Often considered the longest continuous civilization on earth, China has a remarkable history. Notable civilizations around the Huang He began at around 2500 BC, and by 1700 BC, the well established dynasties such as the Shang and later the Zhou, appeared. In 221 BC, the Qin conquered all other states and formed the first Empire in China. Over the next two millennium, the pattern of dynasties falling and rising continued, but civilization was never severely disrupted. Thus, many innovations and inventions came out of China such as Confucianism, paper, gunpowder, the compass; to other parts of the world through the silk road, and later, in the Indian Ocean trade routes. Neighboring regions such as Japan, Korea, and Vietnam, were highly influenced by the Chinese culture, and more or less incorporated it into their own culture [architecture, Buddhism, etc]. For the greatest part of its history, China was one of the most advanced civilizations in the world, but towards the late Imperial Ages, isolationist policies left the Qing Dynasty dangerously behind the west. This and other internal problems led to the collapse of dynastic rule in 1911 AD.

The pastoral nomads are sometimes belittled in historical studies because of their barbarian and warlike nature. However, it's absurd to say that they were not a significant driving force in history. Often times, the Nomads waged war with their sedentary neighbors and in many instances, nomadic hordes such as that of the Xiong Nu, Ulghurs, and the Turuk penetrated deep into sedentary lands such as the Chinese, Roman, and Persian Empires. In the western steppes, for example, the nomadic Huns were a significant factor in the fall of the Roman Empire. While nomads were warlike, it would be wrong to state that they were always at war. In fact, nomads traded as much as they fought. Because of their location, they acted as operators of the silk road. The most crucial period of the Nomads was during the Middle Ages where the Seljuk Turks, Ghaznavid Turks, and Mongols conquered large sedentary civilizations. The Seljuk Turks became the new Islamic power and Ghaznavids introduced Islam to India. The incredibly enormous Mongol Empire, often accused of brutal conquest, left a legacy of world integration and exchange, where economical activity was at a maximum. However, by the end of the period, the gradual development of firearms took away the prominence of the nomadic war machine. Lacking the military edge that gave them their fame, the nomads gradually lost their strength.

South and Southeast Asia are known for their long history of diverse culture. South Asia, commonly referred to as the Indian Subcontinent, was home to the Harrapan civilization in the Indus Valley, one of the oldest in the world. The Mauryans formed the first extensive empire in the region in the 300s CE. At that time, foreign influence had already begun arriving, which over time, resulted in a number of multicultural states north of India. After the 500's CE, no single power could claim dominance over the region for 500 years. Yet during this period of political fragmentation, India was immensely active in maritime trade on the extensive Indian Ocean routes that closely paralleled the land based Silk Road in magnitude. The arrival of Muslim dynasties around 1000 CE, returned centralized rule to India under the Delhi Sultanate. Islam's arrival, only added diversity to the culture of the region, which had given rise to Buddhism and Hinduism. Succeeding the Delhi Sultanate was the Mughal Empire, whose splendor and wealth are epitomized by the Taj Mahal. South-East Asia was the land that slowly became the crossroads between India, China, and later, the Europeans. Some of the most unique episodes in history belong to South-East Asia.

At around 2500 BC, the Polynesians began their great migration across the ocean from their homelands in the Philippines. On mainland SE Asia, powerful states began to form around 500 CE, including the Khemer Empire of Cambodia, and the Srivajayan Empire of Sumatra. These and later states were linked to other Asian cultures through maritime trade routes. Hinduism, Buddhism, and later Islam, spread to the region where they became well established. However, the importance of the region for trading and the lack of extensive empires due to geography, made it an area of great interest for the European imperialism from the 1500's onward. The Portuguese trader, Vasco De Gama arrived in 1498, and other Europeans soon followed. By the 1800s, the Europeans had seized a great deal of South and South-East Asia.

In the years after the death of Muhammad, Muslim armies poured out into the surrounding areas, bringing the lands from Persia to Spain under their control. With this huge amount of land under their control, the Umayyad, and later the Abbasid Caliphates, allowed merchants and scholars to easily travel through western Eurasia, bringing goods and knowledge, which the Muslims greatly expanded through the Caliphate and outward to less advanced regions, such as western Europe. In 751, paper making from China made its way to the West through Muslims. Trade introduced Islam to the Africans. In the Middle East, the success of Islam meant, that culture would be changed forever. Even after the decline of the Abbasid Caliphate, Islam would remain as one of the base institutions of the region. Future states of the region, such as the Safavid, and Ottoman Empires; were Islamic Empires.

By 364 AD, the Roman Empire had been split into two separate states: The Eastern and the Western Roman Empires. The Western Empire soon collapsed under the weight of barbarians, and Europe was plunged into the Medieval Era. Under barbarian rule, civilization decreased dramatically, with only the church remaining as one of the few institutions of civilization. However this period was crucial to western history because modern western nations directly trace their roots to kingdoms of this time period. The Crusades began around 1100 AD and gave root to significant change. Europe became more centralized and activity with foreigners brought back learning to western Europe. By the 1400s, Western Europe had fully recovered politically and culturally. With the advantages of unification, European technology and knowledge in the next period skyrocketed to take the lead in the world.

While the Western Roman Empire collapsed, imperial rule in the East survived the threat of invaders, and the Eastern Roman Empire, during Medieval times, is labeled today as the Byzantine Empire with its capital at Byzantium, which was re-named Constantinople, and was later changed to Istanbul by the Ottomans. In contrast to Western Europe, the cities in the Eastern Roman Empire were centers for learning and culture. The Byzantines were especially important to Eastern Europe, for their influence in art and religion. However, as Western Europe grew more prominent, foreign pressure brought the Eastern Roman Empire to a decline. The Empire fell to the Ottoman Turks in 1453, one of the events that signaled the end of the Medieval Period.

Since the dawn of recorded history, Africa has been the home to empires. The pharaohs of Ancient Egypt built a realm that endured for nearly 3000 years. The warrior traders of Carthage ruled from the Atlantic to Tripoli, and hammered at the gates of Rome. To the south, Meroe and Axum, Ghana and Mali, built vast kingdoms, and traded in ivory, salt, and gold. At one time Timbuktu had libraries and universities greater than any in western Europe. Later, the warrior nations of Ashanti, Fulani and the Zulus built disciplined armies and conquered wide areas. From the middle of the fifteenth century, Europeans worked their way down the coasts, carving out new empires in fire and blood. In the nineteenth century, came the scramble for Africa, with Britain and France, Germany and Belgium trampling on each other, and the indigenous Africans, to build empires many times the size of their respective homelands. Africa has known the tread of Hannibal and Scipio Africanus, Caesar and Cleopatra, Mansa Musa and Shaka Zulu, Henry Morton Stanley and Cecil Rhodes, Kwame Nkrimah and Nelson Mandela. From the grim slave pits of Elmina to the brooding towers of Zimbabwe, from the battlefields of Zama to the blood stained diamond mines of Katanga and Sierra Leon, Africa has known conquerors and rebels, heroes and villains, idealists and tyrants.

Although most of Precolonial North America; north of modern Mexico did not see the formation of large states, Latin America was the home of some very notable empires. Mesoamerica provided a home for cultures such as the Olmec, Toltec, and Aztec. Likewise, in south America, many cultures grew in the Andes, and these later became the basis for the famous Inca Empire, which established control over the entire Andes. Precolonial American Empires were advanced civilizations with an organized social structure that flourished in art, mathematics, astronomy, architecture, and engineering. When the Spanish arrived, their weapons and the diseases they brought from Europe, which the indigenous people had no immunity to, and which also occurred in Hawaii when first exposed to explorers from Britain, brought an end to these empires.

Several events marked the end of the Middle Ages. In Europe, 1453 marked the end of the Hundred Years War. By the end of this war, many things had change since Medieval times. First, the strengthening of monarchies, and secondly, the rise of gunpowder weapons. In the Muslim world, 1453 was the year Byzantium fell to the Ottoman Turks. The Turks fielded massive cannons against the walls of Constantinople, another symbol for the rise of gun power. Around the same time, we see the rise of two other powerful Muslim states, the Safavid and the Mughal. Another thing that marked the end of the Middle Ages was the Renaissance [revival of learning in Europe], and most importantly, exploration and colonization. The small expanding populace of Europes motivated nations beginning with the Portuguese to sail outward. Eventually, other countries followed, and this ultimately led to the massive sea based empires of the Spanish and English. To the world as a whole, this meant that everything-any one place-was an important part of the whole. The Seven Years War of the 1750's was the first global conflict, and a milestone toward globalization and the global interdependency of today.

Continual expansion overseas led western civilization and western imperial powers to stand astride the globe, and during this period of expansion and colonization, one out of every three people on the earth lived as subjects to one of the super European powers that were riding the crest of exploration and colonization, and usually, not by amicable means, using manifest destiny as an excuse to plunder existing civilizations. The few non European states left with sovereignty, such as China, Japan, and the Ottoman Empire, were either verging on collapse or in the throws of massive social and economic change as they strove to adapt to the tide of Western ideas and technology. In the years since 1750, Western power and Western thought seemed supreme upon the world stage. Then, in less than a 100 years, everything changed. Old empires crumbled into revolution or disappeared entirely while new great powers hewed their way onto the international scene.

Out of global empires emerged new nations. The very name of empire and conquest acquired a sinister tone, perhaps an indicator of an evolutionary step where the sanctity of humans and their respective civilizations, no matter how technologically regressed they may be, have a right to exist, be free, live in peace, harmony, joy, and exercise their esoteric beliefs as they see fit for them as individuals in the collective sea of humanity, which I believe will eventually extend to beings and entities of the larger universe____another bridge to someday cross. The rise and fall of empires in the years between 1750 and the present have shaped the lives of million upon millions of people, for better or for worse. They have shaped our world in a struggle for power that is still going on today, and seems to have no end in sight. All nations seem to believe that war is the best way to stimulate the economy of the commercial interests, while at the same time bankrupting the treasury of the nation. If those natural resources and trillions of dollars were to be used for the edification of the environment and citizens, we would begin to see a move toward the paradise that we have envisioned in our minds eye, but have never made it part of our practical world; and never will until we take it out of our illusions and place it square onto our reality, and make it manifest.

We have so many tools at our disposal, if only we would apply them to the higher self motivated efforts that we are capable of. At some point we are going to have to put humanism back into humanity or our existence on this world is not going to mean much for a species that has so much potential. But, we are the universal paradox, and what makes us so, is, the freedom of choice that makes us unique on this planet.

We now posses such a wide spectrum of technology, and are daily being bombarded by some new invention or innovation. I don't really think we know what to do with such awesome power, but that is what happens when we put all our eggs in one basket; and by that I mean that we have concentrated on only one aspect of our capabilities and left our social graces and higher insights in the dust. We are definitely out of balance in our endeavors, putting too much emphasis on those things that accumulate money. Maybe someday we might get over the luster of gold, and rise above it, but until that time comes, we are bound to remain in an unbalanced state, wasting our talents and resources to feed the golden calf.

There can be no doubt that in the period of 1500 to the present, many awesome explorations, inventions and innovations have occurred, some of them very beneficial and inspirational, and some of them more like an ax over our heads. The Renaissance may have brought back to the Western mind, the means to learn and become educated, to move forward with scientific exploration, culminating, in my opinion, the ability to travel to another world in our solar system, even if it is only 240,000 miles away; traversing the void of space is a mile stone in human evolution.

However, the Renaissance did little to curb our appetite for war and killing, and the past 500 years have been the bloodiest years in human history, with the subjugation of millions of indigenous people around the world by explorers, conquerors, and territorial expansionists, mostly with exploitation on their mind. I am inclined to believe that the real and most important Renaissance is still to come, one whose focus encompasses more than just scholastic achievement, but will in the outcome enhance every aspect of the human potential of soulful, artistic, and social achievement. An elevation in conscious awareness needs to be aspired to, where humanity will see the need *For all good men to come to the aid of their planet,* and in so doing, rescue themselves as well as all the other living things____flora and fauna____of this world.

And so, this is my take on the evolution from the Big Bang to the present. A postulate that is in my opinion supported by logic and investigation, albeit with some errors no doubt, due to the immensity of the time scale and the interpretation of the people involved in the tedious and involved studies that have led to these conclusions. I also know that there are people who firmly believe in creationism, and it's not my intent to try to refute their beliefs or argue the question of creationism vs. evolution, for who am I to say, they may be right. I base my belief in evolution, on my own perceptions, intuitions, and study. To Me, the basic premise of this writing does not hinge on the belief of either evolution or creationism; that is just my point of view, but is more about the situation we face now and in the future which relates to our survival as a species, who might have mustered the courage to rise above the mundane and understand how beautiful life is on its own merits.

We have crossed into the new millennium, but the same old yoke remains on our shoulders of not being able to see that we are all in the same boat with basically the same desires for life liberty and the pursuit of happiness. Instead we see only the differences in cultural and social beliefs due mostly, to geographic location, even though we share a common ancestry.

There are forces that would keep it that way, after all what is another human life, where it is so abundant that it seems to be invulnerable to any kind of decline. However, that could come to a sudden stop if we continue to use or misuse our resources and environment. All through human history, once an immediate environment was used up or became to congested, we could just pull up stakes and move somewhere else, usually creating another ghetto in our wake. Well, I think we are running out of places to run to and we are going to have to make it where we are.

Expansion of our species is one of the major themes in this writing, which I think is going to be the linchpin to our survival. We can't continue to tax our world with expanding population forever. Eventually something is going to give, and it will not be pleasant or painless. I understand the human need to replicate themselves in the form of offspring's, it's in our DNA and undoubtedly a major factor in our survival up to about 8000 years ago, when husbandry and the domestication of farm animals became the existence of the majority of the worlds population. At that point attrition of our species began to decline and more humans survived to adulthood and even into old age.

Modern medical science, immunization, and less exposure to the elements, now allows people to live longer lives, which also adds to the problem of over population. Better tools and better weapons took us further from the food chain, and humans began to expand at an exponential rate. 5000 years ago this expansion did not seem to mean much, as there was much room upon the Earth. But, as we enter the age of the Water Sign, we are not quite elbow to elbow yet, but are definitely putting an immense pressure on our Earth, and not with love, but just taking it all for granted, which also means that our environment will eventually take us for granted too. The laws of nature are relentless and can offer succor to the aware, or pain and annihilation to the fool.

Perhaps in the near future our Love will reignite, and we will become aware that our genius can be used for creation of beauty, peace and understanding, and not just for tools of destruction, and thus lead us to a more present moment, where we might realize that nurturing love, awareness, clarity and care for our world, is also a form of science, as is anything we endeavor to accomplish outside of instinct. In subsequent chapters I will endeavor to express my world view, and offer some ideas and techniques that have helped me survive addiction, insanity, and ego mania on my worldly path, with the intent of ascending to higher levels of understanding, something that I believe is going to determine the quality and the survival of this idyllic world and all of its inhabitants.

Despite my optimism, there is a possibility that because of our nature, and our innate resistance to change, we will chose to follow our destiny, even if mean our extinction. There is certainly plenty of evidence around us that extinction is a realty and has occurred right on our world many times since the formation of our solar system, although not by conscious effort, but by the physical laws that govern the universe, and can not be changed. What we impose on our world through the manipulation of those physical laws of nature is of a conscious nature and is within the realm of our control.

However, if I believed that there is no alternative for us as a species, I would not be sitting here writing these words. I believe destinies are malleable and can be shaped through the implementation of our total being, which means not just using our mental intelligence but our hearts and souls, which can act as the a balancing fulcrum on the scales of life. It's not easy, and it's not the path of least resistance, but changing our perspectives, our domestication, world view, and altering our DNA, is well within our powers. Powers that we have been striped of by severe domestication, lay in dormancy, and must once again be rekindled.

Chapter 2

The Wild

From the wild we emerged, and from the wild we still gain some of our strengths as is apparent in our propensity, even as a modern culture to seek the solitude of the most remote areas and wilderness places that remain on this earth. With the present expansion of human population, the undeveloped wilderness areas on every continent are rapidly disappearing, leaving an enormous pressure on the remaining wilderness to support wild life.

I grew up in a rural community, in the late thirties, forties, and early fifties, where wild was just a short walk away, and could at any time of my choosing, escape into a very different world than the one that I was compelled to live in. And, I must admit that the contrast I experienced made life a lot more interesting, and also offered a measure of freedom that is unattainable when your neighbors are only a few feet away from your home. I think that whether we consciously feel it or not, there is always a feeling of being restricted when forced to live in an eighty by eighty foot plot of land, such as we encounter in congested cities.

In the rural environment of my youth, it was by no means a wilderness environment, but it was unoccupied and could still sustain some of the indigenous life forms that had over millennium adapted to those surroundings. However that kind of opportunity is getting harder to come by as the urban sprawl continues to expand at an alarming rate. Development of housing tracts are now being built, not out of any pressing need, which is evident as the the homeless population continues to grow, but is executed for the sake of profit that now plays a major role in our economy, and holds up one of our illusions that there is nothing else that we can do with real-estate but cut it up and force people to live in congested neighborhoods.

One of the major impacts that forced growth has on our world, is the loss of wilderness, and just as important the loss of habitat for the rest of the citizens of this world. I am sure that there are very few people that would agree with me that the wild animals of the world could be considered citizen, but they are, and have shared this world with us through the whole evolutionary process, and have actually played a key role in our survival. We don't need to prey on wild animals any more, since the domestication of certain species, now allows us to fill the counters of our super markets with every variety of fresh meats.

Still some feel the need to go out and pit their egos against wild animals that don't have much of a chance of surviving an encounter with a hunter who is carrying a fire arm that can find its mark at five hundred yards; and we call it sport. You want sport; go hunt grizzlies with a bow, arrows and a knife; now there is real sport! No, we want the easy kill, thinking we have accomplished something special. Of course, how can we expect to value the lives of wild animals, when we don't even value human life, the life of our own species is wasted in the constant warring that humans can't seem to extricate themselves from. We fight at the literal drop of a hat, and most of the time for some ideology that in the end is going to be modified or completely changed anyway, which is the destiny of all ideologies as time moves on.

Not only are animals hunted for sport and trophy, but they are hunted for such ridiculous reasons, as using certain parts for aphrodisiacs that are worth their weight in gold in some oriental markets. Elephants are hunted for ivory and the rest of the animal is left to rot.

Hunting certainly has a big impact on wildlife, but the major reason wild animals are fast approaching extinction, is the loss of habitat, due mostly to encroachment of humanity whose population continues to swell like an over inflated balloon that is about to overrun every thing in its path.

Even in this so called modern age, some wild animals are still being slaughtered because of fear or the possibility they might prey on the live stock of ranchers. The wolf and the coyote are only a few of the species that go by the label of varmints, and no account is taken for their useful purpose in the overall scheme of the environment. Many of the creatures we consider to be pests, are actually helpful in naturally keeping the environment clean. Every time we eliminate some creature from a specific habitat we upset the balance of the natural ecology. For instance, if we eliminate or seriously reduce the rattlesnakes from a habitat, the mice and rabbits are likely to become an infestation. This is the situation that was created in Europe at the time of the great plague, when the population decided to kill as many cats as they could find because they were thought to be associated with witchcraft, thus allowing the rats to multiply in an uninhibited manner and setting the stage for disease and misery that took so many lives.

Many herds of animals migrate great distances with the changing of the seasons, and usually follow routes that have been in use for thousands of years, and some of these routes are being severed by roads and fences or large tracts that have been plowed under for agriculture and farming, again to feed the burgeoning swell in human population whose appetites are growing as fast as their numbers, not only for food products, but for energy. Energy that comes from the burning of coal and oil that are raising the temperature of our atmosphere, which is also going to impact not only the animal kingdom, but us as well, by raising the level of the oceans, possibly flooding all the coastal regions, and changing the weather patterns all over the world, and creating a much more turbulent atmosphere, where winds, tornadoes, hurricanes, and intensified storms could severely hinder our ability to grow the crops that we need to survive. These conditions are being produced by the burning of fossil fuels that power our cars, trucks, ships, airplanes, trains, and electric producing power plants spewing millions of tons of carbon dioxide, sulfur, carbon monoxide and many other poisons into the air we breathe, and the more carbon dioxide that goes into the air, the more heat from the sun that is trapped in the atmosphere.

But wait: aren't trees supposed to take in carbon dioxide and in turn expel oxygen? Well yes! So why are we cutting down the forests of the earth as fast as our chain saws can get to them? Well, it's being done because there is a whole industry that is built around the denuding of mountains or anywhere that trees grow, and further reducing the habitat so essential to the support of wild life, especially where old growth forests are concerned. This also creates the conditions for erosion that washes away the top soil that is vital for the re-growth of the forests.

There is a big demand for lumber of all varieties from countries that are reluctant to cutting down their own forests, or don't have any forests left. Those countries import large quantities of wood, mostly from South America, where the rain forest is being cut down at an alarming rate. Almost every thing we burn, from fossil fuels, wood, natural gas, and even our own bodies, converts oxygen to carbon dioxide and a host of other harmful chemicals. Yes, try to imagine how much oxygen is consumed by the bodies of eleven billion people, plus all the other creature on the planet.

Humans have been burning fossil fuels since the dawn of time, and for most of our existence it was balanced with new growth. It was not until the industrial revolution that all of a sudden our fuel consumption went of the end of the charts. No longer was it on a personal level, but now we had huge machinery to feed, and on a grand scale consume so much coal, wood, and gas that the scales were tipped so far that it will never recover, unless we can come up with cleaner sources of energy which would tip the scale back into balance. This is going to require a whole different mind set, of upgraded values on environmental issues, in order to accomplish a lasting balance.

I have noticed that humans are very good at looking at the past, and scrutinizing history, reveling in our accomplishments, and self congratulating ourselves of our lofty endeavors. However, I don't think we are very good at looking into the future, perhaps its because we don't like what we see there. If history really repeats itself, the future certainly does not paint a very pretty picture for the quality of life.

When we do look into the future, its usually in a fantasy way, and talks about our conquest of space and colonization of other worlds, and its more about head bashing and how we will war against the aliens we encounter; its just more of what we have already set in motion here on Earth. Do we really want to carry that legacy to the stars? Or, do we want to fix our problems at the source, here and now. That way we would have something more viable to impart to the cosmos than we have at the present time. The *Wild* out there as well, but even more pressing here, is waiting for us to make that evolutionary step, where we become aware of everything, not just ourselves.

Its not enough to reach for the stars with only our advanced technology. If our social skills are still in the dark ages, our efforts become only ego and exploitative at best.

Trees are some of the most noble entities that inhabit this world, giving so much and asking so little, one of the most useful species that continues to serve, even after death. Not too many things can claim that kind of status.

When old growth forests are cut down, many species of birds and mammals that do not make their home anywhere else, suddenly find themselves homeless. We have lost more of our oxygen producing trees to the chain saw, for the sake of upholding a very large and powerful industry, that granted, keeps a lot of people employed, but whats going to happen to these jobs when we cut down the last tree? We will probably wind up like the inhabitants of Easter Island, who cut down their last trees, just to use them to roll one more statue down to the shore line, and in so doing, changing the whole ecology of the island that led to their own extinction.

The past hundred years has produced some visionary people, some in government, some in the private sector, who looked into the future and could see how devastating a loss it would be, if our wild places were not protected from those who would mine, clear-cut, and strip-mine anywhere that was not protected by federal law. People like Theodore Roosevelt and John Muir, just to mention a few, acted with unfaltering resolve and energy to create the national park system. Many others have been instrumental in turning large tract of pristine land into wilderness designated areas, where only foot and horse travel are allowed, with no mining and drilling allowed.

As we proceed into the new millennium, that visionary and moral orientation seems to be dwindling, mostly where government is concerned; who are mostly aligning themselves with the concerns of industry. There are many environmental organizations such as the Sierra Club that do have an impact on staying the hands of those who would bulldoze the whole world into a pile of rubble. I belong to several and recommend that everyone with an interest in saving whats left, join and support as many as possible. In the end, it is the individual who will save the day. It will require involvement; making sure that our representatives are clear on what we want them to vote on or against, and if necessary make the only moral threat we can use; our vote.

Life on this planet can not exist without trees, nor can the the animals that have evolved around specific environments. Animal can't artificially adapt like we do to moving half way around the world, mainly because our world and the way we live is one of control. Anywhere we move to is very similar to the one we came from, not in exterior conditions but in interior ambiance. We have the ability to control our environment by building dwellings that protect us from almost any environment we may encounter, and so man is more adaptable than the wild creatures, by way of his ability to solve immediate and complex problems of survival. Animals don't have the luxury of putting on another layer of clothes if the situation demands it, and have evolved to specific conditions of climate and geology.

Some of the wild animals are herbivores and some are carnivores, and some are both, and both kinds are hunted for food or for sport, yet the carnivores seem to engender more animosity and fear from people than the herbivores, simply because carnivore are perceived as a threat not only to man but to livestock they raise. Some of this problem exist because of the loss of habitat by species such as lions and tigers, who even in such a vast continents as Africa or India, are facing extinction because of being bottled into smaller and smaller areas. Again over population rears its head. However, the problem for wild animals is also produced by the creation of huge farms and ranches that are fenced of and made inaccessible to wild fauna, and even if access is gained, the law will support the owner in eradicating any wild life that may trespass on his property, using the excuse that they are going to kill their live stock, not even beginning to understand just how much of the land is being coveted by humans, or the premise that our bounty should be shared by others outside our own species.

For instance, wolves in the western United States, are under constant threat of being shot on sight by ranchers who own cattle, and if it were not for the endangered species act, they would have been eradicated long ago, as they have been in other parts of the country. In my state of New Mexico, the Mexican gray wolf was reintroduced in several wild areas, but have met with much resistance from ranchers and cattle men, and are covertly being hunted anyway, though the number introduced was only a couple of hundred. At last count, their numbers were diminishing rapidly, where they should be thriving given the ideal conditions of where they were planted. Although they are under the endangered species act, there is no way to insure the safety of any wild animal, except the conscience of the individual.

Along with the wolf, the coyote is another wild animal that most land owners consider to be vermin, and considerable efforts have been employed to trying to eradicated them, including poisons, guns, and traps that leave the poor animal to suffer from broken limbs and starvation. However, the population of the coyote has not been diminished significantly, and one study showed that as the population of the coyotes decreases, more pups will be born to the pack, thus compensating, and frustrating the efforts of the annihilators. The coyote thus seems to be able to adjust its progeny to the conditions at hand, which is something that the wolf can't do, producing a fixed liter of pups no matter what the conditions may be.

Wild creatures will, just as we will, suffer from the poisons that are unleashing into the air, water, and ground by the industrialization of the nations of the earth; and all the nations are digging in their heals to catch up and compete for the worlds markets which produce all the amenities that we think we need, some of them are quite useful, and some of them are just trinkets. I am writing these words on a modern computer that I find very convenient and expedient to employ, but I will likely use this operating system until there is no software to support it, which was the reason for my last upgrade. I would probably still be using windows 98, which still did the job just fine. The problem lays in the way that technology changes from one week to the next, and people rush out to buy the latest advancement or so called improvement. Some of these advancements are purposely generated just for the sole purpose of selling product, putting more unneeded pressure on our resources and our energy consumption, and in most cases just amounts to another bell or whistle to occupy our minds and make us feel confirmed to the rest of society with the same mind set of keeping up with everyone else. This scenario not only creates waste of resource and unwarranted pollution, but creates mountains of unwanted instrumentation in third world countries where they decay and bleed their poisons into the ground. This is not recycling, which is what is supposed to be happening, it is nothing more than garbage dumping.

Much of our pollution, not only poisons the air we breathe, and seeps into our water supplies, but eventually finds its way to the oceans where it causes severe damage to the marine life and their habitats. And now there are oil spills to contend with, that have been shown to be caused by cutting corners, for the sake of profits. The safety standards and compliance of regulations that should minimize the possibility of accidents, especially in off shore drilling rigs, are often ignored. The recent BP oil spill in the Gulf of Mexico has created and will continue to create unimaginable consequences for marine life in those waters for hundreds of years, as well as for the habitat that exists along the shore line of the Gulf of Mexico. We will suffer from that loss as well. The oil industry is not about to give up that gold mine, and it is up to us to push the tide toward renewable energy sources.

Not only are we responsible for poisoning the oceans, but we are harvesting the bounty of the oceans edible creatures at an alarming rate, not only endangering the most popular species, but in some cases, reducing the food supply of other marine life. Activities such as whaling are outdated, and the world community should ban together to put a stop to it.

Life in the oceans is going to be severely compromised by poisons that are washed from land based industry, into the soil first, where rain water carries it to the rivers, and the rivers carry it out to the oceans of the world. Industrial pollution such as lead and arsenic not only pollute the oceans but also pollute the ground water that we drink and use for our daily sustenance. There are many shore line fisheries that are not allowed to be harvested or sold in fish markets because of the high toxin content of the fish, and this boundary continues to move further out from the shore line.

There are still countries in the world that think that they can not survive without slaughtering the whale population to the point of extinction. Also, many unwanted species are dragged out in nets that don't discriminate in what gets caught in them, and are just discarded as waste.

Not only are we poisoning marine life, but our navy is assaulting them with high energy sonar that is so painful to marine mammals that they will beach themselves in order to get away from the high intensity of the sound. Man is very careless with his toys. Yes, its just grown men playing with high tech toys; without conscious or empathy for his surroundings.

If global warming is a reality and our atmospheric temperature continues to rise, then many of the species that are adapted to the colder climates are going to run out of habitat due to the melting of the ice caps in the extreme north and south polar regions. This would also cause the oceans to rise and many of the coastal habitation of man would be under water, further shrinking the available land mass, and compounding the problems we already have with population.

Warming of the atmosphere and pollution are also being credited with the demise of many of the coral reefs that's leading to the extinction of some of the most unique and diverse forms of marine life. Life forms that are found to exist only in particular habitats. Something else that tears up the ocean floor is nets that are dragged along the bottom, not only tearing up the ocean floor, but snagging up marine life that is just discarded once its brought up to the surface.

I try to imagine what the consequences of navel warfare has had on the purity of the oceans and the multitude of life that it supports, and it boggles the mind to think about all the ships that have been sunk during battles at sea since the end of the sailing ship era, and all of the pollutants in the form of oil, fuel and explosives that the oceans have had to absorb. There were thousands of ship that were sunk during the two world wars and all the other minor wars, plus all the oil tankers and off shore drilling platforms that have contributed to the total, and it's a wonder that there's any life left in the oceans, and another good reason to end our obsession with war.

Humans don't seem to have any love or compassion for anything outside of themselves, and I think the reason is that we don't actually love or respect for ourselves; which is where it has to start, before we can show any love and respect for anything else. We take ourselves lightly and squander the gifts of the higher self, which are the attributes that make us a unique life form, and allows us to rise above the plane of just living a materialistic existence. The hook of materiality and money keeps us nailed to the proverbial cross, and the illusions of ordinary lies and false pride in systems that except for a very few [one percent], are dead ends for the majority of society, but still we support them.

The oceans are polluted directly, from what washes out through the rivers. Pollutants stays in the oceans, because of the water evaporated from the surface, which will eventually move inland and become rain, leaves most of its heavier pollutants behind, as occurs in all distillation processes. However, when it rains on the land mass, there is a fresh supply of pollutants to wash back out to sea.

Pollution is not the only nemesis the oceans face: the other is over fishing and the unintentional catch of non marketable fish that inadvertently get swept up in the fishing nets, that even extends to dolphins and sharks. Most fish exist in the food chain, and the demise of non marketable marine life denies sustenance to other marine life. I realize there is a very large industry associated with ocean fishing, and much of it is the life line of long standing fishing traditions. Within any industries point of view there seems to exist the paradox that states: that as long as there is abundance, the industry will always support growth. This is either a very short sighted view or the denial that every resource on this planet is finite, and it may be difficult for the individual fisher to see how one catch can make a dent in the population of the vast oceans, but it is the collective catch of thousands of fishers that makes the impact so devastating. Its always been man against the elements, but I believe its going to have to change to man for the elements, that will eventually lead to more sustainable ways of harvesting the oceans.

There was a time, and not that long ago, when sea food could only be found in specialty restaurants. Now it can be found in almost every kind of food vending establishment imaginable. From pizza places, to Mexican, Italian, Chinese, fast food; to everything goes restaurants, sea food can be found on the menu, and it is hard for me to wrap my mind around the demand and the pressure this puts on the marine population.

It would be more prudent for the fishers to protect their precious industry while there is still something to protect, instead of waiting until there is nothing left to catch. Sea food has always been popular with people that live by the sea, but today sea food is transported to the interior of almost every country.

The oceans of the world are like all of our other resources, there is a limit to what we can take out before there is nothing left to take, and there is a limit to how much pollution the oceans can sustain before that ecological system collapses.

Every form of wild life is on the road to extinction from pressures brought about by an uncontrolled human expansion, that threatens to take up every bit of available space on the land, the sea and in the air. This might not be so bad if it were not for the fact that we do not nurture, love and respect what we covet, but only proceed to exploit the Earth for everything that we can extract for the sake of making money, and one of the tragedies is; the people that do most of the work, get the least reward. Once blight and disease attacks a tree or any other living organism, it is just a matter of time before death comes to visit, and our Earth is a living organism that with its own essence produces millions of life forms with no help from us. We however, do have the capability of destroying it all with our heavy handed use of resources that we often aim at each other in an effort to annihilate one another. We have not acquired the ability to love our selves, our neighbors, our kin in the wild, and a world that gives us everything that we need to thrive. In our collective insanity, thriving is not enough, we have to take all we possibly can, even if it means extinction of the wild places, possibly followed by our own demise.

Where have all the hymenopterous insects gone? I no longer see any buzzing from angiosperm to angiosperm, carrying precious pollen from one to the next, pollinating and bringing to life the fruit we eat; everything that pollination enables. There are places on the Earth today where pollination has to be accomplished by the growers themselves, by hand, a very tedious and time consuming task that our friends the bees did with joy and efficiency. Our allies, the bees are heading toward extinction by spraying crops with chemicals that don't discriminate as to what insects they kill. All this is done for the sake of higher yields, but without the bees, there isn't going to be any yield at all.

There are state government organizations that are supposedly instituted for the purpose of protecting the wild life in their countries and states, but most of these organizations cater heavily to the sportsman, and I use the term sportsman loosely. They are mostly interested in the revenues that selling big game hunting licenses brings. Look in any sportsman magazine and all you will see is a great white hunter hunkered over his kill that he made with his 300 Weatherby Magnum rifle, at 500 yards. Where is the sport in that, where the human has such a high margin of advantage. Its just killing that matters, and revenue again. Hunting has built a big and profitable industry around itself, and the only ones who have to pay the price, are the hunted.

Some animals like the rhino are hunted strictly for their horns because of the myth that it contains an aphrodisiac, and brings big money to the poachers, and a grand illusion to the users. The elephant is hunted for its ivory tusk, although, there are laws prohibiting the trafficking in ivory, there is still a lot of poaching that escapes the law enforcers, who in the African wild are too few and far between to be effective. The real problem is; how do we convince the poachers and the users that what they are doing is wrong? I think the only thing that will work is to create employment for the poachers. Turn them into protectors of wild life by paying a decent wage for their services. Most poachers are just trying to make a living, though in a deplorable way. We need to work on bursting the bubble of illusion for those who think a ground up rhino horn is going to turn them into a colossal sex machine.

Tigers are hunted for their beautiful coats, but are also rapidly losing their habitat to human expansion. People with high powered weapons could hardly be considered sportsmen. I have more respect for pygmies who used to hunt elephants by running underneath the animal and jabbing a sharp stick into its heart, and then hoping to make a getaway before getting trampled. Try that one sometime sports fans, and really test your mettle.

The final line is that we really don't need to hunt animals any more, and its seems to me quite ludicrous to kill a wild animal just to hang its head on the wall. An act of pride no doubt, but pride could also be taken in the preservation of the wild kingdom, and I personally think that would be much more uplifting than killing an animal that is already endangered.

Humans have risen above the wild, but it seems to me that we have a very hard time leaving it behind or leaving it alone, and showing some love and respect for the place of our origins. Hunting had its origins at a time when we were still in the food chain and hunting became part of our DNA. Those energies could now be turned toward the preservation of the animal kingdom, the environment, and the ecology of this beautiful blue planet.

Some animals are considered vermin, mostly because they prey on the livestock that humans raise for food, but the reason this occurs is that the natural habitat of wolves, coyotes, bears, deer and elk have diminished to such an extent that it leaves the animals with no options but to feed themselves wherever they can. We have created those circumstances ourselves, and if we don't get a handle on our own population explosion, then nature is going to do it for us.

The native Americans had a more symbiotic relationship with nature, so that when Europeans migrated to the North and South American continents, there was such an abundance of resource to tap into that it created a mentality of over use and exploitation, and an exponential increase in population growth. It was perceived as and infinite place for growth, with infinite freedom with no restrictions that had previously been imposed on them in their countries of origin, across the sea. Well, we have reaped the whirl wind of abundance and are already starting to feel the pinch of diminishing resources, and no one feels that pinch more than the wild kingdom. That however, was just the tip of the iceberg, the symptom of an attitude that was very narrow in its view and its motivations.

We humans move too fast. So fast in fact, that we have no way of evaluating the consequences of our actions. Its momentarily here and then its gone, to immediately be replaced by something new, and it leaves us with a void and no clue as to what just happened, or what the overall effect will be. We are so good at placing ourselves on the treadmill, ultimately running from ourselves and our true destiny. A destiny that takes time to analyze, scrutinize, digest, discuss, ferment, and make an informed decision. I believe that society's current design is to keep us so occupied on the treadmill that we have no time to take a deep breath, let alone take the time to understand ourselves or the situation we are in, or begin to formulate a valid opinion of the path we wish to take.

If we don't curb our appetite for procreation, we are going to find ourselves in the same predicament that the wild animals are in today; looking over the fence for our next meal. Our ability to produce enough food for everyone is already at the limits that the land can sustain, and there are millions of people who are already facing starvation every day; which brings us to the problem of obesity in the more affluent cultures, a problem that is reaching epidemic proportions, and stands as a testimonial to what the effects of stress are in an over achieving culture, where substitutes have to be found in the form of addiction; which include drugs, alcohol, prescription drugs, and of course the most acceptable one; over eating; as if to say to the world; we will make up for what you don't have on your table, and consume it for you. Those last two lines are my attempt at dark humor, prompted by the darkness that I see in many of the facets of our lives, such as politics and money, television, advertising, greed, and our preoccupation with sex. Having taken sex out of the sacred realm and placing it in the mundane and perverted view of; no Love, no Heart, only immediate gratification; its just another form of addiction.

The water fowl and all birds in general depend on clean and unpolluted water just as much as we do, except that wild birds have to use natural collection deposits and have to settle for what ever might be in the water, whereas we in city water systems usually have elaborate filtering systems, and always add chlorine or others substances to the water for the purpose of killing bacteria. People that derive their drinking water from wells have to settle for what ever comes down through the water table, which because of the lack of oxygen is not bacteria, but certainly can be chemicals that have found their way into the water table from spraying of crops, mining, oil spills, and rain that washes the air clean and drains into our ground water sources. Adding to that is the new and improved pollution technique of fracking, which purposefully and consciously injects harmful chemicals into the water table, just to extract a minuscule amount of natural gas.

The avian population does not have the luxury of drinking filtered or processed water, and we came close to loosing the eagles when DDT was being used as the primary insecticide for crops. Of course these chemicals don't just affect animals, but they also have deleterious effect on any biological organism; man included, and most of those chemicals can be considered carcinogens. The birds around my home do have the luxury of clean drinking water, but in many parts of the city they have to drink out of stagnant pool that consist of drainage from city streets that contain particles and chemicals in many forms. Every year the count of migratory birds goes down.

In the late 1950's and through the 1960's, while my children were growing up, we would delight in the observation and identification of some 30 species of butterflies and moths. Now in 2014, it is a rare occasion to spot a butterfly of any kind, and even the migratory monarchs don't seem to come this way anymore. Of course they are in decline also, mostly to losing their habitat in Mexico, and being poisoned along their route of migration. Sprayed weed killing chemicals don't discriminate what they kill, and are also decimating the milk weed that the monarch butterfly uses for sustenance, and seriously inhibiting their migration through the United States.

Somehow, we, the citizens of this planet are going to have to make some serious adjustments to our mod-us operand i, or history is going to look back at us as the eliminators, who with such voracious appetites consumed or poisoned everything around them and left nothing for the survival of the wild creatures. Anyone reading such a history would surely think of it as an era of barbarism. The term barbarism, is not exclusively connected to what we do to each other as humans, but also extends to how we treat all the other living entities we are supposed to be sharing this world with. But, what can the wild expect from a species that can't even get along with itself, and is constantly waging war over nothing more than ideas that are taken too seriously. Fundamentally we are all the same, and at the core of our being we have the same aspirations, of life liberty and the pursuit of happiness; if we could only shed our illusions. Illusions that have been carefully planted there to keep us at each others throats, and in self slavery.

The next time you have the opportunity to see a wild creature, try to see yourselves 2 million years ago, and try to think of what homo sapient might have been like then, and maybe we will find a place in our hearts for our less evolved relatives, who at this point in time, really need our help. Although, if evolution is equated with survival, then anything that has survived to the present is just as evolved as we are.

At the time of this writing, the government is in the process of trying to dismantle the environmental protection laws, and remove many wild and threatened creatures from the endangered species list, in order to drill more holes in the earth, and supposedly protect ranchers and their cattle from predators. Trying to drill more oil wells is ludicrous, and is an industry that is in its final throws, but the industry wants to milk it to the end, and is unwilling to invest in research for renewable energy sources, although their profits certainly could easily support such research. We need to replace all carbon based fuels with cleaner form of energy. Our government at this time is not responding to realistic issues that are going to have a world wide impact. They are responding to the money interests and the pressure of large companies, who don't want to see change. We might as well change the constitution to read, government by the wealthy, and for the wealthy, and lets trample anyone who gets in the way, including the environment. I don't think that is what the governed meant, for their part.

The United States at this time is selling coal to China and India, who have very little pollution controls in their industrial complexes. This country should be a world leader in the race to clean up the atmosphere as well as its own back yard, but it seems that we are fast falling from grace.

If wealth becomes our standard, instead of life, liberty, and the pursuit of happiness, we are likely to destroy all the beauty that this world still has to offer. Some of us have become drunk with power, and like alcoholics, moneyholics are unable to think about anything but their addiction, and like most addictions, they very seldom lead up, they always lead down the path of self destruction. In this scenario, the destruction is going to involve the whole world.

The wild is not just about animals, it includes us as well, and also includes all the flora of the planet. The trees and the great forest are our source of oxygen, an element that is the major progenitor of life as we know it. Without it we cease to exist, simple as that, and yet that simple fact seems to elude people in positions of power.

We are cutting down the oxygen producing forest at thousands of acres a day for the sake of a buck. I know, I am beginning to sound like a broken record, but I honestly believe that wealth has us by the throat, and if we cut down much more of our forests, this choke hold is going to literally extinguish our breathing.

Perhaps science will invent a way of synthesizing oxygen, but can you imagine the price we would have to pay for a service of life giving proportions. Forget about the yearly vacation, we have to pay our oxygen bill. I think most of us would rather use the free oxygen that mother nature provides.

If we don't clean up our act and our environment, clean water is going to be another commodity that we are going to have to pay through the proverbial nose for. If all our ground water is polluted with industrial waste or chemicals that are being used to fracture the strata in order to extract a minuscule amount of oil and natural gas, then the most abundant compound on this planet will turn into the most abundant poison. Drinking water is not the only concern. Water in any form needs to be pure. We can't water our crops with poisonous water and hope to harvest nontoxic foods. We need to seriously contemplate what our future goals are. It helps to know where we are going when we set out on a journey. Like managing a ship at sea; hopefully we won't run aground on our trip into the future.

Chapter 3

A Public Seduced

We the people are under attack or at least, severely pressured from a conglomerate of sales media that is very adept at using psychological choreography to promote the sales of any thing from cars to drugs and everything else in between. Automobile ads are not based on just technical data and a description of the mechanical attributes of the machine, but extend into the realm of fantasy, even depicting machines that seem to have a mind and personality of their own. In reality all cars except for their size, horsepower and appointments are the same in design, and construction.

The different car companies battle it out in multimillion dollar commercials to try to convince the public that they produce the ultimate machine on wheels, while trying to discredit the competition with negative innuendo. Some of these commercials are quite sickening and insult the intelligence of the public with arbitrary and ordinary lies. There are laws for truth in lending, and there should be laws for truth in advertising as well.

There is a real drive for commercial interest and distributors to force feed the economy through high pressure advertising, on television, and almost every publication from magazines to news papers. They try to appeal to the most basic instincts of the human psyche, appealing to the ego or the competitive nature of people, who are usually running full tilt to keep up with the rat race.

Half of the advertisements that we see on television are car advertisements that try to build a mythology around certain makes and models as if the product had the ability to make our lives complete. Completeness comes from within, not from external sources.

Can insults work to sell product? The answer is yes, and it is amazing to me that the way they work is in a reverse psychological mode, by making the target feel angry or inadequate for not being able to acquire the proffered product.

Even more amazing is the fact that a large portion of the public will actually get in serious debt to buy that new car, truck or house, and mind you this is not being done for an actual need, but only to full-fill a false need of appearing to society as an adequate player, in the game of keep-up. There is tremendous pressure to put people in the position of selling their souls for the privilege of getting into debt that is way above their means. They call it the American dream.

For some time now; every time I view a commercial that is trying to ram some product down my throat [yes they are trying to Ram a particular truck down our throats] all I see is a big hook with a big juicy worm on it, and I think, if I was a fish I would be quite inclined to bite and probably get myself hooked. Well that is exactly what business is doing, they are all just out fishing for pocket books, and guess what? It works. But how? We are intelligent people. We do not fall for such obvious ploys. Well, we do and the reason is a thing which has been discovered by business profiteers, which goes by the name of ego, and feelings of inadequacy. This factor is very prevalent among the young who are just starting out. There is no tutoring by parents or educators about the pitfalls that ego can drop us into. Instead they say go for the gold, and so, many mistakes are made along that path, where some reflection might lead to a smarter choice.

In this wide and wonderful world of ours, and at the present time in history, ego is the major controlling factor in most of the intercourse that our society partakes in. So, you say, whats wrong with that? Well I will try to convince you that the unbridled ego is not a friend of the individual, and as a host of individuals we all possess one. I don't mean to suggest that we should try to annihilate our egos completely, or at all, for it is one of the most powerful attributes we have in our tool-box. What I do suggest, is that there is a serious need to control this powerful force. Like all of our other addictive tendencies, such as over eating, alcohol, drugs, and prurient behavior, present society is addicted to the ego high, and uses it as a manipulative force to coerce and control. An unbridled ego is comparable to a wild stallion or a loose cannon.

Perhaps, in the distant past it served us well as a radical warning in the fight or flight situation, and what I am talking about here is mostly in the area of our survival, and in response to a physical threat, which I concede could occur in our modern society. I believe that most of the threats that are perceived at the present time are just illusions that are a product of fear and total separation from our fellow man. This separation is kept alive and reinforced because it is easier to control individuals than it is to control a collective of people who are willing to work together for their common benefit. That is the major reason that unions have been able to elevate some sections of the working class out of literal bondage and are a major contributor to creating a middle class. Unions are also under attack by forces that would like to bring back slave labor. Companies are prone to pay the lowest wage that they can get away with, as is very apparent in the level of the minimum wage, a standard that is below the poverty level, and would pay even less if they could get away with it. All of these things are manifestations of the ego and do not necessarily serve our best interests, and in most cases just creates unnecessary conflict, that could be avoided by just a little contemplation and an interjection of heart into all of our dealings with each other. There is no heart in the system as it stands now, and maybe there never has been, but if we do not begin to work our selves into a more heart felt system, we are just going to continue to prod along as usual in a system that exploits people and makes greed and profit the major goal.

There is nothing wrong with reasonable profits, but it seems that under our present operating mode, the only thing that is important, is to amass as much as possible. This mind set of hoarding is having a direct impact on the infrastructure of the world, that is outdated or worn out from use, and is directly responsible for the lack of funds for research into renewable forms of energy production. We are still bogged down in trying to squeeze more oil out of the Earth. Our world view is stagnating and affluence seems to be the only thing that matters.

So where does the ego lead us to in the purchase of any commodity? Well in case of high power advertisements, it leads us right into the jaws of the dragon who is just waiting to swallow up our hard earned resources; resources that in the case of most working class people was hard won by investing half of their life-time of hard work and servitude.

Purchasing in an urban society is an essential part of survival, since the majority of urban dwellers are only capable of growing minimal amounts of food for their own sustenance, because of constraints of space and the by-laws that govern most city developments, which are put in place mostly for health reasons. I don't think most people would want to see chickens and pigs in the neighbors yard that is situated just a few feet away. So whats left? The *supermarket,* the only alternative for survival. I don't believe that there is any thing wrong with purchasing, but I don't like being coerced into buying stuff I don't need; it is unrealistic and only leads to an unstable economy.

I would like to see advertising that only deals in the specifics of a product, and not wrapped up in a theatrical production that only alerts me to the fact that here is a product that is being pushed hard because of its unnecessary worth. The man on the street, eye witness, or user, are supposed to convince us that they actually use these products and are absolutely thrilled with them, when in reality they are only actors who have memorized a script and are only acting out a part that they are payed well to enacted. Some of the worst offenders of this form of advertisements, are the legal drug companies. They will have some actor exalted about how this particular drug saved his of her life while spewing out the long list of side effects at three times normal verbal speed, sometimes ending with; could cause death. I have been around drug pushers, but never on the scale, magnitude, or pressure of the legal drug companies.

I realize that all these high finance commercials, and its a billion dollar industry that creates them, brings us all the programming that we view on television. However, I consider sixty percent of the programming on television to be of little substance anyway, and much of it is just a re-hash of something that has already been done a hundred times with new faces and wilder special effects.

As for convenience, most of the mom and pop operations have been driven out of existence by the the mega consortium food chains that deprive us of more convenient means of shopping for the small items we may need on a daily basis, therefore creating a need for vehicles just to go and pick up a loaf of bread, creating unnecessary pollution and unnecessary use of fuel. Of course, there is method in that madness. More fuel is sold, more wear on the vehicle, more frequent visits to the tire store, more oil changes, and the list goes on; feed the piggy! The design is impeccable, but leaning heavily to the dark side of our nature, and the only interest here is in the bottom line.

Everything it seems is being designed toward unnecessary consumption, and I realize that our economy is in serious trouble, but that is only because the economy was originally built on the glut principal, where the name of the game is use as much as you can as fast as you can and never mind about tomorrow. The over abundance that we have experienced in the past is not going to continue much longer. Over forced farming methods have taxed the top soils of the world to the point that produce can only be grown by using chemical fertilizers. After plowing under the left-over organic material from the previous crop, the soil should be left fallow for a year or two in order to regain its vitality.

Genetically enhanced seeds are being widely used, and some in the science community are warning us about the deleterious effect this may have on humans. Just the fact that seeds from genetically engineered plant are sterile, puts the users in bondage to companies like Monsanto, and there is a penalty for trying to seek out an alternative if farmers no longer wish to participate. All of these conditions have been created for the sole purpose of cornering a market that represents billions of dollars.

Unless we change our priorities and begin to view our world in a more realistic way, we or our children are going to pay a very high price for our mismanagement of the precious gifts our world has to offer. The buy, buy, and buy some more mentality creates a collision course between the finite amount of resources that are available to us and the amount of population that these resources are expected to sustain, and as quantity increases, quality decreases. I have not experienced too many products that are as good or better than the original, and in most cases appear as cheap imitations of the original product. A product should become better as it evolves into subsequent models, but companies are always trying to see how many corners can be shaved off the product and still make it marketable.

This process seldom produces better quality and would not be as unacceptable if the price of the product was also shaved down in proportion, In reality the price of everything under our sun, continues to rise, and we have to wonder when and where it will level out. This kind of inflation is particularly disastrous for people who live on a fixed income, and even people who earn a salary don't get raises that come close to keeping up with the rise in prices of everything from food, clothing, fuel, which comprise the products that are essential for survival. I retired in the year two thousand, and in just these fourteen years, I figured out that I have lost twenty five percent of my buying power, and there is no end in sight. Every visit to the supermarket reveals an increase in price from the last time we shopped. We have painted our selves into a corner by becoming totally dependent on one source only, but for urban dwellers there are few choices. I have to shop around for the best deals and try to buy produce from the local growers whenever possible.

The loss in *gnp* is the amount of money that goes to foreign markets for goods that were originally produced and sold in the USA, and we are not the only country to experience this decline. Many of these products are being made less expensive and are of a higher quality, which makes them more attractive to the consumer. In the years after WWII, the Japanese people tried to rebuild their economy by manufacturing cheap imitations of products already being marketed in the *USA*, and these products became known as__ made in Japan__ with a tongue in cheek sort of meaning; in other words it was of poor quality. At that point an expert in business practices and production systems, went to Japan and helped them elevate their products to such a degree that they were able to compete in a world market with the best, including making serious inroads into the United States automobile industries domestic sales.

The US automobile industry did not react in time to the demand for smaller cars that would get better gas mileage and by the time they did react, the Japanese imports were well established. Now we are losing more and more of our products to foreign producers, not only because of quality concerns, but also because of the out sourcing of our own industries to other countries, where labor is abundant and the wage scales are much lower.

Business has no allegiance to countries, and has no qualms about sacrificing the economy back home for the sake of added profits. Most of these countries have an abundance of workers whose standard of living is much lower, and are willing to work for a penny instead of a dollar, and that is the attraction for companies to move away from home. The only positive aspect of this scenario is that it might some day equalize into a real world economy, where the standard of living is going to be the same for everyone, no matter where in the world they are located. However, this is probably some distance in the future. Economies all around the world are struggling to stay afloat, mostly due to the shady business practices that have become the norm in recent years, where ethical business practices and just plain common sense have been replaced with the gamblers philosophy of hitting the Wall Street Mother Lode.

These practices are no better than spinning the roulette wheel, with the hopes of making a fortune. Even professional gamblers are smarter than that, knowing when to back off when they are ahead of the game. If their will is weak, then they don't last long in the gambling arena. The point is, no one with a moral compass would use such techniques as the ones that have been used by investors during the last economic collapse. In such schemes, there may be a few that win big, but there are many more who are going to lose, and most are going to be the unsuspecting investor who had no idea that they had put their trust in experimenters who were selling worthless derivatives around the world and using complex formulas instead of sound investment practices.

The success of the gambling concerns of recent years is a testimonial to the willingness of people to gamble on the chance of hitting a big pay off. The hard truth is, the odds are already set and pre-calculated. and they are; by a large margin, in favor of the house, not the players. I can see an occasional diversion, but it turns out that many people wind up losing everything they own. This also happens to many who play the stock market.

There is no place else to go in this solar system and the stars are far in the future, we need to make it here and curb our appetites for everything that is proffered to us by a media that also makes big bucks on forcing everything from soup to nuts down our throats. Sure, the economy is going to see a severe shake up, but eventually will become more realistic and predicable. Yes, there will be lots of moans and groans but it will be nothing compared to the chaotic avalanche that we will have to deal with if the collapse comes because we ignored all the warning signs and we just ride along fat dumb and happy till the run away train collides with the immovable object. We created the monster, we can tame it, or should I say, tame our selves. We definitely exhibit wild tendencies.

Organizations such as Wall Street are just symptoms of the overwhelming aversion we have with wealth, and stand as monuments to our greed. We even support gambling as a hope for hitting the big jackpot and the illusion that this is going to heal our personal problems, and it could be healing, if we could give half of it to the needy. Such unselfish acts would go a long ways toward relieving the suffering of someone else who is not directly related to us. That I am sure is a totally foreign concept to most everyone.

The fair distribution of wealth and services is something we are going to have to deal with, and in the not too distant future. Elevating everyone to the same status is a concept that is going to require a complete metamorphoses in the way we think and deal with each other.

We have been in the me and mine way of separation from our fellow men for so long that its going to take a major evolutionary step to accomplish bringing everyone up to the same level, and its fantasy to think that it can happen overnight.

If real equality is ever to survive, it will have to come about one small step at a time. The first step could be equal pay for equal work: men and women on an equal footing. The second step could be fair wages. Wages that people could actually use to pull themselves out of poverty. Companies like Wal Mart and McDonald's make billion of dollars in profits but pay their employees minimum wage. These people have to seek out food stamps or hold two jobs just to squeak by: this is just plain injustice, and will not change until we can extricate and steer our government away from supporting big money and not the majority.

One of the most inhuman enterprises that is force fed to us is the false need for *war*, only because it keeps the wheel of mega industries turning. Now, there is a waste of effort and natural resources with the sole purpose of throwing the world into turmoil, increasing the separation that already exists in humans, for it is only in separation that the wheels of chaos can endure. Separation is one of the grand illusions that we keep being falsely fed after all the evidence that we are all of the same origin, and the only difference is in the regional beliefs that stem from our provincial location on the planet. If as much effort were made in the course of peace and the restoration of our planet to the paradise that as stewards we should be aspiring to, our efforts would be rewarded ten fold just by knowing that we are doing something to shed light and real purpose to our existence, for we are beings of free will and we have the capacity to destroy or create. The only ingredient that is missing is *Love. Love* of ourselves, love of others, tolerance and understanding.

As long as we live in fear, we will always be on the defensive, a posture that only serves to create chaos in our world. After all, what we fear in others, is what we see in our selves, and trying to fight it externally will never work; we are literally fighting ourselves. When we attack others, we are only attacking ourselves. What we really need to do is to work on our own perceptions and fears, and allow light and reality to flood our minds, and hearts. This is why I consider it so important to nurture the independence of the individuals mind so that we can move away from the present world view that is fraught with darkness and cultural misconception. Those who see a better way, must help those who don't. There is a responsibility to moving forward, always has been, and some have paid a dear price for their participation in it. That is not likely to change until we are whole and of one mind and heart again.

Not an easy thing to do, because we have been living at the whims of our ego for so long that it would seem that this is the only way. We have forgotten that we also have to run our perceptions by our hearts and not let them dwell only in our mind. The heart will not deceive us because it is closer to the source than the mind and will not prescribe conflict as readily as the mind and the ego.

One more force feed is the exploration of space, which sounds very noble, except for the fact that while we are driving for the stars, our home is going to hell and seems to me to be a little premature and immature of a culture that is trying to jump ahead of itself. The universe will be waiting for us with open arms when we are ready and have taken care of business where our roots reside. More research needs to be done on more efficient propulsion systems that do not pollute the atmosphere of our world with tons of particulates every time we execute a launch. It would seem that the only reason for inception of the space program in the first place, was competition with the so called super powers during the cold war. That case of the race to the moon, has now been abandoned for the grander concept of Terra forming Mars. We should first concentrate on re-Terra forming our own home world first, before moving on to an alien world. With our present mind-set, we would probably just create another junk yard on any other world we visit.

Very few, and mostly ardent conservationist have adopted the premise of: if you pack it in, you can pack it out. That has not happened on Mt. Everest and did not happen on the moon. We leave our garbage everywhere we go.

Are we just experiencing the learning curve: are we intelligent enough to acquire the skills for true survival, or are we doomed to wallow in our denial until this structure collapses around us and we are thrust back into a hell that could only be imagined. Some believe that we are born onto this plane of existence to experience and learn, and I tend to agree with that analysis. The only question in my mind is; will we learn soon enough what survival really entails. The premise of survival has changed. It is no longer primarily a physical struggle, it is becoming more of a psychological, intellectual, and spiritual battle for the warriors to try and turn the ship around, before the point of no return. And if you asked me what survival entails, I would have to say moderation in everything. The middle of the road again; the balance point. We are also at the mercy of cosmic forces and maybe we can deal with those maybe we can't, but if the worst happens, at least we don't have to blame ourselves for something that occurred beyond our control. What we do with our choices, is within our sphere of influence, and we have to accept responsibility for what we do.

Buying and acquiring will always be a part of our existence, although imagine what this world would be like if there was no more need for legal tender, and every thing that is produced is available to everyone. Probably sounds too much like socialism to the majority of people that are totally invested in capitalism, which when really analyzed means that it is acceptable to use leverage to gain advantage over others, and once this leverage gains momentum it is practically unstoppable, and creates a chasm between those who have the leverage and those who don't, leading to an accepted form of exploitation. I can't imagine how this acceptance of exploitation and self enslavement has come to be unchallenged, but it has been with us throughout recorded history. One of the reasons for this imbalance is that the laws of the world in general are heavily in favor of supporting the affluent, yet the burden of funding for all community services, including the judicial system, and all governmental institutions, falls on the shoulders of the middle class. We are funding a system that does not support its supporters. In recent times, there is a strong effort by our elected legislators to remove more and more of the tax burden from the richest people and corporations, which means more burden for the middle class. Smells like corruption at the very core of the apple. Money talks and morality goes right out the door. Big money lobbying in the house of representatives and senate should be outlawed. Its just another form of prostitution and should be eradicated.

I understand that money managers are an essential part of any economy and finance institutions are vital to keeping any economy moving and to finance large under-takings. It is only when greed comes into the equation that leverage begins to show its horns, and the investors and consumers get caught in the jaws of a vice that is threatening to squeeze the middle class into oblivion. I have no problem with the service of money lending as long as it is conducted in a manner that is fair to all the parties involved, and the lenders are entitled to some profit for the service they have provided. But as we enter into a new millennium, the scales are tipping more and more in favor of the institutions that have leverage on their side to the point of becoming a global embarrassment that smacks a little of barbarism. Certainly not the course of an enlightened population or a humane point of view that puts us on the same level of importance. But, leverage or no leverage, because what goes around comes around, immoral behavior will eventually effect everyone, including the rich. Any nation that is top heavy rich or bottom heavy poor is in a state of potential collapse. A good example is the economic woes that most of the countries in Europe are going through at the present time. This condition is partly due to over extension of credit, but also a direct result of Wall Street selling worthless derivatives on the world market. When our economy collapsed, the whole world economy was affected, This has damaged the credibility of the United States as worthy of being the worlds monetary standard. Now, there are several major players in the worlds economic market who are actively seeking to move the money standard to some other currency: perhaps the yen. This would have a negative impact on the U.S. Economy, but well, we asked for it.

Yes, we have evolved, but not in every aspect. There is a large imbalance in what we seem to consider important in the areas that we care to explore and develop to the best of our abilities. For instance, in the first two centuries following the renaissance, there was a major thrust to promote music, the arts, and science, and they all flourished during that period. However, in the last two centuries, and especially after the industrial revolution, science is being pushed to the forefront as if science is the only facet that is of any importance in human affairs.

This is totally neglecting the abilities that the human

spirit is capable of. Not that there is anything wrong with science, it is just this imbalance of priorities such as the dwindling of art and music curriculum that is not being offered in some of the public school in the latter part of the twentieth century. This imbalanced push has actually led scientific endeavors to become, not only a burden, but also a subtle danger to our survival. If you really think about it, you will see how our science has led us to such obstacles as global warming, the low quality of the foods we consume, the way we are packed into suburbia, the poisoning of the waters and the air we breathe. Of course this is not a science problem, it is a human problem in promoting this unhealthy situation by not exercising controls in the processes involved in industrial endeavors.

The unbridled creativity and genius of the human has been allowed to charge forward with no scrutiny what so ever, and the state of our world reflects the consequences of our actions. We must begin to realize that in this universe there is no such thing as a free lunch. Every action we take has an opposite and equal reaction, and nothing we do to the environment is going to go unnoticed. In our beginnings, the effect we had on the earth was so small and subtle that it was easy to ignore what our axes and other primitive implements had on our surroundings, and our efforts were still within a sustainable range.

However, our implements, population, and demands for consumption have grown to megalith proportions, and we are well on the road to demanding more than this world of ours can sustain. If we are unable to back off from the world view of consuming as much and as fast as we can, we are going to find ourselves in an untenable situation where there is not enough to go around and no place to go. At that point, nature will take over and hell like we never imagined will descend upon us, with humans reverting to their feral state. We could deal with a collapse if we could come together and face our problems in a civilized manner, but I am afraid humans are too prone to panic, and there would be a barbaric run for what little resources remain.

Our need to curb our burgeoning population is of utmost importance if we are to survive with a minimum of trauma, since I believe we have already passed the point where we could survive unscathed.

There is going to be a tremendous amount of resistance from many sectors. There is a large portion of our population that has not even thought about or is aware that there is a potential for disaster. And, there is a smaller but more powerful portion of the population that only lives for today and would not want to see anything changed for the sake of profits that have grown at the same rate as the population, and for them, creates an illusion that there is no potential problem.

Another area of resistance is the religious sector, that preaches; we are on this earth to procreate with all the vigor that we can muster. They preach that the taking of a life is a sin, such as abortion. Yet they have no qualms when it comes to sending young men into battle to be killed.

Irresponsible procreation just leads to unwanted children that suffer and are not well cared for, and there's a lot of them around. Religion has a very short sighted and outdated view about procreation, but since their authority come straight from the creator, the congregations have a very strong tendency to believe implicitly in what they are told, and they are told to go for it like rabbits.

There really is no need to kill anyone anyway. If we could instill the importance of contraception and the importance of family planning in our existing population. The media could play a very important role in popularizing a concept that has come of age, but the media is also hamstrung by their dependence on syndicated news organization which tell them what they can or can not report on, which is mostly fear related news. The public broadcasting system is the only media that might have a chance of promoting contraception and moderation as a means of population control.

There is one other aspect that adds impetus to procreation. It is the overly and inordinate romanticizing and popularization of sex in order to sell everything from cars to makeup. Everything in advertising has to have sex appeal, and is used as a hook by advertisers because they know the tremendous influence it has on the public mind. They don't miss a trick, but it does lead to obsessive behavior in the sexual arena that is directly linked to casual sex and often results in ignored or unwanted children. People who are involved in casual sex are very seldom interested in establishing a family and just as seldom employ contraception in their casual encounters. But, casual or not, any sexual encounters can produce an offspring if contraception is not used.

Much thought goes into the planning and construction

of our projects, but not much effort is made to appraise the impact our efforts will have on our environment. Mining, oil drilling, and lumbering leave enormous scars on the surface of the earth, not to mention the chemical pollution that is left behind in the wake of these operations. Some processes such as pumping water and chemicals into the ground under high pressure is bound to lead to severe pollution of the water tables. Its hard for me to understand how anyone could even consider employing such a process, when the results are obvious. The real reason is nothing more than trying to keep the oil industry alive, even if the results are so drastically devastating to the environment and the health and safety of people who live in the areas where these processes are being deployed.

Science and the intelligence it stems from is just another double edged sword that cuts both ways, and can be used to make life better or destroy whats left of our world. It will all depend on the choices we make in the next few years.

What if anything can we do to turn this addiction of irresponsibility around? I believe, if change is to come about and awareness of our situation is to happen, it is going to have to come in the form of individual transformation. We have been led to believe that we only have power if we are involved in a collective effort, and most of us don't realize that we also have personal power to act as individuals, in what we do and in what we think. Yes there is power in the collective, but it also has a tendency to drag people along with it that are unwilling to disagree with the collective because of pier pressure or fear of being ostracized, especially if they disagree with the views of the majority in the collective. Before we can be effective in a collective situation, we first have to be individuals, otherwise, what, of any value can we possibly bring to the party. It boons nothing to unconsciously agree with issues that we seriously disagree with, and could possibly lead to our demise. If you don't think we are heading in that direction, just look at what is happening to the wild kingdom all around us. What can happen to them, can happen to us, as they are just a symptom of where we are headed.

There is no amount of politics that is going to solve the problems of the people at the grass roots level. Just check the tract record of politics over the past five thousand years and you will see that the people have only been subjects in the organizations that are supposed to be working in our best interest, and who we ourselves have elected and support, or in totalitarian regimes, have no choice at all.

The problem is that governments have a tendency to bloat, and become unmanageable by the constituency, and become inaccessible and as remote as the moon. The only reason that government by the people worked in the thirteen original colonies of the United States to a satisfactory degree, was, that the whole structure was small, and everyone was involved at some level. As governments grow larger and larger they become more and more remote, even though we can vote in the elections that occur every two, four, or six years. Once the elected official is installed in the nations capital, that official then comes under the influence of other forces that might have a totally different agenda than what the voters might have envisioned, or expected. Size, is the key word, in that governments only seem to work below a certain size, where the constituency can get directly involved. I believe that this is the reason that so many people don't vote. They feel that it is an a exercise in futility, and to some extent they are right to feel that way.

Another form of attack comes in the subtle disguise of pride, patriotism, and ego. Pride to me is just a form of self adulation, and if you are a proud person, any one who wants to push an agenda forward, can put us at odds with ourselves just by appealing to our pride, and compelling us to do things that we would consider appalling, such as taking up arms and killing people that we don't know, or know nothing about, and have not threatened us directly in anyway. Pride like our appendix, is an outdated structure. I would rather say, *I love being an American*, than saying I am proud to be American. The latter immediately gives us a cross to bear, and we all know what happens then; eventually we get nailed to them.

Patriotism to me is a way of looking at all the good things that are associated with America; the beauty, the freedom of movement and speech, the Constitution and The Bill of Rights. That said; I don't delude myself into thinking that we live in a perfect bubble. I know many people that take patriotism to the extreme and exclaim; my country, love it or leave it, as if there is no room for improvement. As long as there is human fallibility there will always be room for improvement.

Insults are another form of attack. I have come to

understand that insults are a means of venting frustration by someone who finds it very hard to say what they mean in a more direct and pro-active manner. Someone who hurls insults at anyone is afraid to speak about the real motive that is behind the attack, which is usually fear and is something that very few individuals are willing to disclose about themselves. Fear to most people is considered a sign of weakness, when in reality it is one of our strongest allies. However, the fear I speak of here is not the fear that comes to warn us of danger, but the fear that we hold on to even if there is no eminent danger or is triggered by some past experience, or belief. This kind of fear is what produces insults, and before reacting in a hostile manner I would prefer to try and reassure the person that I am no threat, and this usually helps to defuse a dangerous situation. Insults show the distress of the person doing the insulting and have nothing to do with me anyway. Don't give way to cheap shots.

This is a premise that is hard for most to accept, because we are taught that we are totally separate individuals and that we have no connection with each other. This is an erroneous belief. We are connected by the source of the cosmic creation and what we do to others we do to ourselves. We have a hard time accepting this postulate due to our participation in the collective insanity that is plaguing our world at this time, and is obvious by the effect of post traumatic syndrome that most soldiers suffer after returning from a war. A mental trauma that comes from having to breach our basic beliefs about killing and all the other atrocities that we experience in battle situations. This trauma is less pronounced if the war is justified and the reason for participating is prompted by a real threat, but we haven't been involved in a justified war since the end of World War II. The less justified, the more heinous it appears to the psyche, and the more mental trauma it will inflict on the victim.

People at this time are very ungrounded, and it is easy to divide them from each other, eliminating the possibility of any kind of united front, and unity is the only way for people to push through any kind of agenda of their own. Political parties conduct caucuses in order to come to some agreement about their motives and to consolidate their efforts. Well, the general citizenry should also have caucuses at local levels, and then representatives of the local levels could go on to participate in national caucuses. We are too fragmented in our political participation and there is no cohesive mind that speaks for us. Our congress and senate are supposed to accomplish this representation for us, but again there is no united coalition of the citizenry to speak loudly enough to counter balance the voice of special interest groups that also have the advantage of big money on their side.

Ego is certainly another form of self attack, unless we learn to put it on a short leash. When the ego is in full control, there is very little intellectual or humanistic control over our actions, and our true heart felt feelings are totally compromised. The ego is an instinct that comes from a time when we were not yet capable of making fully informed decisions, and the need for quick action in the face of danger was imperative. That instinct is still with us, but does not always serve us well in a sentient world society, and can create more damage than good. We need to recognize that, and learn to engage our consciousness before we turn the ego loose. We can always free the dragon if the situation calls for it, and we will feel good that we were able to control this powerful entity that resides within us, who when analyzed, reveals itself to be our killer instinct personified. This is not an easy task, as I can personally attest to, and requires practice, a constant vigil, and awareness to be able to jump out ahead of the ego; it is very quick and can move beyond our grasp at lightening speed. So be aware all the time, its just another challenge in the long list of challenges we face in our daily lives.

It is one thing to be attacked from an external source, and yet another to be attacked from within. how many times in our lives or even during a day, do we relive situations that we would in retrospect, have handled differently, or made a different decision. These can become a constant source of irritation and self denigration when our memories return to a certain situation, usually triggered by something that reminds us of that time and place. Some of these can be what we might consider major decisions, while some may be a lack of response to something that was said or done. If we visit these painful memories enough times, they can become obsessions that haunt us like a predator, causing serious damage to our self esteem, and eliminating any chance of well being, and sometimes leading to depression, that can eventually lead to physical problems as well.

This mental reiteration of what could have been, can

certainly lead to psychosis. No one has the ability to hurt us more than ourselves, and in reality, believe it or not, we are the only ones that can hurt us. Some of our problems may have been strictly circumstantial or out of our control, but the wounded mind seldom analyzes its way to a logical conclusion or solution. I believe that the ego has a lot to do with keeping us nailed to the proverbial cross and seriously hinders us in finding a way out of the psychic maze that has an entrance but no exit. Until we come face to face with our fears and obsessions, and understand that there is something we can do to relieve our pain, we will be constantly reminded that we screwed up, and continuously reminded of our failures at every available opportunity, drawing the curtains and shutting out the light, and in the darkness of our regrets, we stagnate.

There is a shamanic ceremony that is called stalking, and I describe it in the chapter on Religion. In brief, the painful situation or memory is relived during the ceremony and the full impact of the memory is felt, not with the usual fear, hate, and loathing, but with intense emotions that will bring it to the for front of your perceptions. At this point, the offensive situation is offered up to the quantum intelligence of the universe that you have already established contact with in the preliminaries of setting up the ceremony. The result is, relieving the mental burden from the mind and removing one more of those rocks we all carry around in that sack on our backs, we refer to as our unwanted baggage. This baggage is energy that is then returned back to creation, and for us it produces pure relief. Energy that can now be employed in a more joyous manner. I have experience this relief and joy myself, and felt the buoyancy when a weight is removed. This ceremony can be performed over and over until all the garbage has been eliminated, and is recommended to be performed daily, or as often as possible, since as fallible humans, we can accumulate bad experiences on a daily basis, especially if we have to interact with our fellow human being on a regular basis, such as work or even at play. I might note here, that there are other methods that can be employed for never having to absorb that kind of attack at all and are covered in the chapter; My Path.

Attacks come at us in many forms and degrees of intensity, from subtle innuendo to sharper and more stinging comments to outright physical abuse, but they are all intended to do damage to our self worth or put us on the defensive. Many of these attacks can be defused instantly if we are in a state of awareness at all times. We have to realize that attacks are not about us, but are telling us something about the attacker, who is reacting from a fear, hate or prejudicial base. Empathy for an attacker can help us by understanding that they are acting from a chaotic and painful state of mind.

Attacks of any kind only serve to alienate people, and don't produce any positive results, and only serve to alienate people. Relatives and family members are notorious for attacking each other, mostly verbally, but it has the same impact as a physical attack. Some times comments are made, maybe in the form of gossip or directly to an individual, possibly because they don't agree with the course a family member has taken, or something they don't like about them, something in their personal lives. We forget the proverb: Let he who is without sin, cast the first stone. Most often we attack in others what we see in ourselves, and don't like.

We even attack our own children when we are frustrated at their behavior. The problem with attacking people, is that there is a malicious intent behind the action, or even anger. Certainly there is no love, compassion, or understanding involved. Children do not respond well to attacks from parents or anyone else. It is also mentally injuring. If a lesson is to be imparted successfully, the only thing that is going to keep the channels open, is a moderate approach, one executed with genuine concern and an amicable demeanor, and also show that we can follow our own advise. Don't say one thing and do another.

A big percentage of the people in prisons or on death row are there because they were physically or mentally abused in childhood, and the lack of interest in the penal system of instituting rehabilitation programs just make this number rise by the day. There are many offenders that are not hardened criminals and could be helped, but once they are subjected to the influence of seasoned criminals, the doors close on any kind of salvation. We put people in prisons and then try to forget about them.

Now prisons are going commercial, a business, and like any other business needs inmates to make a profit, and so being a criminal becomes a way of life. It is not that criminals are inherently evil, they are just a product of where they are coming from. Some one with a criminal background can not be returned to their original environment, they need to be helped to start a whole new life, with love and understanding. There should be facilities to re-educate and facilities to help criminals purge their minds of the anger, fear and animosity that they hold for the society that created them in the first place. I understand that this approach would not work with all criminals. Some are too far gone or insane, and can no longer be reached, but there is a significant number of offenders that are not yet case hardened, and could be helped back to lead crime free lives.

The United States has the highest number of people in prison per ca-pita, than any other country in the world, and a lot of these offenders are imprisoned on misdemeanor offenses, such as possession of small quantities of marijuana, petty theft and other crimes that should not be prison offenses. All of this constitutes forms of attack, from and by people that are totally disconnected from each other and from source.

Our God of Love says, Love thy neighbor and thine enemies as you would Love yourself. Well lets start there. Most people do not love themselves, which in turn makes them incapable of loving anyone else. I would surmise, that is where we are going to have to start, in the recuperation of our own humanity by accepting and loving ourselves. Again, only something that the individual can accomplish with his will, intent, and any useful process that he might find along his path.

Religion in its simplest form could help, but more often than not, is embedded in contradiction and ideology, only creating more separation between the different religions and its adherents, and only creates a field of competition that has very little to do with the salvation of humanity. That is why I so strongly advise the individual to scrutinize his or her beliefs, in order to come to more heart felt conclusion.

Help is only going to come from within. That is where the Ten Commandments came from, within, from our hearts and best intentions not only for others but for our selves as well. Salvation from outside ourselves will never come, and if there is a God, it works from within, from the soul level, from what to us is the unknown, but may someday be revealed. We really don't need to idealize the universal workings or intentions of God; It is written in our DNA and is accessible to everyone.

Does it always take a calamity to get the attention of people? I hope not, or rather I hope that we are evolving to the point where we begin to see some light before the hammer falls on our heads and it's too late to salvage this blue jewel in the void. We still have 5 billion years of sunlight left according to science, but at the rate that we are attacking this planet with our avarice, there is not much that is going to be left in another millennium for future people to enjoy. It took roughly five billion years [we are half way through the expected life of our sun] to get to the point where we could walk upright and begin to use primitive tools, and only about three hundred thousand years to advance ourselves to the point we are today. If we continue to follow this exponential curve of expanding our population and using up resources, we are going to exhaust our finite supply of raw materials in a very short time.

I have read scenarios about the possibility of mining other worlds of our solar system for metals and other resources, and I suppose that its not impossible to accomplish. But, can you imagine the cost of such an undertaking, and the added impact on the ecology it would create. Simple metals such as bauxite or copper would become as expensive as gold is now, or worse. Unless a more efficient and less polluting means of propulsion is invented for our space born vehicles, the consequences to our environment would be catastrophic. I realize that it is the dream of some people to strike out into the void, as explorers and colonizers of other worlds, which in my youth I entertained as well. It is a dazzling and alluring concept for our imaginations to entertain. Now that I am older and have my feet more firmly on the ground, I realize that we are going to have to set our house in order before we entertain the possibility of shooting for the stars. And, we are going to have to come up with a better and more efficient way of slipping the surly bonds of earth. One that does not cause tons of pollution every time we step outside of our atmosphere.

We need to quit attacking everything that comes within our grasp, and pause for a few moments in geological time and take some soundings on what it is we are doing and why. It won't hurt us and may serve to ground us, and make us realize that there are still many challenges for us to sink our teeth into, right here on planet earth. Space travel at this juncture in time is tantamount to putting the cart before the horse. If we can't clean up our own house, what are the odds that we will take care of other worlds. Although, exploitation would probably be the true motive for anyone financing such a venture at present.

Challenges abound for us. Our transportation is in serious need of an efficiency expert or hundreds of them, that can solve the problems of fuel consumption or alternative methods of propulsion. I stated this previously, but I reiterate, if we run out of bio fuels, our flying days are over, but I suppose airplanes would make great recyclable material. We may actually have to go back to sailing ships. In sailing days we had the perfectly ecological means of transportation, and an engine could be installed in case we run into the doldrums. I know, that would be considered regression by most people, but sometimes backtracking to find the right route is not regression, it only means that we got lost and are now searching out a better path. Sailing ships certainly make use of a very renewable resource; wind. This would probably put and end to the mega cruise ship and wind powered ships would probably have to be limited in size.

One area of research needed is, the matter of mass land freight transportation. It would be so much more efficient to transport large quantities of goods by rail, than to have a million eighteen wheelers on the road, traveling from coast to coast using million of gallons of fuel, and creating hazardous conditions on the highways. Of course, the oil companies love this excess, since this mode of shipping uses up more fuel. Just another form of attack on the environment for the sake of profits.

We the people need to attack these problems with the same zeal that created them in the first place. We have the ability to turn our enthusiasm in any direction we want and use our insatiable drive to solve our problems.

We evolved and survived because of this drive and enthusiasm, and it meant driving as hard as we could just to stay ahead of what nature was confronting us with. However as we became less vulnerable to forces that surrounded us, I think something important slipped by us: We need to adjust our drive as we rise in our status out of the food chain, and not drive as hard as if we were still in our basic survival mode. We have survived nature so far, and so, we now need to survive ourselves. If war is a historical indicator, then we are becoming our own worst enemy, but, we can change that, and become our own best friend by starting to feel a connection with the earth and to each other.

Chapter 4

Religion

Since the beginning of time, man has looked outside himself for a higher power that would define his existence and give us a purpose, and guide our existence, and a possible road to what we define as our higher self. It is also the possibility of moving from chaos into harmony with our surroundings, and our fellow man. Unfortunately it has not always worked that well, and in many cases has caused more strife than harmony, especially when different religious beliefs collide. Its a hallmark of the inflexibility of humanity, and our inability to see similarities, and only look at the deviations that exist in dogma. It is another testimonial to mans ability to go to war and killing his fellow human beings for the sake of ideology that in most cases changes with time as the culture evolves.

Religious doctrine in books such as the Christian Bible,

Islamic Qur'an, Jewish Torah, Hindu Bagavad-Gita, and the Buddhist Tipitaka, are an amalgam of the spiritual and social values of a particular region, and though supposedly these writings were inspired by the divine hand of a supreme deity, a lot of the content of these books reflect the laws and social order of the people they pertain to. It would probably be difficult to ascertain whether the motivation for social order and stability came before or after the need for the spiritual and religious aspects of humanity, or possibly evolved hand in hand, with social order, establishing the laws of community, backed by the omnipotent power of a deity.

Organized religion takes the basic spiritual beliefs of a group of people or region and with time works those beliefs into dogma, which usually become the inflexible guide lines of the religion. The councils and hierarchy in any time period will render their interpretation of the dogma and what that particular deity represents, which in early man, were elemental in nature. Most modern deities are monotheistic [the belief in one God], along with a retinue of aids; angels, etc. Dogma will always be subject to reinterpretation by the subsequent leaders of the religion, and usually reflects what their point of view is, that over long periods of time may not even resemble the original belief system.

Have you ever sat ten people down next to each other and whispered a sentences in the ear of the first person in the line, and ask them to pass the message down to the next person until the message reaches the last one in the line? I have never seen the original message faithfully repeated through the chain, and in most cases the message does not even resemble the original at all. This is a fun parlor game to play, but imagine what happens to a message that is passed on down through several millennium, where different leaders of a religion as it progresses through time attempt to interpret a scripture, or attempt to change it for their convenience, or the convenience of the state. O course, this would only apply to an oral history, and most religious texts have been written down for thousands of years, so that any changes were deliberate, and not the result of our parlor game.

Religion and the state have never been as separate as we would like them to be; not since the Roman Empire embraced Christianity, where the church and state went hand in hand. Contrary to the original intent of saving people from damnation, they usually wind up as institutions with the aim of controlling the population, so it makes sense that the church and state would more often than not, embrace in their common goal. Of course the bible and the other books of religious law are supposed to keep that particular faith constant, but as it turns out, even those texts are often rewritten to suit the beliefs of an individual or group of people. This is particularly true of an autocratic society.

What I am going to disclose here, is my personal belief, and many other people in the modern era: that religious beliefs should be left to the discretion of the individual, after all, that is who they are going to be serving. This does not mean that an individual cannot participate in an organized order of ideology, but having the freedom to agree or disagree with the interpretation and the teachings as set down by and supported by the leaders of a religion.

Some would call such an action heresy, but I would call it freedom of religion, giving us the power to choose what we believe, and not placing our beliefs in the hands of someone who is supposedly the true representative of god, since I believe that we all are true representatives of the divine. This would be another step in moving towards being a true autonomous individual, which is something that most organized structures find repugnant, since it undermines the authority and control over the populace. No doubt, ego plays a role in those who try to undermine our humanity. The real need is within ourselves and that is the only place the warrior has any hope of accomplishing anything positive.

I believe there is no need for dogma. For instance: the Christian beliefs are based on the preachings of Jesus Christ, and I see no need to re-interpret his words with any of our own meandering thoughts.

The interpretation factor is strongly illustrated; taking for example the fractures and factions that have splintered off from the Christian religion, and I don't think its because of the basic teachings of Christ; its because of the added fluff of dogma, with the rules and regulation that are mostly inventions of man. Most religions around the world have their spin-offs, or have changed the dogma because they did not agree with its content. There is nothing wrong with changing something to suit the practitioner, we could even say this is one of the basic forms of freedom and evolution. We have to sift through our prescribed religious dogma, what ever that may be, and and take in what fits and makes sense.

Organized religions have a tendency to become over convoluted and cumbersome. Religions that are thousands of years old, have a lot of time to throw ideas onto the pyramid and create a megalith where the basic truths get buried, never to be seen again.

One aspect that I disagree with is; a religion that supports unlimited procreation from its flock. It may have been a good idea two thousand years ago, but today and in the future, it is going to be a serious threat to the survival of the human race. Many will argue that we are just lambs in the flock of the divine, to be led to salvation by the interpreters of the scriptures, who are only men, regardless of the station or elevation that we the lambs have accorded them.

It has been my observation that people are very prone to allowing someone else to tell them what to think and believe, and I think it goes back to the power that we instill in people who claim to be closer to heaven than you or I, when in reality we are all powerful human beings that don't know that the individual in an ocean of individuals has the same power and vulnerability as the next man, no matter how scholarly they may be. We have a tendency to elevate others over us and then we complain that we don't like the way things are going, and this is never going to change until we realize that we are all the same and are all connected to one-another via the heritage of coming from the same source.

There are other sources of dogma. When the Romans adopted the Christian concept, and because they were then a very powerful nation, they did every thing they could to discourage the original Christians from practicing or spreading their beliefs. This was usually accomplished by force of arms.

I think this tendency to elevate others above us, comes partly from the fear of damnation that has been kept alive down through the ages and has been so effective in the subjugation of the masses throughout much of our history. It is either the fear of God or the fear of our neighbors, and it all comes from somewhere outside of our selves. It is very effective, mostly because we have relinquished our self determination, or because we have a strong propensity to be apathetic or just plain lazy in thinking our way though the maze of information; we believe only the scholarly can interpret. We are bombarded daily with so much information and misinformation, that it keeps us so busy, we have no time to reflect on our own perceptions.

Turn off your television sets or don't watch as often. Believe me, you are not going to miss much. Every escape we try to find in life, can turn into an addiction, just like alcohol and drugs; something to fill in the precious time that could be used for real contemplation. In my opinion, the media is not designed to illuminate or even inform, but to keep us occupied and in fear.

More and more people are living in urban communities, with homes that are spaced just a few feet from each other and affording very little opportunity to commune with the natural world or any of its wild creatures, or really free inhabitants, and the beauty that can only be found in such surroundings, where the breath of our original spirit can be found.

Man originally made deities of many of the occurrences in nature, such as the wind, rain, thunder, lightning, water, as well as mountains, trees, rivers, and too many to mention here. Some of us still revere them to this day; not in the form of deities, but as wonders of a creation or an evolution that can stir the soul when encountered in their pristine majesty.

Early man, as he became more conscience of his surroundings, must have been in such awe that he was compelled to create Gods of everything in his surroundings because it exerted such a powerful impact on their lives. As man became more able to think outside the box, they probably took these deities and organized them into complex structures that would eventually evolve into organized religions, and would eventually lead to the belief in one creator.

One of the first belief systems to surface was more than likely the Shamanic culture, where one man or woman was trained by an already established Shaman in the ways of healing, contacting the spirit world, finding spirit helpers, advising, using herbal medicines and many other services that were all for the purpose of helping a tribe or village to sustain a healthy mind, body, and spirit in an environment that very often offered overwhelming challenges for survival. Evidence of Shamanism has been discovered in all parts of the world, and it has also been observed that the tools and techniques used in ritual, healing, and journeying are very similar no matter where they were discovered or uncovered. This gives Shamanism a distinctive validity, which seems to endows the practice with a fundamental universality that so many of the modern religions don't seem to attain.

The validity of Shamanism probably stems from the purity of service that was required of the practitioner and his or her helpers. An effective Shaman was a powerful member of a tribe and was revered by the people they served. They were likely, one of the first roles of true service ever established. In order for true Shamans to be effective; meant that they could not abuse their power within their community without loosing the connection and respect of the people, and there by loosing their effectiveness. The Shaman acted as the link between his clients and the spiritual realm and was able to lead his people to a place where they could then begin to effect their own healing, as I believe that every human being has the power to heal themselves, if some of the stumbling blocks that hold us bound to negativity, doubt, guilt, and self recrimination are removed and cleared away so that the light of truth can shine through, opening and enabling us to tap into the power of our own bodies healing system.

The Shaman to me represents one of those quantum leaps in evolution that periodically mark the advancement of the human species in its upward assent from animal to sentient being.

This is a practice that has survived to the present day, and actually has had a resurgence in modern times, mostly I think, because of its ability to produce real results in our quest for healing, enlightenment and clearing our minds of useless clutter, enabling us to *see*. It is very difficult to *see through*, if the mind is bogged down with a lot of useless or outdated ideas that no longer serve, or ever did at all for that matter. *Seeing* is very different from just looking, and when someone says to me, I *see*, I take that to mean, that this person has somehow been able to move past the barrier of ordinary lies and internal dialogue that presents a wall that blinds us to reality, and can now access the truth.

It has been said that one mans lies are another mans reality and visa verso, but I do not agree with this conclusion, mostly because I believe that down at the core of our being, we all know what is right and what is wrong, and are only able to fore go the truth, because of all the miss information that we are programmed with from the day we are born to the day we die. Concepts that are offered to us at a very young and impressionable age are very hard to change later in life. That is why I am of the opinion that some of the most important concepts that define us as humans should be taught at a very early age, thus giving our offspring the foundation of a broader view and their place in the cosmos. What we think is what we are destined to do and manifest. Otherwise we follow our destinies, never knowing that destiny can be changed, thus altering our course, and making a positive difference in our walk through this existence.

At the core of all religions we would find a theology that is sincere in its efforts to instill the concept of God essence in its adherents and also exposes people to the commandments of a particular religion that mostly reflect the morality that has grown with us as we have attempted to become more civilized. Commandments are usually based on common sense and how we would prefer to be treated by others. We would certainly not want someone to kill us, steal from us, accuse us falsely, profane us or our deities, etc etc, and in general do things that would make life uncomfortable or down right dangerous.

In the Christian view, the ten commandments fall a little short of describing that which we should do and not do to each other, but a lot of those commandments would fall under the category of rules that allow us to have some measure of peace and security as we interact with one another.

That is why I so strongly believe that these basic concepts should be taught, not only in places of worship, but also in our schools. One hour a week is not going to instill morality in anyone, and what is the use of over emphasizing science and mathematics if all the scientists turn out to be mad men and women {someone without conscience, or moral guidance}.

No religion in schools you say! Morality and good social practices have nothing to do with religion. These are the basic premises of a healthy society and should be taught in the home first during the most impressionable age [before school], and reinforced in the classroom, where we are first introduced to society.

A note here from my son who is a middle school teacher of English and knows what he is talking about when he requested that I mention that he believes strongly and by direct experience as a teacher: "that if our young people were balanced, physically, mentally and spiritually, academics, which now represents and insurmountable proposition to a great number of students, would become a cake walk, and only those with true mental disabilities—a very small number—would require special services or special care."

I believe that our children today are swimming in a world of contradiction, with very little to anchor them to any worthwhile reality. Cell phones and cars don't replace a strong and loving family environment, but its the only thing that they have to latch on to when the parents are not willing to be a viable influence in the upbringing of their own children. At present it is all being dumped in the lap of the teachers, as if they were responsible for the total upbringing of the young, and they might be a positive influence if their hands were not bound by the law. How can a teacher maintain discipline in the classroom if they have to walk on broken glass, its impossible. Yet, the administrators seem to be blind to the real problems teachers face, or in most cases only care about test scores and how they compare with the rest of the world.

I believe that we emphasize scholastic achievement because it is an external discipline, and we don't have to look inside our spiritual nature for any of the answers, we only have to employ the use of that super computer that sits on our shoulders, ignoring the imbalance that we are creating for ourselves and for our off springs.

A balance can only be achieved by putting equal emphasizes on every thing that we have discovered. Life is like walking a tight rope, a middle of the road exercise, and a vantage point from which we can view all possibilities. Which ever way we fall, right or left, we can no longer see the other side. At that point we become entrenched, and is at the root of all conflict, being unable to see anyone else and their condition or point of view, and not being able to discern that what we dislike in others is the same things that we dislike in our selves. We pick up our swords and try to root out the problem, never realizing that the problem is in us, and that is where the healing has to begin. No one has ever healed anyone with the stroke of a sword, inevitably, that just adds more weight to the load that we are already carrying on our shoulders. More baggage.

There are people who call themselves atheists, and believe that there is no such thing as a God or higher power in the universe as far as they can discern, and they could be right. I respect their right to that belief, but I suspect that at least some of these people have had a bad experience with organized religion, and think, any thing that can become corrupted to the point of killing other humans for the sake of an idea, can't have anything to do with a supposed God of love, and realizing that what takes love out of the God equation, is man himself.

In the Christian religion there is the belief that there is a Devil out there, and most other religions believe in forces that try to mislead us on our altruistic path through life. I believe that there are dark forces that try to pull us from a path of love and light, after all, we do inhabit a universe that functions on the principles of opposites, such as positive and negative, light and dark, love and hate, sickness and health, up and down, and the list could go on and on. Could this be the reason that we have the capability to make choices in what ever we do, think and say? And, a choice we do have.

Something that in my opinion we do not exercise enough. It is easier to stay in the groove than to jump of the track and risk the encounter with the infinite possibilities that riding on a track cannot offer, or lead to change. Evolution always means change, if our volition is engaged. We have, however, from childhood, been taught not to rock the boat, and it is not surprising that we don't think for ourselves, since the consequences are often traumatic in the use of mental or physical abuse that can even be lethal; such as burning at the stake.

There is no doubt that religious fervor has led to some of the most impressive architecture that exists on the planet, with cathedrals and mosques that reach to the heavens, and are more of a monument to the creative nature of the human spirit than an offering to God, for God resides in ever thing that surrounds us in the natural world, including all the flora and fauna, and I can't think of a more magnificent temple than that of the human, the temple that is home to life that is animated by spirit, the energy of the cosmos, and the place, for us, from which all perception stems from, be it spiritual or physical.

Places of worship are meant to awe the congregation, and rightly so, for most of these places of worship, especially in the classical style are quite spectacular and ornate, or in in the case of the more modern churches, less ornate, less stuffy, but always with very impressive appointments.

As a child, I was the only Presbyterian attending St. Joseph's Catholic school, because my mother thought that they practiced more discipline than the public school in Taos,

New Mexico. Nevertheless, I was still required to go with the rest of my class to mass on Holy Days, and I could not help but be in awe at the splendor of the ornate alter, the gilded castle like structure behind the alter, all the bigger than life statues of Christ, Mother Mary, all the saints, and the beautiful stained glass windows.

On Sunday morning, my mother and some of her family would go to the First Presbyterian Church for Sunday school and then services, and I would think how austere our church was, but to me our church had a warmer feeling than the cathedral, which was much more ornate, but to me had a feeling of intractability and severe consequences. I love to sing, and one of the attributes of our church was the singing of hymns between ten minutes of preaching. I also felt that this institution was more accessible and more fluid, and forgiving. Later in life I did become a Catholic, because of marriage constraints, but by that time, knowing that religion is mostly external, and that any religion I was moved to participate in would not change what I was at the core of my being.

Religion has been at the core of many a conflict, and remains the impetus of conflict to this day. Not all wars are fought over religious ideologies, but a big percentage have, and by people who have been taught from childhood that killing is a sin, so at age eighteen, we stick a gun in their hands, train then how to use weapons effectively and ship them off to some foreign land to kill other humans that they don't even know or know about, and then wonder why they come back home mentally twisted, when they just violated one of their core beliefs, instilled in them at a very early and impressionable age. One of the Ten Commandments states, thou shalt not kill, and has no amendments to it with regard to whether its an enemy or a perceived enemy, and Jesus is quoted as saying; love thine enemies as you love yourself. Something else that I was vaguely aware of until recently, was the alien concept of; love and honer thy self, which is the spring board for loving an honoring others. If we do not love, honor and respect ourselves, then we have no basis for applying it anywhere else.

Wars of politics and ideologies are seldom fought by the instigators, but are fought and financed by the general public, who had very little to do with starting the conflict in the first place, and who are usually seduced by pride and ego and misplaced trust in their leaders. People would like to believe that once elected, their representatives are going to honor their campaign promises. Without the constant and watchful eye of the constituency, who might have to face these representatives and look them in the eye to make them understand that we are serious about our intentions, trust is misplaced, since there is, an overwhelming amount of influence from special interests. We allow our representatives to do as they please, and then wonder why we are always getting kicked in the backside. Government by the people, says it all in the first four words; it's an interactive game and we can't win if we don't play.

Morality and altruism needs reinforcement, and seems to occur naturally only in a very few individuals. The darker side of the human psyche seems to dominate us, even when our original intentions were good. Its probably because the darker side is more seductive in that it feeds our greed with the material wealth that we have so come to worship in this modern era. Toys abound, some of them useful, some of them just toys that only feed the bottom line of industry, Tomorrow a new model will be available with one more bell or whistle, and your old one will be tossed in the great heap of outdated technology in some remote eastern country, where the seepage of toxins will pollute their environment. We don't realize that polluting anywhere on earth is still polluting our own environment. Eventually it will get back to us.

Back to the subject of war, I don't want to give the impression that I believe that all wars are unjustified. There are wars that are thrust upon us, where freedom and annihilation are so eminent, that there is no choice but to take up arms and fight back. World War ll, in my opinion, is one example of a justifiable war, where one very intelligent, charismatic, and insane person that has totally lost touch with their humanity, motivated by hate, vows to subjugate the entire planet, there is not much of a choice left but to fight back.

However, since the end of World War ll, propelled by the shear inertia of a war that saw such a massive build up and mobilization of men, arms, and technological advances, the two super powers that remained standing, did not seem to have been able to put their foot on the brake pedal, and continued head long into one conflict after another. One of these super powers has had to back off because of bankruptcy, and the other one is rapidly heading in the same direction, with a national debt that is reaching astronomical proportions while our esteemed representatives are trying to cut what little benefits there are for the middle class and the poor. At the same time giving themselves exorbitant raises and benefits, leaving me to ponder the sanity of such a government. My observations are; that most institutions, and governments included, eventually become self serving. I guess its easy to loose sight of a lofty goal when there is so much wealth and power passing through the hands of only a few.

So what has all this got to do with religion? Well! There have always been those who worship the golden calf, whose God is affluence, and who put pedal to the metal when it comes to amassing wealth. Religion is not just about God, but can encompass anything that we humans can do with religious fervor and conviction. Granted, it does take some intelligence and perseverance to attain a state of wealth, but I believe that it is more a matter of greed and desire that promotes mega wealth. It really is not that difficult to achieve, since it is one of the baser traits of humanity, which could be elevated by the distribution of wealth on those who are responsible for supporting the structure by means of their labor and life commitment. One man can not amass wealth without the support of a broad base of loyal employees, and consumers. It is ridiculous and a slap in the face, that only those at the top get the big bonus; the biggest going to the top dog who needs it less than those at the base of the pyramid.

The problem with amassing wealth by one individual is that it cuts out the opportunities for thousands of others to make a business for themselves, because amassed money has so much leverage that the only option the masses have, is to work for the money people for a very small percent of the profits. Small business and mom and pop operations are being systematically eradicated from the world stage by mega corporations that despite their claim to serve the consumer with lower prices are not really meeting this claim, with inflationary prices in commodities continuing to rise every time we go to the store. But again, as with most all other matters of human interaction, there is the matter of perception and awareness, which I am only stating here with the hope that these words enables a change in the way we do business, and the reasons that might lead to a more cooperative way of living, equitable to all.

As far as religions are concerned, they need to practice what they preach and a need to inject more love into their practice, and not so much fear of retribution from a supreme power who is supposed to be a God of Love. I personally don't believe that God judges us, we judge others as well as ourselves, instead of employing forgiveness and moving on to some equitable solution of our problems. We don't realize that conflict always happens for a reason, and we never ask ourselves, what part did I play in creating this scornful circumstance.

Judging others is just a way that humans use to hide their fears and insecurities. There is no good or evil. Everything happens for a reason, and those we consider to be evil are just a product of where they are coming from. Something happened in their formative years to twist their minds and create an imbalanced human. Childhood abuse is one of the biggest contributors in the creation of insanity in humans, assisted along by social rejection, denied human rights, unwarranted criticism, bigotry, and all other forms of mental cruelty. All of this is a product of our fear and insecurity, and because of the lack of Love for anything, including ourselves. If we were to be taught from a very young age to nurture and expand our innate Love, we would be less likely to wind up living in fear, and conflict would eventually disappear.

In recent times there has been a break with the larger and more organized religions, and has been labeled, the *New Age*, which I think could also carry the label of *Old Age*, since it employs rituals and practices from some of the oldest and more spiritually based belief systems of the old world. They include Shamanism, Hinduism, Buddhism, Native American practices, and Wicca. I believe these practices are more grounding and allow the practitioner to adopt, and choose, what turns the key in the lock, to move the participant in realizing that some significant change or effect has been made in his or her life, in the form of freedom, joyful living and enlightenment. This can lead the individual to a tailored set of beliefs that work for that individual, which no organized religion can offer with their hard and fast dogma, that if violated can lead to being ostracized or worse, being burned at the stake. Not that this practice is used any more, but being burned at the mental stake is just as powerful, but still a form of torture.

These are not Gods rules, they are mans rules, and organized religions are not about to allow any form of free thinking that would lead to loss of control. They say: we have all the answers and all you have to do is pay your dues. Humans have a very strong tendency to follow doctrine or to believe that someone else knows what is best for them. I think it is apathy and lassitude, with no interest in seeking out the truth.

What *New Age* practice proposes is not anarchy, but it does suggest autonomy, where the individual takes responsibility for their well being, beliefs, and consequently, for the actions they take. A well grounded person is the result of connecting with spirit directly, and gives one the middle of the road view, where all things are possible, and all points of view are observable. No judgments are rendered because the observer can *"see"* that there is no evil and there is no devil sitting on our shoulders prompting us to commit crimes against humanity or the environment.

What is recognized, is a faulty program that is running around in our heads that was installed when we were at a very young and impressionable age, and therefore very hard to change after we have reached maturity. There are methods, especially in Shamanism that can allow us to change that programming that in most cases is based on false hoods or social norms and prejudices that only add to the separation of the human race, from each other and everything else in creation.

One of these methods is called stalking, and it entails stalking one's self for those occasions and situations that have caused us pain. Some wounds are so painful that it can drive us crazy or totally insane. There are even those teachings that state that we are here to suffer and only by suffering can we atone or gain redemption. I don't think I ever subscribed to that one, when in actuality we were born unto paradise, and if it seems to be all muddled up its because we have fallen from graceful ways, where lies hold more power than truth.

Stalking therefore entails a ritual where by the seeker brings to the surface, painful memories and misguided actions, and he or she offers it up to the quantum reality of the universe and creation to be dismantled and lifted of the shoulders of the seeker, thus relieving him or her of part of the baggage that we all carry around in our daily lives which only serves to burden us down or make us suffer. These rituals can be learned by anyone and are taught by qualified Shaman that are willing to take on apprentices. Stalking is similar to what psychiatrists do, by facilitating the patient in bringing up deep seated memories of pain and deception, to be analyzed. The problem with this method is that once that pain surfaces, there is no place for it to go, no way of getting rid of it once and for all, and this is where stalking goes the final step to dissolve the problem from our personal existence. The memories don't go away, but its akin to a bomb that has been defused. The energy those memories once held is removed and returned back to us in a pure form.

There are many rituals in Shamanic practice that are effective for healing, both physical and mental as well as spiritual, and mostly work because they effectively lead the seeker to self healing by clearing away the obstacles that have led to sickness; by stress, depression and all the social pressures that we seem to put so much importance on. The body will heal itself, once the path becomes joyous, less encumbered and light is allowed to shine throughout ones perspective. There are guides and power sources to help with these endeavors.

Of course in the world as it stands today, we not only suffer from mental and spiritual depletion, but also the air we have to breathe, the water we have to drink, and the food we eat, all play a very important role in our health and happiness. That is something that the present and future citizens of this world are going to have to address, or we are either going to poison ourselves or wind up as a race of chemical mutants.

In the last few decades there has been much said and written about the advantages of food that is grown organically, which means no chemical fertilizers, and no hydroponically grown food. It means food grown in rich soils enhanced by mulch of organic material, and the use of organic fertilizers. How many people put their leaves out by the curb in the fall for the garbage trucks to take to the dump site? Well, most people do not realize that this is going to cause the depletion of the soil on their properties. Composting should be a priority for everyone, and can be effected with very little effort or cost.

Religion is supposed to give us the tools for salvation; but not in this world. As long as we consign our efforts for salvation to another existence, we are bound to continue to suffer in this one, and as far as I can tell, this existence is the only one we have substantial proof of. Is Heaven for sure or is it a hope prompted by our own desires. Well I for one will not dismiss the possibility, but for sure I do know that this world is real as long as I am alive, and a major portion of our religious beliefs are upheld by pure hope and faith. Faith to me is a form of manifestation, so why not have faith in ourselves, and re-manifest a Heavenly paradise right here where we know for sure we will reap joy and happiness by the product of our own co-creation.

We can't continue to take and never give back anything, for we already know what that produces, and in nature it goes by the term "critical mass", and we also know what comes next; a chain reaction that would alter our reality so much that it would not even resemble what it was before, or ever hope it to be.

In such a scenario, some would survive, and maybe learn the lessons that would permanently change the way man thinks and acts, but what a loss to those who do not survive and the possible pain that would ensue in that chain reaction. The physical world and the universe can survive without us, but we cannot survive without it and the conditions that make life possible. We evolved from a balance of conditions and without a choice nature would maintain that balance for us, and did up to the time that we developed the ability to choose.

All of evolution from the Big Bang to the present, pivots on a fulcrum of balance that if upset leads to extinction, which has occurred many time in the life of the Earth. Since humans have removed themselves from the balance that the natural world imposes, then, by our choices we can move that fulcrum in our favor or disfavor. Something intangible plays a large part in our decisions, other than our intellect, its called the ego [yes the ego again], and since all things in creation have a purpose, then it must be of use to the human who all posses one, although ofttimes seems to be counter productive in our dealings with our fellow humans.

Ego definitely has the proclivity toward grandeur and manifests itself in the colossal works of art and edifice that we produce, but sometimes creates a paradox in our social dealing; domestic, national and international. I believe, ego comes directly from our past when survival was more; act now and ask questions later; when any delay meant annihilation. However, in a world of idealism the threats are not physical, but we seem to perceive them that way, and we jump out with our swords in hand, ready to do battle when a more amicable solutions would have sufficed.

Perhaps the ego is one of the parameters of being human that we need to get a handle on, and become more aware of when it is needed and when to subdue it. Its like the taming of a wild horse. I don't think we have ever considered taming our egos, even if it is obvious that it sometimes leads us astray, and to acts that we later regret. This is an instance where our intelligence can serve us well by making an informed decision before acting; we can always let the tiger loose if need be. We may be coming to a place where we are outgrowing our ego, the same way we outgrew our appendix. I personally believe that our ego will always be useful to us, we just need train ourselves in when not to use it. We need to be able to recognize instances when the ego is damaging and when it can aid our creativity; in other words, we need to domesticate our ego and turn it into a friend, another step in civilizing ourselves. All this needs to occur on an individual basis, but will never come to fruition if we are not aware of its potential. Getting a handle on our fear, would go a long ways toward taming our ego. Fear is a powerful trigger for the ego in many of our conflicts.

The fact that there are so many religions in the world, with so many factions within, and breakaway splinters, with dogma that covers such a wide spectrum of ideologies, confirms to me, that humans have lost or don't have any idea what or who God is or what his plan for us might entail. Of course, this isn't God at work, its just man running around in circles.

In the course of conversations and discussions, some people have said to me that we do not need to believe in God to be a good person, and I agree with them implicitly. For, it is my contention that God can only be found in inner space, and resides in the hearts of every living being, We are the house of God, and that applies to everyone, so why all the diversity of ideologies? Well, beliefs in dogma change and spin-offs are compelled to change things to suit themselves, and it only means that we have not arrived at any truths.

There are many people who profess not to believe in a Creator or higher power, but still lead good productive lives, with cooperation and no more rancor than people who do believe in God. Such people also live loving and inspired lives because whether they know it or not, they are listening to the voice of their hearts, the voice of spirit, the voice of the creator. People who do not believe, and can still maintain a loving relationship with society, actually have an advantage: they do not have to be confused by the myriad of religious philosophies that exist in the world, conscripts that are solely designed to satisfy a whim.

Believing in a Creator, in Spirit, in God, or not believing, is a very simple matter. It is the unbridled human intelligence that has a tendency to run off the end of the world with any concept that tickles our brains and opens avenues of creative thinking, and this applies to the concept of God as well. However, this is a concept that is so basically powerful, that it needs no fine tuning or manipulation by us to make it more valid.

The problem is that we have either forgotten, or are simply too lazy to pay attention to what our higher self is telling us. I believe that we all know what is right and what is wrong at the basic core of our existence. I have observed a strong tendency in humans; to be told what is, and what is not the truth. Of course, what we are taught at an early age, usually overrides the voice of our conscience because we are not taught to listen to ourselves. We are taught to listen to the voices of authority, and it is these authorities that create the dogma we are fed, and what our hearts tell us, takes a place at the back of the bus.

Well, its time to start to listen to ourselves again, and it is time for our teachers, wherever we might encounter them to teach the young to listen to their higher selves. In the

Christian religion for instance, young people are taught to implicitly believe in what the dogma prescribes, depending on what branch of Christianity you are in, ignoring the fact that the bible and other religious books [of any religion] are more in the vane of history books than spiritual texts.

The new testament of the Christian Bible, is to the best of our knowledge, the words and deeds of the life of Jesus Christ on this planet, and is also supposed to represent the driving force of the Christian Religion. But I find very little semblance in the overall practices of Christians to the examples that Jesus Christ exemplified in his actions and his teachings, primarily the exercise of Love in all our words and deeds. Love again has its seat in the heart, and is part of that voice whose purpose is to temper the power of our minds, and our egos, which without that tempering effect, can run off in any direction it chooses, often to our own self made destruction or lowering us to the status of a computer, whose only choice is in the dictates of its program. Our brains are computers, but we as human beings have souls and a connection to the infinite possibilities that the cosmos has to offer. We are the pinnacle of life on this planet, and with that comes an awesome responsibility to honor everything that surrounds us.

It is hard for me to think of God as a being who sits on a throne somewhere, and oversees and judges the actions of humans, and really this depiction seems to be more earthly than heavenly in its acumen, and, if I am to be honest, I could not realistically describe God or Heaven except in earthly terms, and that is what I believe most religions do.

Our Earthly perspective is the only one we have to go by, and we are correct in describing Heaven as resembling some of the most beautiful places on Earth. Deep in the depths of our being, I think we instinctively know that we inhabit a veritable paradise that we are rapidly converting into an artificial landscape of concrete and tarmac, blowing off the tops of mountains, drilling holes everywhere to extract the blood of the Earth, with not even an ounce of gratitude for the abundance that surrounds us.

Where does God reside? Well, for sure in the hearts of all human beings. That is where the voice of reason talks to us, and acts as our guide, moderator, and conscience, and can also be seen in all the marvelous wonders that the universe has to offer. What God is remains a mystery to humanity, and that opinion is based on the myriad interpretations and attempts to quantify the existence of a supreme being and creator.

It may turn out that God is the sum total of everything; that we live in a micro cosmic part of a larger entity, which would suggest that the quantum field is infinite in all directions. In the macro end of the scale, this entity would then be facing the same dilemma we are, with the same questions about his creator and his purpose in his universe. In the micro end of the scale, the atoms and molecules that comprise matter as we know it, would in essence comprise other universes for sub atomic creatures, who would also be pondering their place and purpose in the whole of creation.

My personal view of God is in the life force that gives me the ability to think, question, reason, understand, feel emotion, and most of all the ability to Love. If God is out there observing his creation, it would appear to me that he is of a non interfering nature, and has given us freedom of choice to see where that takes us. Humans have a strong sense of what is right, but to balance the paradox of choice we are also endowed with greed, hate, pride, and ego, which I consider to be lower traits of our natures, and the highest being Love, and compassion. What part of our natures we decide to use as our model for living, lays in that most powerful of attributes: Choice.

I have just begun to understand that within myself, there is a shear rock wall that I have had to scale, a rock wall that represents my ego, fear and chaotic nature, a barrier that if not vanquished will forever hold me back from experiencing harmony, joy and love in my life. How many people do we know that seem to travel from one personal disaster to another. Some will attribute their misfortune to bad luck, usually something that is affecting them from without and which they have no control over. My belief is that we make our own luck by the path that we take. In our course through life there are many forks in the road, some leading up and some leading down, and I believe we have a strong propensity to choose the path of least resistance. Sometimes we are shoved down some of these dead end roads by circumstances beyond our control, and sometimes they are of our own choosing. Either way, back tracking is difficult but not impossible. It also entails scaling the precipice from the very bottom to the top, where we can at last get a clear view of our plight. From the top of that precipice we can begin to dismantle the tangled and convoluted ideologies that keep us in fear and chaos, allowing us the straighter path of love and light, and the only means to freedom, personal evolution, joy, happiness; this is what real salvation is.

Many paths we could consider destiny, because they are the accepted modes of our own culture and can be followed with the faith that they might be a valid path. And sometimes we never stop to question or deviate from anything that we have been led to or taught. The prescribed path of any culture is usually supported by the belief in a deity and the fear of transgressions against God. These are usually instilled in us at a very early age, and become second nature in our make-up.

We, however have the ability to question our values and should do so on a regular basis. This is one of our gifts and should not be wasted. Many of societies norms and values are handed down from one generation to the next, and become so entrenched that it is difficult to swim against the tide. Many well meaning people have been turned into martyrs for trying to introduce a new idea into the system, and by living the life they feel is right for them.

The only one I can change is myself, and evolution starts with one step and then a second and so on. I am one of the steps along the way to enlightenment, and I feel compelled to reach out and try to engage with others that might be feeling that a change in our course and perspectives might be in order.

I feel that I am fortunate to have encountered and later sought out teachers and modalities that have set me on a path to an open way of thinking, by clearing much of the clutter from my mind, that used to delineate my way of thinking and controlled many of my actions. Now, when I look back on the person I was, I see how most every reaction and act was dictated by the program that had been installed in me as a child, as a result of the domestication process that took place early on. I feel like I was operating in automatic mode in my younger years of life, and I realize that I made many mistakes as a result of going against myself, even when it did not feel good to pursue a certain course of action.

Domestication is a powerful force. It guides us on the accepted and prescribed path of ideologies that our respective societies adhere to. And, we have the choice of staying in line with everyone else, or stepping out and reevaluating why and where this line is heading.

My parents and my teachers, wherever I might have encountered them, felt so strongly about not only their beliefs, but their prejudices, hates and misinformation, that they, without any conscious consideration of the consequences, passed them on to me, and I, not knowing any better, took them to heart.

I don't mean to lay blame on anyone, since this is the formula that most of society subscribes to. I know my parents did the best they could with the information they had and where they were coming from. They came from a generation that did not rock the boat, and the prevailing philosophy was: you adhere to what you have learned about the so called truths up to the point of maturity and beyond. This is not to say that they did not learn academics, it just means that their philosophy on life did not change after a certain point in life. I remember my parents not deviating from their domestication through-out their entire lives. It made them rather predictable and easy to dodge. I certainly am not condemning everything I was taught as a child. Some of it I will keep forever and feel it was quite valid, but I want the freedom to weed out those premises that no longer serve me, or my interaction with the rest of society.

I now understand that there are very few truths in life. Most of what we call truths are just fabrications from ideas that we use to justify our actions, for good or ill. There are only a few truths that apply to our survival. We have to eat, sleep, and breathe in order to sustain our physical being. Everything else we do is an invention of our minds or something that we have been taught, and the point is, we have a choice in the final character that we decide to model in our lives. The human being is bombarded by so much information that it is hard for us to make sense of all or any of it. The best way is to start with the basics of our existence.

The first truth: we have to eat and drink water to sustain our physical well being. It necessitates finding a means of obtaining food, either by earning money to buy it, or be able to grow ones own food. The latter is the best, but not an option for us who live in a city, where cultivation is minimal at best, so we have to try and create a career that will give us the monetary resources we need to survive. Of course what we eat is of the utmost importance to our health.

It would be very beneficial to those involved if we could all acquire a plot of land large enough to grow our own produce and possibly raise some farm animals. The benefits of organic growing is the recommended way of working the land and insuring the purity of the crops, eliminating the need for chemical additives. Many of societies health problems stem from the impurity of the foods that we consume especially in the high tech world, where herbicides and insecticides, and genetically engineered products are preferred to organic farming, mostly in the interest of super high yields, and profit.

The second truth: we have to sleep, which leads us to many more aspects of our resourcefulness in securing a comfortable domicile, and again leads us back to the aspect of acquiring finances. The owners of a plot of land could build their own homes, another obstacle to people living in a city. It can be done, but city codes have to be adhered to.

The third truth: we have to breathe, is an immediate truth that we can not ignore for more than a few minutes. We can go without water for an extended period of time and food even longer. The purer the air the better for our health. The air we breathe has never existed without some form of pollution. There have always been volcanic eruption and forest fires to taint the air we breathe, but since the onset of the industrial age, we have added a significant amount of pollution to the atmosphere and it just keeps escalating as the population increases, and more cars, transport vehicles, and more heavier than air craft take to the skies.

Everything else we do are extensions of these three truths, and have their roots in the time of the first humans, who began by inventing crude tool and weapons for hunting, and who also started to clothe themselves in animal furs. They also started using natural shelters, such as caves for protection from the elements, [fire being one of the most useful tools until the invention of the wheel] allowing them to move to less hospitable climates. Then came the invention of social order, where it was discovered that the power of a group was many times that of an individual trying to survive on their own. And so inventions, including our religions, were built on previous inventions until we arrive at modern times.

Everything outside the three basic truths are born out of our vulnerability, fears, insecurity, ego, and the need to ease the burden of survival. But, for every action there is an equal and opposite reaction, as is exemplified by the performance of the propeller driven airplane or one using a jet engine, where the compression of air by the propeller {the action} produces a vacuum {the reaction} in front of the engine, and the engine is then pulled forward to fill the vacuum. This principle means that every thing we do outside of nature is going to cost us something, and much of this payment is so subtle that most of the time we think we are home free and that the consequences of our action are not relevant, or minimal. However, minimums have a way of adding up, and I believe we have arrived at a time when all our action and consequent reactions are beginning to have a big affect on our world ecology, at first subtle, and eventually becoming a hammer fall. We are already experiencing harsher weather and a more turbulent atmosphere, and with the melting of the polar ice caps will come the rising of the sea levels, and the flooding of much of the coastal areas, leaving us with less land mass and an increasing population.

Pollution is the reaction of our industrial action, and if unchecked will continue to poison the air water and the oceans killing life on the land, in the air, as well as life in the seas, and what does not perish from pollution we will probably consume, leaving us a lifeless planet unable to sustain any kind of life, until nature again reestablishes its self again as the dominant force.

Examining the three basic truths of life might lead us to examining our own belief system and begin to modify our outlook with a more realistic view of the future in mind. I know by experience that its quite comfortable staying in the grove of what we perceive to be our unmitigated truths, thinking that there is no other way to approach life except the ones that we have been indoctrinated with. Many civilizations have toppled because they became entrenched in their outdated philosophies, unable or unwilling to change and adapt to what time always bring with it; change is another of those truths of life that we have no control over, and stops for no one.

Resistance to change has always been at the core of civilization, and I see and hear it from friends and acquaintances who defend their beliefs with worn out cliches and ego rhetoric. Evolution by its very nature dictates that we stop periodically and look around to see where we are and where we are heading, first as individuals, then as a whole community of Earth citizen. The impact of pollution and global warming are going to be felt world wide. I believe that this is a very good point for everyone to re-evaluate and modify their core beliefs. We are on the verge of monumental consequences if we don't open our minds to more than the mundane pursuits that are keeping us occupied and steeling away our awareness. We are not going to accomplish anything of significance if we continue to stay on the tread mill that has become the accepted way of living in modern times. We are accomplishing a lot, but it is a dictation from an anonymous source, a source that could care less about the final outcome, as long as the bottom line shows profits. We all need to wake up from the sleep of the sheep, and start to take responsibility for our actions, and most importantly, sifting through all the hypnotic lies, political or commercial, in order to make more informed decisions.

My religion. How do we even begin to clear our mind of unwanted and useless clutter? The first step is to stop the internal dialogue that is our constant companion, and is continuously reiterating those core beliefs, whether they are about the world at large, other people, or what we believe about ourselves. The latter can be uplifting or a self made hell.

Stopping that constant dialogue in our minds is not an easy thing to accomplish, but it is feasible with practice and dedication, in pursuit of real independence. It is impossible to *see* [meaning to uncover real revelations or perceptions] if our minds are constantly hashing and re-hashing our beliefs or our struggles, in our lives, present and past. One way to begin is to adopt a regimen of meditation, where one can sit with eyes closed and just observe our thoughts without actively participating in them. In this mode, our thoughts drift by and we play the part of the observer, not latching on to any particular thought. If this is done a couple of times a day for a half hour, eventually the mind begins to clear, allowing our true perceptions to surface, and could be equated with sweeping out the cobwebs in the attic. This of course does not mean that we forget everything, it just means that we no longer let it dominate our actions. There are many outstanding books on the subject of meditation and its value.

There are ingrained thoughts that only serve to give us pain and block out the light. We constantly judge ourselves and others, never realizing that there is no sin, and everything that happens has a reason behind it. We judge in order to build a wall against the fact that we all have the potential for acts that are of a benevolent or malevolent mature, and what we don't like in others we see as a possibility within ourselves, and it scares us.

There are other effective ways of purging painful thoughts and memories that originate from painful situations we have experienced along our path in life, and just like our internal dialogue only serves in keeping us from walking a liberated path in life.

The choice for liberation is ours to make, and no one can make that decision for us. In fact the way of the warrior is fraught with obstacles and resistance that is caused by trying to clean our minds of superfluous and harmful thinking, but also the way we have to fit into a society that is rigid, unbending, with no fluidity, thus limiting its options. We call people on the path to enlightenment warriors, because we are waring with ourselves to remove the mental barriers that keep us chained, and also keeps us from our full potential. Humans are more powerful than they realize, and I believe that most humans are more afraid of their own potential than they are of dieing for lost causes.

There has been a lot said and written about the new millennium and in particular about what is to happen after December 21, 2012, ushering a new era in the Mayan Calender. Some of it is probably speculation, with some things that have been written about this new era, do propose major changes in the ways that we deal with our world and each other. These changes would have to come in the form of higher consciousness of mind and spirit, where we would actually take to heart our action and their consequences. Of course, some of the scenarios are of doom and destruction, such as portrayed by Hollywood, but I think that this type of view is just business as usual and a continuation of what passes for entertainment these days; fear and ego based.

And then again, nothing may occur, and we will be left in the bulldozing mode, continuing to defile all the natural wonders, and leaving a very sorry legacy for posterity.

It is all going to depend on how many people become independent and sentient enough to begin to mentally effect the collective conscientiousness of the whole human race. If enough people orient themselves in the direction of peace and prosperity for all the citizens, the restoration and clean up of our planet, the voluntary control of population, the rest will follow. And, I don't think that it would take a majority to effect the change.

If we are to be effective in making a major change in the way we look at our environment, we are going to have to work on our selves first, by seeking out modalities that are going to promote enlightenment and not leave us stuck in the quagmire that we find ourselves in today. We don't have a lot of time in which to accomplish an about face in our attitudes and beliefs, certainly not as much time as our ancestors had, since the wheels of our so called progress are gaining speed at an exponential rate. That means that what took ten thousand years to accomplish in the distant past only takes one hundred years to accomplish at present, and that includes changing the face of our world into a landscape of desolation.

Organized religion can't help us in our real time of need, because of the their dogmatic stance which is intractable and not fluid enough to offer any realistic advice to an ailing world. Religion can't be a one fits all suit, and there is no such thing anyway. Our educational system is the same, trying to force every student into the same mold. This kind of thinking can only lead to failure, because we are individuals, not assembly line robots.

There are some of us who are artists by our very nature, and science does not speak as loud, just as the science oriented individual would consider music of secondary importance. And yet, there are some who can juggle them all. I am one of those individuals who identified with science, but also tried to express my love of music, arts, and crafts. It is the diversity that makes the human race great, and is going to have to be embraced if we are to cease cranking out neurotic citizens. There is a basic problem in the scales of compensation for what we do, creating workers that are only in some field because of the money, when in fact they would rather be doing something else instead. How effective can a square peg be in a round hole? Its just a job, is what I hear. It pays the bills, but it does not feed the soul.

At present, society is trying to push the sciences to the forefront of the educational system, and is ignoring the humanities, arts, and literature, creating an imbalance. Many of the school programs in the arts have been suspended or completely deleted from the curriculum, and only because someone thinks that science makes the system more profitable, and creates the need for more industry and the need for more raw resources.

Science the new religion. Unspoken but still there.

Chapter 5

Population

Standing room only: I am reminded of a Star Trek episode where all sickness, poverty, and hunger had been eradicated from the world portrayed, and no one was in need of anything. All the population had to do was to enjoy life and multiply. And apparently they did, because the population had gone so out of control that there was standing room only.

I realize that scenario was a very extreme and a fantasy depiction, and probably a collapse would ensue long before such a situation could occur on any world. Just feeding such a population requires unlimited resources of not only food, but staples of every kind imaginable. Unless they had the technology to synthesize common dirt into usable materials, the natural resources would soon vanish. Even common dirt would not last long; diminishing the size of the planet and there fore creating an exponential effect where now instead of standing room only, they would have to get up on each others shoulders because of the diminishing size of their world. This scenario definitely portrays utopia and hell occurring at the same time.

We on planet Earth are not even close to solving our health issues. We can't even feed that portion of the worlds population that is starving. We have actually created more health problems through our industrialization, through the pollution it produces. and our current sedentary way of living.

For me that episode, when first viewed took on a somewhat humerus aspect. As I became more aware, I realized how devastating this could be if it were to come true and somehow we on the planet earth were to come to such an end game. That particular episode did try to convey a message, of what happens when a world is over populated, and no effort is made to cub procreation.

I would like to raise the question of how keen our awareness is of where we are heading in our head long quest for expansion that takes and never gives anything back, not even a thank you.

Awareness of our surroundings has always been a key to our survival, and knowing what was coming at us from anywhere is a cardinal endeavor to staying alive or becoming some wild animals lunch.

So in light of that last statement, I would like you to consider this writing as a deep abiding love and the awareness for the condition of our world. This love creates at the deepest levels of my existence, a consummate concern for this beautiful world and all the inhabitants, be it flora or fauna. This love should be completely universal and encompasses all matter, living or not. According to our present standards of perception, our concerns are rather narrow and based mostly in the me orbit.

Considering that all matter, whether organic or solid has to abide by the same molecular laws, whether it is an animal, a tree, or a rock, it has the same molecular action taking place at the atomic level. It is only in the combination of these atoms and molecules that all the myriad of possibilities exist. So, what I am trying to say, is, that its hard for me to define what is to be considered life and what is not. I find it hard to draw that line, since I see most everything around me as life in some form or other. I offer this perspective, because my attitude directly effects the way I relate to my surroundings. Our attitude plus issues and circumstances, lead us to our destiny; which in turn has an effect on everything around us.

I have heard some people say; you can't change or cheat destiny. I see that as a rather erroneous view of the control and guidance we can offer our selves and our environment. We may not be able to cheat destiny, but I believe we can change it if we make the effort. Destiny will take us where ever it will if we just stay in the same old groove, content to allow someone else to set the course. All we have to do is to follow the carrots on a stick, to where ever we are being led, and most of that has nothing to do with saving us or our world. Unless we are willing to stop and analyze what we are doing and why, we will just continue to walk a path that is not really our own. After all we are perfectly designed to make choices, which might require us to push against the envelope, and might eventually lead to fruition of our intent and desires, if indeed we have any desires to see this world flourish, instead of diminishing, as our present course is taking.

If we can resist the temptation to use undo force, that only creates more enemies, we might actually be able to establish meaningful dialogue among the different nations and factions of the world. An alternative to the methods we have been employing through out recorded history. To use the premise of Love instead of harsh judgment and brute force when dealing with others, unless there is absolutely no other alternative, could go a long way in creating a peaceful and just world. Now is the time for all good men to come to the aid of their planet, by adding Love and Understanding to our tool boxes. Only our higher selves possesses the power to take down the highest and strongest walls.

The carrot on a stick path is the easiest to follow and offers the path of least resistance, so that most of us follow blindly, keeping our places on the path that has already been laid out, mostly for someone else to reap the harvest, since not all in this world are sheep. There be lions here also. I believe we have to balance those two forces and be part lion and part sheep in order to remain balanced.

There seems to be a social acceptance, that its justified to amass fortunes with no responsibility to those who helped create the fortune; in most cases the consumer. It feels like a missing piece in the puzzle, or a glitch in our DNA.

DNA from a time when hoarding increased our chances for survival, but even then, any abundance was shared with the community, which indicates that we were more in the *us mode* then. I believe that we went from us to me when farming and husbandry became the accepted way of life, thus creating marketable abundance. At that point we lost some of the grace of community consciousness. Profits are deserved, but greed gives much of what we do a bad flavor.

I have stated before, the ego, in a civilized situation is not our friend and is only there to increase the gap in the separation that already exists between us and everything else. In order for me to hoard, many have to sacrifice and what is so insidious, is that the more we hoard, the more removed we become from reality, and the easier it is to accept that separation that is the cause of much of the conflict that exists on this planet. The separated, the individual, the island unto himself, the me against the world that has been plaguing us with war and chaos since we started to consider ourselves as civilized.

Having tried to clarify my reason for this writing, I move back to the subject of population, and having invoked a few outrageous examples of possible outcomes, and solutions, I would like to point out that as outrages as these examples may appear, I see us heading in that direction at an ever alarming pace. The need for basic resources is increasing by the same ratio as population.

Where our use of resources began at a slow pace, it has greatly accelerated in modern times. I can also see how in our early stages of development we could easily take our natural world and all of its abundance, for granted. We were like one grasshopper in a world of green. Now, we are heading towards becoming a cloud of locusts in a world that is turning brown. No other animal on this planet has the ability to unbalance the ecological system like man. We have become energy addicted, and that energy is produced by burning million of tons of coal and oil.

Two million years ago, in the mode of hunters and gatherers, the prime motivation was very likely survival and propagation of the species. Propagation seems to be something that the mechanisms of nature prioritize and heavily invest in, and with good reason, considering that the circle of the food chain. It means that any abundance in the propagation rate, no matter how voluminous it might be, will eventually be soaked up by predation of any species that might have developed a taste for the nutrition that is represented. Most mammals, birds, insects, fishes and reptiles still live in this predatory mode that is as ancient as life itself.

We humans, so far are the only species that have had a significant amount of success in removing ourselves from the food chain. Not that we don't fall prey once in a while, however those instances are few and far between and will probably get even rarer as the predators continue to decline in numbers as a result of human expansion.

Our numbers are increasing by leaps and bounds, although I might point out that we still use our predatory instincts [even in the most modern situations] on our selves and on each other to gain advantage. Since we do not exist in the wild anymore, it seems that we turn that predator instinct on each other, and basic survival instincts are the strongest, which also indicates that we are not as civilized as we think we are or would like to be. Or perhaps, we are just totally out of balance.

Our ancient ancestors did not have to worry much about conservation of resources. Everywhere there was abundance and their numbers were few. Not that they did not face their own unique challenges, just in fighting the forces of nature and living in a predator dominant environment; an environment that kept any particular population in check, including humans.

So who is going to keep us in check? The only answer that I can think of, or makes any sense, is ourselves. Otherwise the impersonal forces of nature, will exercise their influence on our environment with swift strokes that adhere to the laws of nature. This force is not going to look back and say; oh those poor humans, they did not know what they were doing, and so I will take some pity on them—not likely, since the forces of nature are as true as what created them, and adhering to: ignorance and apathy are no excuse. Even our sun-star will super nova in five billion years. It has no choice; but being at the pinnacle of evolution on this world, we do have a choice.

I believe that the real measure of our sentience and our intelligence is about to be tested to its maximum limits, and our decisions in the next century or so will determine how well or if we survive. Yes, how well we survive is key here, since some will always survive any particular holocaust that may occur, but probably in such diminished numbers, it would be tantamount to starting over, and in having to start over, and with the burden again of basic survival, it is likely that all the hard lessons that brought about the collapse, would probably be forgotten in the wake of struggle. Hopefully the lessons would be remembered and carried forward.

This would be a very traumatic and painful way of curbing our burgeoning population, for we live on a world of finite resources that are not inexhaustible, and which we have in just a few thousand years, made a significant inroad into. We might even have to resort to mining our waste dump sites to recover a major portion of material that have been discarded and thrown away when they could have been recycled or reused. Recycling is a whole new industry that could spring out of the ashes and create a whole new job market, and I think we would hear a big sigh of relief from our over burdened planet.

There are many examples in nature of rampant increases in population that illustrate the negative effects of eating one's self out of house and home. One that comes to mind is the locust, who can multiply itself millions of time and can invade an area resplendent in lush vegetation and completely level every thing that grows, leaving only the stocks and stems in its wake, and then moving on to another area to do the same, until there is nothing left within reach, and finally succumbs to starvation, where in the hoard dies out completely. It seams that under these conditions, this species of insect would eventually become extinct. This does not happen because, everywhere they go they lay their eggs, which will lay dormant until favorable conditions reoccur. The eggs can then hatch and start the cycle all over again, insuring their survival. In unfavorable conditions, not all the insects will die, leaving a few to propagate until the vegetation can recover.

Humans could face such a calamity if we insist on ignoring the exorbitant rate of growth in the worlds population. Valuable farm land is being paved over for the sake of building urban housing, while our expansion is also diminishing the available habitat for the other inhabitants of this world, who do not seem to carry much weight in our cognition. I do not think that many people understand, that if we can allow the extinction of the animal kingdom, then the next one's in line are us.

One of the most obvious conditions that occurs because of over population, is the over crowding conditions of cities, where people are literally living on top of each other. I know that originally people flocked together in villages and then in cities for the sake of protection and safety in numbers, but I believe that reason has turned around on itself and is creating more hazards for its residents than benefits, in the form of stress and the lack of natural surroundings. This is probably the reason that the more affluent members of our society seek the solace of the less populated areas of the world to live in, where there is more breathing room and grander vistas of the natural world, but not all citizens have that option.

There is one aspect of over population that I know is going to sound crude and unconscionable but which I believe will have a bearing on the over all development of our species, and that is: the human race developed out of struggle of diverse conditions, where survival of the fittest was in every aspect of the word, the prime component and reason for the rise of a dominant race of beings. Dominance can work both ways, it can be benevolent or it can turn malevolent.

Now don't get me wrong, I do not advocate pulling the plug on everyone who is or will be in a hospital or anywhere else on life support, I just want to illustrate the role that medical intervention has had on population growth for good or ill; not judging, just stating a fact. I do believe that a large percentage of people on life support are kept alive even when there is no hope of recovery, which means that there is some other motivation at work there.

It is no longer survival of the fittest, which is due mostly to our advances in the medical field that speaks highly of the intellectual prowess of the human species. What escapes us is the fact that we have to compensate for this massive injection of population that is the direct result of medical advances. There are many more aspects that have contributed to population increase, such as better protection from the elements and higher yield in food production, although there is a large portion of the worlds population that is starving, and our constant preoccupation with war has not made a significant dent in our population, mostly because the child bearers don't go to war. They stay home and replenish the population. Smart.

One aspect of science seem to me to be somewhat of a travesty, and that is in the area of cloning. I realize the lure of such an accomplishment, but don't we produce more than enough people by the usual biological method? Knowing the lofty and sometimes misplaced aspirations of science and governments, who shoulder some of the heavier funding of research, I would dare to state that the real reason for cloning research is to produce a more perfect being, which borders on the insane. Mad scientists are not just in the movies. I have always been an admirer of science, always, from youth to present, with astronomy being my greatest interest, but I also acknowledge the fact that scientific endeavors have a tendency to run of the deep end especially when fueled by the fear and paranoia that governments can generate. Since we are unable or unwilling to reach out to a potential enemy, such an action being considered weakness by the ego, who has almost total control of our world at this time, then the only alternative left is to build a bigger and more potent weapon.

Over population is probably one of the hardest aspects for humanity to control, and since we are no longer vulnerable to predation, most of our progeny survives, and in their turn create large families, and the beat goes on. It has not been that long ago [and especially in the Americas] that large families were very welcome and also practical, mostly due to the expansion of the European settlers that moved here after Columbus's discovery of the new world, and it has only taken four hundred years for the population of the Americas to reach saturation proportions.

I think the only ones who might be in favor of population explosion, are those who stand to make a profit. The rest of the population does not put much conscious thought into the process of procreation. In contrast to the native Americans, who once lived on a more natural level of existence, population for them was not as much of a problem as it is for modern civilization. They definitely co-existed with the flow of nature much better than the western philosophy of creating a need for exploitation of everything that we perceive in our environment.

The real conundrum of population is; that the largest families in modern times are created by the poorest peoples, and who are the least likely to be able to support their off springs in the very basic needs, such as food and clothing, least of all, education. There are millions of people on this planet now that are literally starving, and yet the parents keep on having children, seemingly with no awareness of the suffering that this appetite for procreation is creating. Procreation is one of our strongest natural instincts, and the hardest to curb. Perhaps some day we will evolve to where we can curb any instinct, but in the mean time, there are many effective means of contraception that can be employed to reduce the size of families.

Religions and the righteous minority are always waging war against birth control, family planning, and are even against contraception. Yet they have no qualm about sending young men off to fight in some punitive war. Maybe they are just trying to make sure that there is enough fodder for the next war.

There was a time when disease, natural attrition, and harsh living conditions, claimed the lives of a significant number of our offspring's, and certainly affected the adults as well, where people living to age forty were considered ancient. That is no longer the case, but the exception, and we need to consciously adjust for it.

I realize that not every one on this earth is socially evolved to the same level, and by that I do not mean the evolution of the mind and intelligence, that I believe all humans possess, since we are all just branches of the same tree. What I am talking about is the conscious awareness that what we do as individuals has a definite impact on our environment, as well, and really more directly, on our offspring's. It seems to me that those implications would be quite obvious to the casual observer.

It appears as if some segments of the population have given up on thinking about what it is they are doing, which almost feels like a desperation due to the critical circumstances that some people are forced to live under. Some of these situations are caused by the invasion of foreign cultures on indigenous cultures who might possess a higher level of technology, there by exerting dominance and creating a total imbalance in the indigenous way of life, which can create feelings of low self esteem, at which time, reality can become, if not totally, partially pointless. This situation has played out all over the world countless times. We don't just push wild life out of their habitat, but humans also do it to each other. It is of course the separation that exists between people, that produces this antithetical attitude between cultures. Again no Heart, only mind is involved, and of course ego and appetite.

What are some of the underlying causes of population explosion? Some come from the deep seated beliefs of many of the world oldest and powerful religions that offer the dogma of go forth and multiply, and not just replace yourself, but have as many children as you possibly can. Maybe that was a good idea once upon a time, but as we move into the age of Aquarius, this attitude will just exacerbate the tremendous pressure we are already placing on the resources of our world. One of the problems as I stated before is the large population of earth citizens that live below the poverty level. What could over population possibly mean to some one who lives on the verge of starvation and whose total energy is expended in just trying to maintain the barest of living conditions. Where are the governments that are supposed to be helping people that are in dire need? Of course they are only supporting the people that support the government by their taxes, so that the real problem lays with the people who support the government, and I know most people would say that that is only fair. But until everyone on this planet is well fed and at least fundamentally educated, and can lift their heads above the water line, they are not likely to participate in any kind of meaningful global affairs, no matter how large or how small. As the economy of the world continues to be mismanaged by greed and surfeit tendencies, it is likely that this section of humanity is just going to keep on increasing, with no awareness or world view other than survival.

The resources for uplifting the status and consciousness of everyone on this planet are still available, if only we could get our priorities strait about what kind of world we want, and again it is a matter of the disconnectedness that exists. In our present society, the have's ignore the have not's, except when it comes to exploitation. Consequently, we never give those less fortunate a hand in bringing them into the main stream, where they could then be a more productive portion of the whole society. I think, the point that eludes most of society, is that intelligence or any other human attribute has nothing to do with what segment of society we inhabit, which is just a matter of circumstance.

A good indicator of an over burdened population is; how many people are left out of the main stream and don't have any opportunities to extricated themselves because there are no viable opportunities left. Of course, we could go and kill rhinos and elephants for the horns and the ivory, but that is just another symptom of people that have nothing viable to do to make a living, and is not going to last long anyway, as is apparent by how close to extinction rhinos and elephants already are.

One major contributor to unemployment, although technologically advanced, is: mass production. Humans that could be working, have been replaced by robotic machines that don't require a pay check, health insurance or retirement benefits, and are a boon to those who's only concern is the bottom line. Even if we had the desire to employ everyone, the opportunities just are not there. Much of industry is heavily automated, making humans obsolete. What if anything can people support themselves, if no employment is available. Before automation, an increase in population automatically meant an increased employment base, but since automation began to the present, more and more humans are being supplanted by machines, I believe that what we do to others we do to ourselves, or what we do not do for others we do not do for ourselves. The world is becoming a smaller place—literally and figuratively—so that what may seam like a very distant occurrence in the world, will still have repercussions of varying degrees on all of us, and certainly with respect to the condition of our environment, where everyone is affected by what we pump into the air, ground, and water. What goes around eventually comes around, and the effects of over population do not discriminate.

Somehow we the citizens of this world are eventually going to have to take responsibility for the conditions that affect all of us, and that includes, in my opinion, trying to slow down the rate at which populations is increasing around the globe. A snow ball can not grow in size forever, and at some point it will collapse under its own weight. The same thing will happen if populations continues to escalate at an exponential rate, and when the snow ball finally collapses under it own weight it will be likened to nuclear fission, where the weight or compression of the already unstable fissionable material reaches critical mass, and an untenable conditions occurs, with a holocaust of an explosion that will affect every living soul on this planet.

The problem is not an easy one. There are nations that have tried to limit their population with very limited success. I believe this failure is due to a lack of information and education for the populace, and unless people are well informed and begin to see the light in the message, they are not likely to pay attention to laws governing population control or use contraceptives on cold winter nights, or any nights.

Only a systematic informational effort to reach the public on the problems of over population and the use of contraceptives, will work. People have to be instilled with awareness because we have a tendency to ignore laws that try to effect our personal pleasures. That is why prohibition didn't work, and the drug traffic can't be stopped.

There are many aspects and conditions that have created this problem, and I will try to list some of them below.

1.} We are no longer totally bound by the survival laws of nature, although there are many conditions that we will never be able to control, such as earth- quakes, tsunamis, volcanism, violent weather conditions, and objects falling from space. The Earth based catastrophes, if violent enough, could have minor or significant impact on populations, and have been minor in recent times. Whereas, falling objects from space have caused mass extinctions many times throughout the course of the worlds history.

2.} We are no longer in the food chain, and are no longer subject to predation. Being the dominant species on the planet, and given our early invention of tools and weapons, we progressively became less vulnerable to attack from other predators, although man always remained a predator himself. Hunting is still popular in many countries, and is viewed as a sport, and in most instances is not a necessity for survival. Those who could really benefit by hunting {the less fortunate}, can't afford the license or equipment required of the modern day hunter, however, some poach game, disregarding the constricts of the law and is the subject of another chapter. The Wild.

3.] Going from hunter gatherer to domesticator of the land, and husbandry of animals, gave man the advantage of making a more predictable and sustainable way of insuring their survival, especially with the invention of irrigation that allowed man to increase his chances of bringing in a crop at the end of the growing season, and all of this was originally carried out in a very organic manner, and did not tax the environment, except for the clearing of the land and the cutting down of trees.

4.] When we moved from caves to houses, we moved up another notch on the survival scale, where it was probably much easier to heat a house than it is to heat a cave, with fire pits and later in fire places. Much wood was need for heating and the construction of housing which probably came from the clearing of land for farming. Now we cut down forests for the sole purpose of building. Some wood is still used for firewood.

5.] One of the biggest boosts to survival was the initiation of caring for the sick and injured. This was originally carried out by the shamans and healers who discovered the healing properties of certain plants and mineral and which would eventually evolve into the medical profession. The shamans not only tended the physical aspects of healing, but also the spiritual and psychological aspects of the human condition, giving man a point of reference for his place and purpose in the cosmos. I believe that early man had a more fundamental appreciation of his surroundings, and knew that waste was not going to serve him well because everything at this early point was hard won and not to be taken lightly. The initiation of the industrial age has removed man from the equation of con-server of resources, which now seems remote to most people because of the distance between consumer and manufacture, who's interest is in producing as much as possible, and the bottom line.

6.] Modern food production has certainly created a horn of plenty, although there is still a large portion of the population of the earth that are starving and living in squalid conditions, and until we are able to bring these people out of this abhorrent condition, we can't expect them to respond to such things as climate change or the need for population control.

These are just some of the reasons for our prosperity and proclivity for over population, and will no doubt be a hinge pin to our survival as we would no doubt envision it to be; without the pain of a holocaust that would propel social order into anarchy.

One of the illusions that propels over population is our appetites for the sexual relationship that goes under the guise of making love. Well, love is love and sex is sex, and you can't make love, it is either there or it is not. Sex is strictly an instant gratification of the physical senses, and I don't think there is anything wrong with sex, as long as we understand the difference between the two. Everything in modern society is infused with sex, mostly in advertising because the designers of ads know that it appeals to the basic instincts of man, and a very powerful instinct it is. The question is are we willing to give ourselves over to such a hook, and have someone reel us in like a fish. Advertising has become a very powerful force in the way that individuals handle their resources, their finances and even their personal behavior, and in a circuitous manner, over population, and also the squandering of our natural resources.

Back twenty or thirty years ago, one would hear in various media, the proponents of population control, but in recent times nothing is said anywhere about this important subject. Maybe global warming doesn't like to share the lime light with anything else, and it seems to be the preoccupation of all of the environmental sciences and the media, when over population is involved in using more energy and more resource, along with the glut effect of misuse of everything we require from nature. Population is a significant contributor to global warming all by itself. Just the breathing of so many humans will use up a tremendous amount of oxygen and produce the same in carbon dioxide.

Nothing is allowed to get old or ware out, it must be replaced way before that happens, and that applies to cars, houses, clothes, and even food that we allow to spoil in our refrigerators. This is a product of over manufacturing and over selling, and not to meet the demand but to create it.

Fashion and Style: now there is a subject for the hook principal. The hook principal is anything that is impractical and most of the time outrageous, that is proffered to society as a must have and must acquire item and society hooks us into believing that we can't do without it. Why do styles change so rapidly? Well, there is a whole industry that has grown up around the belief that we need to dress differently at periodic intervals, and if we don't we are nowhere and no one to even bother about. I have noticed that the less there is to a garment, the more it costs, but its just the result of pretzel logic, and again the fashion industry uses the lure of sex to sell their products to a totally manipulated society. Fashion is just another of the many bloated industries that keep society from thinking about the real problems that face us.

There may be a few schools that are beginning to teach some courses on the subject of the effect of mans foot print on this planet, but by and large, the education system seems to be more interested in its ratings as compared to other nations, than they are in teaching children to become good citizens on a valid path that would enhance their lives and leave a legacy of having made a positive impact on a world that started out to be paradise but is slowly turning to ash under the constant pressure of its human population.

Television could be such a powerful and positive influence on our children and their world view. However most of the programs that appear on television are so twisted and amoral that some one that might be watching from somewhere in space, would certainly think that we as a global society have gone insane, and they would not be that far off the mark. I do have to give some well deserved credit to the public television stations for making a gallant effort to bring quality programming into our midst. The only exception I take with public broadcasting is in the programming for children, which is on every week day, and portrays children in adult situations as crime fighter or fighting some dark entity. Its like watching mini people in a soap opera. This time could be used to inform and educate children about the environment and what is required of a steward of a healthy world.

Most of everything that appears on the tube is so infused by maniacal ego and conflict oriented material that it has a deleterious effect on the minds of all who watch, and especially on the minds of children, who are at a most impressionable age. But lets face it, that is what it is designed for, that and making money at all cost, by appealing to our darkest instinct and imaginations, keeping us angry and in fear. Right now, sitting a child in front of a television set just to keep them occupied and out of the parents hair, is only going to give that child a twisted view of reality. Education in any form is so important for the young, that parental guidance is of the utmost importance.

Parenting was once a community endeavor, where children would get an average input from everyone they came in contact with, and everyone had a stake in what the values and insights these children would acquire, since someday they would be the adult members of that community. That type of parenting no longer exists, and what I hear most now is; no one is going to tell my kid what to do or think, and parents get upset when someone else try's to correct their children. Parents apparently don't realize that they can't be with their children all the time and that there are no grand parents or uncles and aunts to guide the child. Children feel free to misbehave when there is no significant other around to keep and eye on them. One example of the effect of undisciplined children is; the abuse and chaos that teachers in our schools have to endure because of not being able to apply discipline in their classrooms. There may be cases of abuse, and could be dealt with on an individual basis, but by and large I believe that the majority of teachers have the students best interest at heart. Chaos in the classroom deprives those who are interested in learning.

As a student for most of my younger life, and with a very independent bent, there were very few times that I did not deserve the discipline and guidance that I got. School was a different place altogether when I attended, and most teachers were quite good at keeping the class environment rational and conducive to learning. Children are quite good at knowing who they can take advantage of, and if the teachers hands are tied, the purpose of the classroom is compromised.

Is it a run away train with no solution in sight, or can we still put on the brakes? I think the answer lies in whether the collective consciousness of humans is elevated to the point that we can approach these compelling subjects with clarity and resolve to improve ourselves and save the only home we have, and I might add, it must be in the very near future. If we can rise to putting men on the moon and building space stations, surely we can say: *Now is The Time For All Good Men to Come to The Aid of Their Planet*, and I believe that all men are good at their core. We [in my opinion] all have the creators essence at the core of our being, all we need to do is emancipate it, for what we think and what we do, is what will be. I am of the firm belief that humans are capable of anything they can think or conceive, and it is in the quality and intent of that conception that the crux of the matter lies. If we can invent destructive ideas and devices, then there is no reason why we can't allow ourselves the joy that nourishing our world would give us, after all, it is we the people that are going to benefit by this obvious act of love.

There is a tremendous amount of inertia to overcome in changing the way that we think and what our priorities are to be, now and in the future, concerning the subject of population. It boils down to, what kind of world do we want to leave for posterity to deal with, or what kind of world do we want to live in ourselves. We need to stop and think about our situation and its implications and take a real interest in what our present course is doing to this world we call home: The only home we have and the only home that we are likely to have. If we could rip our focus away from the mundane and every day distractions of the treadmill, and elevate it to our higher understanding, I know that we would arrive at different conclusions of the role of society as stewards of the blue planet. However, the social order as it is designed at present, keeps everyone on a treadmill that does not allow time for reflection of anything but keeping our heads above the water line. If we are not at work we are propped in front of the television set, which has very little in the way of social value or enlightenment to offer, or we are out doing something to keep our minds occupied, but always on the same old treadmill that only leads to tunnel vision, and does not allow for any time to think of the issues that will determine the future of our world.

Without an elevated consciousness to push us toward self determination and autonomy, issues such as overpopulation, global warming, deforestation, poisoning our environment and loss of habitat for all the other inhabitants of this world will just fall by the ways side, and we will continue to consume until there is nothing left. I will address the subject of consciousness and how to gain a different perspective in an other chapter, and proffer some of the the techniques that have had a profound impact on the way that I now perceive the entire cosmos. We are part of a tremendous cosmic symphony, and not just an isolated speck of dust, whose only choice is to follow their predetermined destiny. A destiny that is controlled by those who do not believe in balance, and that mass consumption should be our priority, when one of the most powerful attributes of man is that we are quite capable of changing our destinies. However, we will not change an iota until we become the free thinking individuals that we were meant to be. By that I don't mean that we can just step all over everyone else in this process of changing, although I would venture to say that that is exactly the way our society works now, with those who have the leverage to ignore those who have nothing. By thinking that we deserve it because some how we are superior, when in fact it is just a matter of circumstance, and where we happened to be born.

In that context, I am grateful for the circumstances that I was born into: A rising middle class of the 1938 era, middle class being a middle of the road perspective, that allowed me to see the other two extremes of our global society, and in my opinion is the place where we should all be, the middle of the road, with the implication of being a balance point. Where nature and the cosmos have to exist in balance, so should we, if it were not for our high level of intellect which allows us to move outside that balance, proving that intelligence is a double edge sword that can cut both ways. Everything in nature has to follow the dictates of balance or extinction will ensue, but, either by the creator or evolution we have been endowed with the power of choice, and the responsibility that comes with having that ability.

The only choice that I believe we have, and would make any sense, is to seek a way of moving our whole society back into a mode of balance, that would probably entail a modification of the way we view life, and what it is that we hold near and dear. What is it we fear? Mostly we fear change. With the creation of governments and big religious institutions, humans placed their well being in the hands of others, and in most cases follow blindly or by coercive means, such as patriotism or the threat of hell. There is no hell waiting for us after we die. Hell can exist right here on this plane. If you don't believe it, just think about the countless people that suffer poverty, hunger, physical, and mental abuse every day. That is hell for them, and what goes around, can come around. The problem is, we believe in hell, and by doing so, manifest it. There is also paradise in this world. So, which one would we want to manifest? Humans are so adept at going to extremes, and both hell and heaven are extremes. What we need to visualize is a balance between the two extremes, the middle way, the fulcrum, the point where everyone is included in the process.

Can people come down out of their heavenly ivory towers, and can people rise out of the ruts of hell to meet in the middle and say, good God, look at the way we are growing. Our population is bursting at the seams, and if we do not take action soon to stem this tide, we will be left to face the hell of collapse. In reality, if we could arrive at a balance with what our minds tell us and what we feel in our hearts, there would be nothing to fear. Someone said, all we have to fear is fear itself, and it is fear that keeps us at war with each other, not only on a global scale but I see it within neighborhoods where people should be somewhat socially bound to each other. If we could reduce the global population by a significant amount, there would be plenty of opportunity and a niche for everyone. Economies would boom.

As it is now, there is an over spill of humanity that can not be fit into an over burdened world that has reached the limit of how many people it can support. People don't seem to see that what we need now is quality of life, not just quantity, and a move back to self sustainability, where a major portion of the population could create and maintain sustainable energy sources such as photo voltaic and wind generated electricity. It is also essential that people begin to orient themselves toward growing some of their own vegetables and fruits. Most soils could be organically enhanced, and instead of growing and mowing a useless lawn, that water allocation and lawn area can be used for food production.

Something is missing from our educational system, both at home in our schools. Nothing is taught on the subjects that make up our humanity or the impact that our way of living has on our world. I don't think it is moral or practical to try and force people to limit the number of children that they can have, but if young people are exposed to the possibilities of overpopulation and the benefits of birth control, they would pick up on these ideas and at the very least think about their role in the outcome of the future. Nobody seems to want to talk about pressing issues that touch those sensitive nerve endings that relate directly with our survival, such as overpopulation, recycling, global warming, loss of habitat for the wild creatures, and the massive collective foot print that we humans make. These issues should be at the forefront of the collective consciousness, being publicly addressed and discussed. Instead, the most powerful media source we have is clogged by ego driven programming, backed by massive sales and consumerism advertising; a waste of such a powerful medium. A medium that reaches into the majority of homes in the world. This powerful media could produce programs to educate and elevate the consciousness of the public, instead of the demoralizing effect it has now.

Laws that address some of our more pressing problems will never be considered, much less enacted, until we can eradicate the insidious lobbying that has taken almost total control of our legislative system. The average constituent does not have the mega-buck capital that the special interest concerns have to buy their way through, and that is not the way its supposed to work anyway. Its just a measure of the total imbalance we face in our future, prompted by greed and fear, and a resistance to change.

There are various environmental organizations that try to address some of these issues, but don't seem to be able to make any kind of inroads into the main stream consciousness of the majority of the population, and I believe that the reason is that they spend their energies and resources on trying to influence governments, instead of running educational campaigns that would reach the general population through the most popular media around; television and radio. That would directly influence the population and the younger citizens. Environmental organizations operate more on a corporate level than at a grassroots level, after all, governments are not going to legislate any thing that might lead to the death of the Golden Calf. It is the well informed citizens that is going to make a difference, in what they consume and how much they consume or how much is wasted.

I don't think that the average citizen understands the power that the collective can wield and the pressure that can be brought to bare on our governments, corporations, and lending institutions to bring about permanent change that would start to level the playing field for everyone. The majority has the power in its hands, but does not know it, or is kept so distracted and pinned under the weight of survival and plain old propaganda that we don't have time to think about what is happening to us, or how we are being manipulated. Manipulation has been honed and refined to a razors edge, and makes its cut without ever being felt physically. Those who wish to push their agenda on the global population, have learned from history, that if you push too hard, you wind up with revolution on your hands. So now the new paradigm in control, is to push a little here and a little there and wait for the wave to subside, and then you push a little more, gaining at every push. What the heck, let them eat cake. This method is subtle and hard for most people to perceive, and the loss to the average person is small at every juncture. But, over time the losses in freedom and rights become significant.

Historically, it seems to take an over whelming amount of pressure to motivate people into taking a stand on the loss of life liberty and the pursuit of happiness. In our present society, the thumb pressure is very subtle, and sold to us as a benefit, instead of what it really is; a push toward higher capital gain, at any cost to the environment and our natural resources, which also includes humans. We are now categorized as a resource along with all the other materials that industry uses to manufacture product.

Overpopulation in my opinion is one of the most significant challenges that modern man is going to have to face in the immediate future. If we continue to ignore the problem, the consequences are going to cause a total collapse in our ability to supply everyone with the basic means of survival, or we will crush our environment to the point that it is no longer friendly or nurturing. We have the ability to turn this planet into a toxic waste dump that can no longer support life as it originally evolved, we also have the ability to turn it back into a paradise.

Population is not an easy thing to control, especially in a free society, where every couple is free to exercise their free will on procreation. There are few people who actually plan their family or set a goal on how many children they want to bring into the world. A large percentage of pregnancies are accidental, with no previous intent on conceiving a wanted child, and shows a lack of responsibility on the part of potential parents, and even less responsibility among casual lovers, whose goal is only instant gratification. Many of the unplanned births are accepted into a family unit, whether the birth was planned or not, but many wind up as neglected or abused children whose lives end up as a living hell from the start. Nothing can justify that kind of unconscionable cruelty, and just goes to show how unloving humans can be, when they can't take responsibility for their most basic instincts and actions.

We are programmed to procreate, not only by nature but by society and religion, but I believe it is time to take a serious look at those teachings and modify our actions with an eye on the future. Surely the people that hold sway over millions of followers, can see the consequences of an unlimited population in a limited environment. Its hard to believe that the clergy is so bogged down in their dogmatic beliefs that they can't apply some common sense to their preaching.

There are many humans in the world who love children and caring and providing for them is a top priority, and would it not be wonderful if everyone who is a parent felt that way about their children.

However, in an ever expanding population, the competition for jobs and financial security is going to escalate, and there are already signs that even if you have a college degree, it is not going to insure the acquiring of a good paying job or a lucrative place in society. The fact is, that as the population increases, coupled to the mechanization of industry, there are fewer jobs for people to fill. Our basic resources have to be stretched farther and the population can outrun the infrastructure with need outdistancing the supply and opportunities . At some point in the future where resources and supply of basic needs have been taxed to the limit, everyone is going to feel the vacuum created by too many citizens with too little left to work with, and this effect is going to be felt by everyone.

What I am describing here may not be felt for some time to come, although I believe that the writing is already on the wall for those with eyes open enough to read it. We do have time to set a different course, and there are so many readily available and inexpensive means of contraception that it is not that difficult to start the reversal that our voracious appetites and irresponsible ways have created. I know, I am going to burn in hell for expounding such heresy, but like I have stated before, I don't believe in a hell where we are supposed to burn forever, condemned there by an all loving God who forgives our sins. This is not God talking, this is man and his fear talking. Right here and now, this is *Heaven*, or this can be *Hell;* it depends on what we co-create.

Want a big family? There are millions of orphaned and abandoned children in the world that need a stable home environment, and adoption would help relieve their suffering. I know that foster children are sometimes hard to deal with, not because they are inherently bad, but because of the circumstances of their abandonment, of either having lived through a chaotic, unstable, or abusive home life, or living as wards of the state. Life is not easy for anyone, when there is no love to smooth our the traumatic vagaries of life.

However, here is an opportunity for many to show the true humanitarian side of our nature and at the same time relieve the suffering of a large portion of the worlds children, and also begin to slow down the rise in populations around the planet.

There are, whether we acknowledge it or not, other citizens on this planet that should be considered right along with the human population. These citizens are all the other creatures that exist in the wilds of our world, and don't have a voice and very little support among the human population. Yes, they kill, but never for sport, never for vengeance, only to survive. We humans not only kill to survive but we kill for sport, as in; for the fun of it.

Hunting was once a very important aspect of our survival and I myself was brought up with the idea of hunting for sport. For early man, hunting was more of necessity, from which they acquired much of their sustenance. Those were considered elite among the tribes and clans for their efforts in supplying the whole community with meat and all the other by-products such as pelts, rawhide, sinew, and even the bones were use for utilitarian purposes. Not much of an animal was wasted by early man, and what was not eaten was used in the making of tools and other implements for the hunt.

To early man, most of the animal kingdom was revered and held in high esteem because of the role they play in the survival of our species. Those hunters had to develop a fine honed skill in understanding the movements of their intended prey, as well as skill in the use of the hunting implements they used. Many of those early hunters did not survive the hunt, since the instinct for survival is strong in all animals and will not yield easily, and the hunters had to be in close quarters to the hunted.

Hunting and predation was the way of life for humans even before there was any sign of civilization, and I realize the intense instinct we possess toward hunting. I also realize, that the combined effect of hunting and loss of habitat is driving animals toward extinction at an alarming rate. I still fish and love to eat the fish I catch, and at least there is considerable effort by fisheries to replenish game fish in the rivers and stream of the states in America, otherwise there would be no fish left in the streams and lakes. Our oceans are vast, but are already showing signs of depletion, by way of the high demand for sea food.

One of the most obvious effects of human overpopulation is the squeeze out and loss of habitat for all the rest of the creatures of the world. What good is it to be an intelligent creature if we can't see the overall picture, a picture that demonstrates very little love, compassion, understanding, or intelligence for all that surrounds us; an outlook that cannot see any beauty in anything outside of our own machinations;

an outlook that has no respect or love for the living essence of everything that surrounds us.

Evolution is knocking at our doors and asking: Are we ready to take on the responsibility of our actions and hold ourselves accountable for our own survival, and the survival of all the other life forms that co-exist with us? Are we ready to take that next major leap in our evolution and begin to trust ourselves to make those individual decisions that will demonstrate what true intelligence, tempered by love, compassion and understanding can accomplish? I have to think we are more than capable, or I would otherwise have to give up this effort as futile.

Chapter 6

Governments

Governments are like trees, they usually start out as strong sprouts, growing a strong centralized trunk that would in this case represent the constituency; then growing branches to better serve and nurture the whole that is now supporting those branches, with leaves that gather the energy that benefits the whole tree.

This of course is an idealistic view of a government that is young and just starting out, and whose motives are for the most part altruistic and with a strong sense of serving the governed, especially in a new formed country such as occurred in America some two hundred years ago. Most newly formed governments are initially run and administered by those who formed the ideas and principals by which the new country is to function, and also fought in a revolutionary conflict.

There are few really new governments that are going to spring up, since most of the world is already settled and governments are established everywhere. New institutions may arise due to the over-throw of an existing one, or one nation conquering another; could radically change the previous form of government.

In any case, without the efforts of a good gardener or tree surgeon, our governmental trees seem to eventually get out of control, growing and growing, as most institutional structures do, putting undue pressure on the supporting structure. As it grows out of control, it also creates a lot of dead wood. Branches that have outlived their usefulness and only serve to ad weight and suck energy out of the useful structure, and need to be trimmed away, making way for a healthier growth. There should be a branch of government whose purpose would be to review the laws of the land at periodic intervals and delete out dated laws, with the approval of the constituency of course.

Sometimes these trees fall under their own weight and of course bring everything down with them. Many of the classic forms of government down through history have crumbled. Some because they tried to hold more in their grasp that they were capable of, some try to grow too fast, and some because of corruption, or all of the above reasons occurring at the same time.

One of the biggest follies in the pantheon of human endeavor seems to be in the constant attempt to establish governments that work for the people, who are supposedly the focus of said government. Many different forms have been tried, but none seem to be able to survive with their original intent in tact as time passes.

I do not believe that this failure is due to the philosophy or structure of the governments, but is due to the entrenchment that occurs when the people serving in the different departments have been reelected too many times. There is also an imbalance in the cross-section of the people who represent us, which mostly come from the ranks of successful business men or people that can afford the exorbitant price of campaigning for public office. There is a need for a broader base of representation, and it is my contention that there are many more people qualified to serve in government, than just wealthy business people and movie stars.

If governments fall, whether they be democracies, republics, monarchies, confederations, fascist, or tribal, they have a tendency to crumble due to losing sight of their original goal, corruption from with in, self serving motives, and the influence of money or special interests on the legislative sectors. Money talks, and it talks big, and is such a big hook that there does not seem to be many that can resist its sway or rise above it to perform their duty to the electorate with strait vision and the morality they professed when they were sworn into office; after all we are only human, and there lays the loop hole in morality.

Once we make that statement to ourselves, we leave the door open to all forms of intrusion, and coercion that will eventually lead to the compromise of our highest ideals. Not that compromise is bad, and is essential in the settlement of matters that may range from simple family disputes and personal relationships to situations that could lead to holocaust or global war. The compromise I speak of is when we sell ourselves for a dime. And, its not that I think that business and corporations should be left out of legislative consideration, however all the indicators point toward a severe imbalance toward the money interests on the scales of legislative decision making, and the middle class is caught in the squeeze of the vise of greed and out of control profits at any cost. Plus, the governments propensity to uphold lending institutions whose practices amount to the roll of the dice, and whose schemes have led them to bankruptcy. The only way to insure good and realistic business is to let the gamblers fall and cull them out, Of course they are usually using money that belongs to someone else, just as government uses tax payers money without any kind of consensus from those who put up the money in the first place.

So who is going to step up and be the tree trimmer for our fine tree, to keep it healthy and in balance____to make sure that there is no dead wood and that every branch is serving the whole. Well, I think that chore is going to have to fall squarely in our laps. Who we nominate and elect to represent us is going to make all the difference in the quality of service we receive, and if government is not there to serve the constituency, then why do we need it at all? I surmise, that's why we bother to establish governments in the first place?

It has been said, that those individuals most qualified to serve as representatives of the people are the ones who are less willing to serve, and it makes sense, since the ones who are willing and eager to run for office; at least in this present era of politics are either wealthy, business owners, and highly ambitious and motivated people who already have an agenda in mind when they decide to run for office. In all fairness, I do know of some public servants that try to do the right thing on vital issues concerning the environment, and the less fortunate people of the country, but at this time are in a minority that is dwindling by the day.

People whose standard of living when compared with say third world countries, would be considered rich, but when compared to the standard within their own country, are considered to be below the poverty level and can't afford decent health care or proper nutrition because of an over inflated economy where the true object of worship is gold, not a higher power, not ideals, not morality, and certainly not a heart felt concern for the well fair of anyone but themselves. There is no understanding, that we are all connected and equal in the eyes of the cosmos, and what goes around, eventually will come around, sometimes, not in an obvious manner, but the exchange of energy is one of the basic and implacable laws of the universe; some call it Karma.

However, the public servants that do have good intentions do not stand much of a chance, mostly because they are severely out numbered or eventually wind up in compromise that is not in any way favorable to the constituency. After all, some view the general population as just another brick in the wall, just part of the financial infrastructure that feeds the economy, that feeds the glut. There by the term, consumer, someone whose sole purpose is to absorb every bone that is thrown at them no matter its validity or usefulness. That stigma will remain with us as long as we adhere to this mode of self slavery; unless we become the free thinking self actuated beings that we were meant to be.

Just as a side, and to elaborate on the term "self slavery": Four thousand years ago, a high priest in Egypt, while over seeing a construction project, noticed that the slaves were carrying only one brick at a time, and at a very slow pace, despite the whip of the drivers. It was then that the light bulb went on over his head and a possibility occurred to him in a flash of insight. What if, he thought, I promise to pay these slaves a few coins a day and possibly raise their incentive to work harder, thinking themselves to be free men at last, by feeding their self esteem and ego's. And so he implemented his plan, and low and behold, the slaves now called worker, started carrying several bricks at one time and actually competing with each other to see who could do it in the fastest time. The Priest was so delighted and all the hierarchy were delighted with the results, and so began the era of self slavery, which is with us to this day. For a pittance we work our fingers to the bone and waste our live on trivial per- suites that hardly give us any personal satisfaction. This is not what we would chose to do, but we do it because that is where a particular industry that is popular at the time is betting its money.

The differences in a consumer and an accumulator are made quite obvious by the difference in the wages that are offered. There is no doubt that educated people and persons with high responsibilities should be compensated for their efforts, but the gap in wages, is, in most cases astronomical, since it is my belief that every person in a company that brings forth a marketable product, is essential and vital in the chain of production, and if any link is removed the wheel stops and output comes to a halt, thus making everyone an important part of the whole. I believe that companies that are owned by everyone in the company are more equitable and create a better environment for creativity and a higher quality product, because the individuals involved have the incentive to do their best.

It takes tremendous amounts of money to run a campaign these days; that fortunes are spent on trying to be elected, and the media makes out like a bandit. Is public office for the wealthy only? Are the Scrooge McDucks the only ones to be able to attain public office and administer to our welfare? Well, Heaven help us if that is the state of affairs. Of course, the answer to both of those questions is a big No. In reality, if we lived in a real world, every one would be compelled by law to respond to responsibilities of public service, with a cross section of the public interests being represented. I just heard a big grunt from the professional politicians, who consider themselves sophisticated people, and who in most cases could be, but its not a given. What we need is a cross section of representation, of doctors, lawyers, Indian chiefs, plumbers, brick layers, sanitation workers and the list goes on, and lets throw in a few street people in order to get a true perspective on our real situation.

Yes, street people. Some are actually educated persons who have given up on a system that only serve some and ignores others. I believe that eighty percent of the people in the USA are qualified to serve in public office, and could be selected on a lottery basis. After all, if we the people can shoulder the responsibility of serving on a jury and make life and death decisions, or compelled to serve in the armed forces and risk life and limb, then what is to prevent us from shouldering the responsibility of government. Some preparedness would be essential, but those fundamentals could be taught in the public schools and should be mandatory, along with language, math and science, and also part of the credit curriculum.

Much of what is taught in schools at present are superficial and idealistic. The ways in which our government should work if everyone had an idealistic intent. Some of the more realistic processes that take place, such as, the effect and the power that lobbying and palm greasing by big money and special interest has on the outcome of any particular piece of legislation, that is voted on, are not addressed at all.

In the United States, we live under the influence of a two party system where the voters are led to believe that they have a real choice in the political process and the direction that any particular administration will take, when in reality the candidates are selected by the parties political machine and are usually picked because the party is already sure of what their predilection is going to be, and the voters are left with the choice of the lesser of two evils, not that I believe that candidates are evil, they are just playing the game by the rules of their own party, making promises and proposing ideals that are soon forgotten shortly after the election. There is a large percentage of the voting population that does not participate in elections and won't vote simply because they can see the futility of the exercise; the real choice has already been made at a subliminal level.

Another fantasy that the voters put undue stock in, is in the power of the president, and probably comes from the times when monarchs ruled the land, where a benevolent king could make the country prosperous, or a malevolent king could cause chaos. I see the importance that people place in the election of the president, as if that single person is going to satisfy all the desires of the electorate, when in reality it is the legislative branches that make the decisions. The president can propose and veto, and can lead the government in a particular direction, if he has the support of congress and the senate. Our present president, Barack Obama, has been literally black balled by congress. They have made every effort to undermine his administration, and I think what congress is really saying to the voters is: alright, you wanted this progressive president; we will not support him because we know he will propose legislation that will benefit the common people and undermine our special interests. Who needs legislators who have sold their souls for gold? The money interests do.

Another problem is a government that is split apart by factions and parties and all that takes place is bickering and a total log jam in the work that should be taking priority. Not only is the government divided, by issues, but by some nebulous ideology of belonging to this party or that one. I believe that the only reason for political parties, is to split the voters; divide and conquer is the real motive here, since there is not that much difference in the two major parties. Political parties that do have different ideals, don't stand a chance because most people are afraid to take a stand, even if they agree with the philosophy of a third or fourth party.

We the people should pick those who are to represent us, not the political machine, and it needs to be done at the local level. The more local the better. We can not trust anyone that we can't reach out and touch, for once someone is out of our reach, they are free to do as they please or worse, be influenced by propositions that don't reflect our best interests, and we should have the power to say what those best interest are.

Representatives become entities that are very hard to control and usually wind up remote and very hard to communicate with. They certainly don't make time to listen to every one of their constituents, and I believe that this is the reason why so many of the less influential citizens feel left out on the limb that is being sawed off the tree by those with enough capital and clout to influence the decisions made by legislators.

Representatives were originally vital to the function of a government whose citizen were scattered over long distances and with no other means of communication, and would carry the desires of the people they represented to the legislative branch of government. However, we in this modern era don't have any problem with communication, and it would not be difficult to implement a system by which every citizen could vote on every issue that is proposed, and probably would not be any more prone to corruption than the present voting system is now, although corruption can occur in any system and always depends on the integrity and moral standards of those who implement the system. It would definitely be harder to coerce a broad base of voters, than it is to influence a few hundred legislators.

This system would still require representatives to assemble and clarify any proposed legislation, and then present it to the voters in a form that could be understood by everyone. The real question now, is, would the average voter take the time to review the contents of a bill in order to make an informed decision on how he or she would vote. I don't think it would be an overwhelming task if we could some how tear ourselves away from some of the mindless television programming that the world has become so addicted to, and channel our energies toward gaining more control over our own lives.

The headlong pace of governments and the affluent world has accelerated to such a degree in the last hundred years, that I think most people caught up in the frenzy of daily life, don't really know where they are going or why. We have worked ourselves into an almost frantic race with life, where we don't even have a chance to catch our breath, much less think about the future or what kind of world we want to leave to our children. The designers of our present mode of living, and make no mistake there are those in this world with the power to pull the big strings that can channel the flow of life in what ever direction they want it to go. But, the kicker is, they can't do it without our submission or cooperation to the will of that small minority of the worlds population, and it begins in the Hearts and Minds of those I am trying to reach. Our next leap in evolution is waiting for us, but its not going to happen without our awakening from hollow dreams and promises that are only going to drive us over the edge of the precipice.

Money and Science are not going to save us, not that they are evil in themselves. As long as we don't continue to worship those two human manifestations, we may someday reach a balance between our fantasies and our realities, of a heart felt mission of stewardship for everything we encounter on this beautiful and diverse world we call home.

The next leap in our evolution when it comes, will not be fought in the battle field with weapons or the spilling of blood. That kind of revolution is of the past and has not accomplished any permanent change so far, its just another war, and evolution does not come from the development of bigger weapons, in fact that kind of exercise sets us back. This battle will be fought in the minds and hearts of all the individuals on this planet, hopefully with an elevation in consciousness and a clearer understanding of the only possible deliverance from our self imposed *slavery__Love__Love* is the only thing that we can truly trust .

In America as well as in most democratic countries in the world, we supposedly subscribe to the principal of rule by majority, where the minority are supposedly able to say, alright, the majority has spoken and now it is time for us to work together for the good of all. Is majority rule nothing more than a hollow ideal? Has it ever worked in reality? Because, in recent political events, just the opposite happens, and the result is; battle lines are drawn and everyone draws their swords and a division occurs where the true purpose of legislation is totally ignored in the chaos that ensues, and nothing of any significance is accomplished with regard to the voters initial intent.

Re-iteration: To me, it should be obvious to the casual observer that the true purpose of a multiple party system is to divide and conquer, and the conquered turns out to be we the people. If we look closely, we will find that there is not that much difference between the two parties involved, and certainly, not the difference of day and night as is proposed. In their misplaced fervor, the supporters and volunteers that align themselves with a particular party, get so caught up in the battle at hand that they forget about what the issues really are, and are usually swept away by the energy of the moment, thinking that they have won a personal victory, but the victory belongs to the already picked candidate.

There will never be cohesion among us as long as we allow special interest to drive a wedge between us. Lobbyists, by way of their deep pockets are the major influence in our political system at this time, and since the constituency doesn't have the time or the monetary resources to pay for legislative enactment, it leaves the majority out in the cold. Politicians are heavily funded in their campaigns for election or re-election, leaving them in debt to industries that could care less about the environment or the quality of life of the average individual, as long as we are there to consume their products. These industries spend billions of dollars trying to shove drugs, cars, insurance, and every other product imaginable down our throats, which also includes influencing legislation.

At present, running for public office is something that only the rich can afford, or those who are supported by special interest, who know they will be favored in the decisions made on capital hill. Only those who can afford the exorbitant price of mass media coverage have a chance to reach the public mind. This needs to change. A limit needs to be set for how much can be spent on trying to be elected, thus giving those without deep pockets an even chance. Also, the media should be available to anyone who needs it on an equal basis. Of course, if all of the constituency had to serve in public office, it would eliminate corruption in campaigning for public office.

During these inter party wars, there is something that is accomplished: Legislators give themselves unmerited raises and secure their personal futures by appropriating lifelong retirement benefits for themselves, even only after having served one term, and all on the backs of the tax payers whom they are supposedly serving. Where is the justice in that. This selfish attitude is prevalent in all governments of this world in varying degrees from minor to extreme. For instance, a ruling dictatorship where the leader and his top officials make the laws and in most cases horde all the wealth of a nation for their personal use. This leaves a major portion of the population in poverty, with no say in policy making and the distinct possibility of being imprisoned or killed if anyone has the gumption to criticize or oppose the regime in any way. This is very extreme, of course; but is alive and well in the 21st century, and reflects a lack of imagination, heart or concern for the governed. Where as, in some parts of the world the population is held in a desired place by very subtle manipulation, of ego, competition, jealousy, nationalism, patriotism, and misplaced ethics, which still lead us to the same condition of self imposed slavery.

The Constitution of the Unites States has all the provisions for establishing laws that would insure the rights of citizens to freedom of choice in all aspects of their lives, as long as it does not trample on the rights of others, but it takes strong and insightful leaders to implement the ideals proposed by the Constitution, otherwise its just another piece of paper. We can reiterate our beliefs all we want, but if we don't take action to make those beliefs manifest, we will never reach our goal of being truly free people. And, I am not speaking revolution here, the true resolve is going to have to take place at the core of our being. Drawing battle lines and shooting at each other has never worked and will never work, as it just leads to the subjugation of others and only creates latent enemies that are only waiting in the wings for their chance at retaliation. It is impossible to create a peaceful world by battering, cheating, or maligning each other, and only friendship and Love is going to take us to a higher plane of existence.

Just as a for instance; how did Jesus Christ move a major portion of the worlds population to believe and adhere [not always practiced] to his teachings?

Well, it wasn't with bigger guns or lightning bolts from above, it was all accomplished by being what he preached, and he was just one man, so imagine what an impact we could have if we all joined hands and said, we want a better world, not just for the lion, but for the lamb as well. This concept is 2000 years old, isn't it time we started giving it more than lip service.

This evolutionary change is going to have to come from within, and existing governments are not going to be happy about it, nor will the minority whose dynastic legacy it is to skim the cream off the top and leave the curds and whey for the rest of us. But well, we are now, and have always supported that kind of behavior, thinking that this minority is deserving of their status and rewards because they are smarter or more intelligent. That is just one of those ordinary lies, and the truth is, they are not smarter, just more ruthless and separated from the rest of humanity.

The separation I speak of is a construct of ideas that states that as individuals we must stand alone, act alone, as if there is no connection or commonality between one human and the next, and only serves to keep us powerless as a collective conscious force that is united and pulling in the same direction for the good of the whole, not just for the good of the few. Under present conditions, our separate efforts can bring the individual rewards, depending on how concentrated our efforts are, and this kind of behavior is lauded by those who are on their way to being well healed and have surpassed others in that nebula we call status. This requires the ability to ignore the plight of others. Intelligence is definitely at work in our present social condition, intelligence that is strictly of the workings of the mind, the super computer that sits on our shoulders, the seat of the ego, that will jump up and defend the machinations of the mind.

However, humans are much more than that, possessing the noesis for compassion, love, understanding, and the ability to view more than the blinders that self adulation permits. Without the connection of the mind and heart, the tempering of these two human abilities, we become loose cannons with the willingness to commit acts of violence before all other possibilities have been explored, and the same happens with governments as it does with individuals. As above, so below, in our imbalanced social structure.

Governments are domestic institutions and very similar to a domestic fruit tree that needs constant monitoring and care and trimming and feeding, but not too much; just enough to keep it healthy, and hopefully produce some healthy fruit. If we wanted a fine tuned government that keeps its ear to the ground to listen to the heart beat of the nation and the aspirations of its people, then we would have to go to a more technical and tedious processes. The process that a bonsai grower uses to grow trees that are aesthetic to look at, but require concentrated attention. A beautiful and aesthetic bonsai tree does not turn itself into a work of art all by itself. It requires the intelligence and love of the grower and groomer to become an aesthetic masterpiece. Our government tree will requires the same kind of attention as a bonsai tree if it is ever to flourish. We have already let it get out of control and like any other tree that's left alone, it just goes wild. Roses are a very good example of what happens if proper pruning and care are not done. Usually, in no more than two seasons, they revert back to the wild plant that it originated from.

We have become negligent in our responsibilities of keeping our government pruned and healthy, thinking that the constitution and all the other devises that are in place will hold the show together for us without our intervention. Well, it doesn't work that way.

Paper can hold a record of our ideals, but it is still people that make those ideals manifest, and people by their very nature need to be constantly monitored and reminded of who they are working for. Being a legislator is just a form of employment, and as employers, we need the option of hiring and firing as needed. As far as government is concerned, the tax payer is the employer, like it or not.

My take is that most people believe that they can elect government representatives and just turn them loose and expect them to carry out their expectations, by believing the campaign promises that are made before election. Well this is never going to happen, and unless we can implement a system as I described earlier, where we can vote on every major issue, including when we are ready to commit our lives and resources in order to go to war, the elected officials will go their own way, mostly due to the vast resources that special interest have at their disposal, which can and does erode the moral fiber of government. Not all representatives are vulnerable to the lobbying force, and I believe there are those in government who try to do their best, but I think they are in a shrinking minority, and, it's a product of thinking only with our heads, which will always tell us to take advantage of every situation possible. We have to stir in Love and constant care into the mix if we are to produce a healthy tree.

What ever happened to united we stand, regardless of race, color, religion,or social standing? Everything turns out the way we as individuals really believe in our heart of hearts, regardless of what the law states or what is written in the constitution. What goes on in our minds is what is going to dominate our actions. That is why it is so important that we teach our children from the youngest age possible, the principles of what it is to be a civilized individual, and I will restate my belief that civilization is a taught thing, and not yet a part of our basic make-up. I believe that most people think that because we are technologically advanced, that our social evolution has also progressed at the same rate. It has not, and a lot of our technology stems from our warlike nature, producing instruments of destruction, albeit, high tech, which then filters down to the commercial level. It can work the other way also, where something is invented in the private sector and is then incorporated and further developed by the military establishment, something that our government, and most governments of the world lavishly spend tax dollars on.

Governments by the thousands, of every flavor and orientation have risen and fallen since history has been recorded, and they all seem to have one common thread no matter what their original orientation was, and that is their propensity to expand and conquer other nations, sometimes in the name of God or to spread an ideal such as freedom or democracy or just plain: I like the land you are sitting on and I think I will take it from you. This scenario has played out thousands of times in our world history and does not seem to have an end, even in our modern situation.

I think we have to address this problem from the perspective of those who start wars, and are usually the head of some government, needing the resources of a nation to promote such an endeavor. My point here is that in most cases, the people within a government that is preparing to wage war, should have the consensus of the citizenry, since it is their money and resources that will pay for it. Sometimes the nation is placated by means of patriotism, pride, hate, fear or lies [weapons of mass destruction for example] to support the war effort. The only instance I can see where the commander and chief would take immediate action is; if we were attacked directly, and immediate action is necessary to fend of an invasion. Of course, there are those times when it is obvious that a defensive posture is eminent and is the only choice left, such as the case of WWII. The second world war was definitely supported by all the citizens of the US in every way possible, and stands as strong indicator that everyone knew that an all out effort was needed, or else we would be living our lives in tyranny, or worse, put to death.

The problem is that being in the military, and especially on the front lines of a conflict, changes people in ways that no longer mesh with society in general. This factor alone should be enough to convince us that we need to put an end to war. Not only are we killing people physically, but mentally as well, manifested by the contradiction of war. The contradiction of killing people we discover to be the same as us, and the realization of the breakdown of civilization that occurs when in that kind of situation.

Somehow we have to generate a better way of creating a livelihood; in place of military service. The only thing that is going to work is, leveling the playing field for everyone, and the resistance will come from those who have an insatiable need to be in a position of feeling that they are above others, or somehow better than others, We are all equals, and the only thing that keeps us from accepting it is fear and the twisted programs that are running in our heads.

The big question is; can we devise a form of government that can reach out to all of its citizens, whether they be civilian, business, military or governmental. I believe we already have such an institution established. I suppose the next question is do we have people with enough principles and morality to carry the institution to its proper conclusion of serving the interests of every one under its umbrella. At present, government seems to be bogged down in useless bickering about the balance of power between the two political parties, again reminding us that the multiple party system is only good for splitting and disrupting the legislative process. Democrats against Republicans, and visa versa, is not what government is supposed to be engaging in. Don't these people realize that they are wasting the resources of the nation, and in effect passing legislation for the sake of partisan designs, instead of the good of the nation.

If there is one thing that governments are good at, its spending money. Money that comes from the hard earned wages of the tax payers, unless you happen to be a million or billion heir, then you can pay taxes at a much reduced rate than the tax payer that makes under 200 thousand dollars a year. Who do you think financed that bit of legislation? Certainly not the middle class. The government agencies always wind up paying more for services, tools and equipment than companies in the commercial sector, mostly because their buyers do not bother to make a competitive comparison of what those parts would cost in the commercial world. For example, it has been discovered that some government project wind up paying an exorbitant price for a simple wrench and others tools that would otherwise cost only a few dollars at your local Ace hardware store.

One of the enigmas of government, is to send help in the form of money, goods and food to foreign countries. I make this statement, not because I am against helping people in need, I think it is a very noble attitude. However, there are millions of people in our own country that are starving or are in serious need of help, especially in this time of economic depression that was mostly initiated by greed and sub standard business practices by wall street and the mega banks. Our government in turn rewarded them with billions of dollars for their transgressions, on the premise that the whole economic structure would collapse. This ruse was probably on the same level as the Y2K snow job, since the economy collapsed any way.

Foreign aid to impoverished countries, especially in

money form, usually goes to the government in power, who more than likely is responsible for the sad condition of the country in the first place, and the condition of the citizens improves very little. When aid is offered, it should be monitored, to make sure it is used for the purpose it was originally intended.

The economy is like a snow ball, it can only grow so large, and then it falls apart under its own weight, especially one built on speculation and creative manipulation, such as derivatives or complicated mathematical expressions that are supposed to insure greater returns. Its nothing more than playing games with other peoples money. At this time money manipulation is so ungrounded and so insidious, that it is bound for disaster. The invested gives the investor the privilege of investing their money in stable ventures that are likely to bring a good return on the money invested. However, greed dictates that the investor will not look at this as a privilege, but as an opportunity to heel themselves and take any risks they wish to take, after all, its not their money if its lost. Ours and other nations economy will never work until we learn to balance debt with cash. When debt severely out weighs tangible assets, the economy may give us a false sense of rising with no limit, but eventually the debt comes due and we find ourselves in the teetering situation we are in now, with no way to go but down. But take heart, most nations past and present have gone the same route, if we can take much solace in that, if not, we should take the lesson.

Economies are expected to grow by significant percentage points every year, which is supposed to translate into a better standard of living for the citizens. I believe that this is attainable if a nation is young and just starting out or is beginning to develop its resources. But, as any economy grows, it is bound to reach a saturation point, since there is no such thing as infinite resources, and that is coupled with a finite demand for products produced. Manufactured goods would be in high demand at first and would taper off as the demand was met. The only demand that keeps growing as the population grows, are the commodities that feed us daily. All other products only need to be replaced when worn out or severely outdated and can be replaced with safer or more efficient products. Realistically an economy would eventually taper off and stabilize at some level, and fluctuate around a mean, but this doesn't mean that profits can't be derived. The only reason that economies are expected to bloat year after year, is a greed for all that extra gravy that comes with a growing economy, and economic stability has nothing to do with stagnation.

However, no economy can grow forever. Eventually all raw materials would be exhausted and the economy would collapse all at once. Some are willing to take that chance and are only thinking about the immediate gratification of keeping an economy growing until it collapses under its own weight. Its up to the consumer to regulate the economy of a country and not be compelled to snatch at every hook that comes along. Bloated economies are designed to strip consumers of all their money and leave very little for savings. Speaking of savings! The interest that banks are paying these days, is an insult, and if it were not for security, we would be just as well off, putting our money under the mattress. Banks charge outrageous rates of interest on credit cards and loans and then turn around and give us the fickle finger on interest for our savings.

Most people these days are in severe debt, some of it comes from over use of credit cards, whose interest rates are so high, that it makes it impossible to pay them off once the principal reaches the maximum level. My advise to people is not to use credit cards at all, or only use them in case of a dire emergency. The exorbitant interest rates that credit cards charge are a form of legal robbery. Might as well be dealing with a loan shark. Even students that are coming straight out of collage are already in serious debt that is very hard to pay off, especially if they can't find a job, and that is happening more and more often. Credit card interest should be regulated by law, and should not exceed ten percent. The scales are tipped in favor of the banking institutions, where interest on loans is high and payed interest on savings is low; virtually non existent. Regulation of banks and other services will never happen until our government gets over the gold fever it suffers from now, and government officials need to be held accountable for the massive debt that was incurred without our consent. A debt that threatens to break the backs of the tax payers.

Another unfair governmental practice is the way the tax laws are structured, with loop holes for the rich, and snares for the poor and middle class. To begin with, taxing is unconstitutional, but if there is to be a taxing, it should be fair for everyone, the middle class, the rich, and the corporation.

There are corporations at present that pay vary little tax or no tax at all, although their profits are in the billions of dollars. Is this the real world: I am afraid it is. A real fools paradise. The poor should still have special consideration since taxation is a bigger burden for them. Taxing everyone at a fifteen percent rate would create bigger revenues than are collected at present, especially if those with big profits are made to pay their fair share.

Our present situation is a result of the insanity that occurs when gold gets a hold of our minds and chokes of the channel to our hearts. It is something that we share as a commonality with all the worlds citizens. Integrity is missing from almost everything we do where money is concerned, and it also carries over to what we are doing to the planet as a direct result of the hypnosis we are under. We are now willing to lie, cheat, steal, and even kill for fortune to show us the green wizard, or is it really a monster. It certainly seems to bring out some of the worst in humanity, and we have a strong tendency to forget that its only a tool and should be balanced along with all our other aspirations. Money alone is not evil, only its worship can make it so.

Governments seldom, if ever, look at their citizenry as equals, and seem to favor the wealthy, as if they were the ones that needed the help. There is something missing here that is kept from our view. What is missing; is what the people do not get to see in the lobbying process. The money that goes under the table or the financial support by wealthy companies for campaign purposes. These transactions are not made public. We can only scratch our heads and wonder why the scales of legislation are so imbalanced in favor of the wealthy. There should be a media channel whose sole purpose is to record everything that goes on in our governmental process, and it should be unlawful to do anything behind closed doors. It should be made law that all such underhanded transactions have to be made public, so the constituency can clearly see what is really influencing their choice of representatives. There is a reason that all this lobbying is kept out of the public eye. No one in their right mind would re-elect such a candidate, and re-election is all that matters to some, or most.

Again, it boils down to integrity of the individual and what it is that we want our demography to be: An outdated dog eat dog world; or a balanced and just world where everyone counts equally. And, that is why I believe we need a cross section of the population as representatives in order to begin to balance the scales of government for everyone. There are many questions we need to ask ourselves about the efficacy of the system we are now living under, and how we can change it for the mutual benefit of everyone.

Chapter 7

Energy

Energy can be felt and seen in every part of the universe, from the subtle cosmic background radiation, the residual from the Big Bang and the creation of the universe, to the incredible output of light, heat, and radiation from a blue giant star, and every thing in between, such as our own supplier of life supporting energy, the star that we call our sun.

All sources of energy are natural phenomenon, even the ones that we have learned to harness and use for our own purposes on Earth. Some forms of energy are still a mystery, such as gravity, which sets up the conditions for the formation, and destruction of most of the celestial bodies and stars in our known universe. One of the most mysterious being dark matter and dark energy, which can not be seen, and only measured by the effects it has on visible matter.

Its as if we are blind to certain forms of energy in the same fashion that we can only visually see a very narrow band in the visible spectrum of energy.

One of the first energy source that early man learned to use, was fire, although fire has always been present, man at some point learned to make fire at will, which opened many new avenues in our evolution. Staying warm on cold winter nights added to the odds of survival, as well as cooking food in order to eliminate parasites and render food more digestible.

Since the discovery of making fire, many other sources of energy have come to be employed, such as oil and its refined by products of gasoline and diesel, Also coal, natural gas, and in recent times, nuclear, wind, and solar energy. Some are considered clean and some dirty, depending on how they impact the environment with pollution from the by-products of transforming matter to energy. Most of what we extract from the Earth to use as energy sources are carbon based, and whose composition comes from organic matter that lived millions of years ago, some of it animal and some of it vegetation.

All of our sources of energy are used to produce heat that in most cases are used to produce steam that turns the turbines that produce electricity. The heat is produced by direct burning of coal, oil, natural gas, or thermonuclear devices.

Oil products as well as coal when burned to produce energy for various uses, such as the internal combustion engines, and electric power plants in the case of coal, release carbon dioxide as well as other poisonous by-product and gasses into the air that we have to breath. There are ways of reducing these emissions that pour out of the smoke stacks of coal fired power plants, but either the laws governing pollution are weak, or the enforcement is not implemented. At the present time, some legislators are in the process of trying to turn back the clock by revoking the few environmental laws that exist now, instead of doing the right thing and coming up with more stringent laws for protecting the environment.

As far as our automobiles are concerned, the manufacturers have come up with a real tricky way of reducing the emissions of cars, by burning the excess fuel that the inefficient engines produce's, in the catalytic converter of the exhaust system, instead of designing a more efficient fuel delivery system that would burn this excess gasoline in the engine instead of wasting it in the tail pipe. Well, it's just a band aid and a way of copping out of the real problem of inefficient transportation, that is really controlled by the oil industry, who don't want to lose the billions of dollars of profits, while being subsidized by the taxpayers, through Uncle Sam of course. We get blown off. We pay at the pump and then make a balloon payment at tax time.

I hear car commercials today, that offer cars that do 35mpg, as if this were a major breakthrough in car engineering. Well, where is the big deal in that? I owned a 1985 Chevy Nova that got 35mpg, and it used a carburetor and not fuel injection, which most modern cars use, and is supposed to be a more efficient system. I don't think we should get wide eyed until we start hearing 100mpg plus, and I am sure that it's not an engineering impossibility.

Car manufacturers are definitely lagging in designing cars that meet the needs of a world that is in the clutches of global warming. There is no doubt that we are significant contributors to the amount of carbon dioxide that is pumped into our atmosphere every day by the burning of fossil fuels.

If the gasoline were to be turned into a real gas [instead of a liquid as is applied now] before it reached the cylinders of an engine, the efficiency and gas mileage of an engine would sky rocket, because most or all the fuel would be burned in the cylinders.

Although much has been said and even promised by political campaigners before getting elected, not much has been done to steer us in the direction of alternative sources of energy. No federal money has been allotted to research or to develop any of these sources of energy. What the government does push is more oil drilling in off shore sights or in places where the ecology of a pristine area would be severely compromised. There is probably no way to asses the damage in the Gulf of Mexico's marine ecological system. We will probably be seeing the effects of that spill far into the future, and there is the possibility that it may never fully recover.

What is going to happen when the last drop of oil has been extracted from the ground? If we do not have some alternative for energy already in place when that time comes, and come it will, every thing on this planet is going to come to a screeching halt and chaos like we have never seen before, will commence.

Oil like all the other resources on this world, is finite, and there is no oil being re-created at this time, nor is it likely that any will be created in the future. Maybe science will come up with a way to synthesis oil, but that would only mean that our environment would continue to suffer from co2 emissions until it finally collapses from the atmosphere becoming too hot and too polluted to sustain life.

It would be much more intelligent to prepare now, before our supplies are completely exhausted. Most of the consuming machines of fossil fuel were invented at a time when we were naive enough to believe that the supply would never run out, and so we marched on constructing bigger and better ways of consuming this precious resource.

One of the biggest problems that I see, is the outright waste of not only petroleum, but of most of the other resources we employ. Have we not yet seen clearly how abundance can turn to scarcity and leave us flat on our faces if we do not posses the foresight to prepare for the future.

Nothing is being done to increase our efficiency of transportation of industrial goods to the door of the consumer by increasing the MPG of industrial haulers. At an early stage in the industrialization of America, the railroad played an important role in the delivery of goods to the nation and was and could still be a more efficient method of transporting good for long distances, whereas today there is a massive fleet of highway carriers that do not have the carrying capacity to be considered viable competitors with trains in the vain of efficiency.

Certainly, some of the railway systems have fallen into disrepair, but that is just one more aspect of transportation that needs to be addressed and dealt with. There is also, in my opinion the overuse of personal transportation; the automobile. No one is willing to walk anymore, even for short distances. This is not only using excess fuel, but is affecting the health of the individual, by denying ourselves the simple but effective means of cardiovascular exercise and burning up calories that contributes to over weight and obese conditions, something that is on the rise around the world, and is even affecting children, exacerbated by the consumption of fast food.

One of the cleaner sources of energy is, electricity produced by nuclear power plants. This source does not pollute the atmosphere, but comes with some very tricky problems of its own. There is the matter of the waste product and how to get rid of it without contaminating the ground or our water supplies. In the beginning of the nuclear power production era, the waste was re-refined and reused, but this process has apparently become financially prohibiting, although I suspect that it has more to do with profits than it has with feasibility. Well, just load it on a Delta rocket and shoot it at the sun, and we don't have to deal with it anymore. Of course, we face the same problem that we had with oil, uranium is another finite resource, and once we mine all there is available, we can turn our nuclear power plants into museums, although it would probably take a long time to exhaust all the uranium on earth.

Another aspect of nuclear power generation is; they have a tendency to melt down if any thing goes wrong with the cooling system, such as what happened in Chernobyl Russia, at Three Mile Island, and recently in Japan, where an earthquake and the tsunami that followed created the conditions for a melt down. Of course, some of these disasters are due to design and location. When designing such an edifice, I think it would be prudent to make the design and the construction to the highest standards possible, with the intent of making it last at least as long as an Egyptian Pyramid. Research on the best possible location as far as the stability of the terrain, would be of prime importance. It does not make much sense to build a nuclear power plant next to a fault line.

And now we come to wind generation, probably the cleanest form of power generation. My only concern is that with our overwhelming appetite for electricity, we would have to cover half the Earth to satisfy our need, and we would also be at the mercy of the wind, although as the atmosphere warms up, it will probably become more turbulent, more windy and unpredictable, with more violent storm, stronger tornado's and hurricanes.

The real problem is that even if we quit pumping green house gasses into the air right now, it would probably take several hundred years for our atmosphere to return to normal, whatever normal is, if we are indeed a major contributor to global warming. The reason I say this, is because the Earth has been through many climate changes, and it has been gleaned from archaeological data, that it does not take much to upset the delicate balance between the energy we receive from the sun and the energy we retain, and my point is that there may actually be some natural variable that is the major contributor in this situation. There is strong scientific evidence that there have been many mass extinctions that were produced by severe changes in climate.

Even if the cause is natural, it does not mean that we have to contribute to the problem, and there is no denying that we are killing our environment on many different fronts. *There is such a thing as over achieving.* We are going to extract all the energy resources that we can get to. We are going to overgrow until there is no top soil left. We are going to fish the oceans until there is nothing left to catch. We are going to poison the land, waters, and air, and we are going to over populate the earth. Something is going to give somewhere. We can only stretch the rubber band so far, before it breaks.

That brings us to another form of energy production: solar. This is another clean form of energy, but it could stand to be a lot more efficient, as it is now, it would require a tremendous amount of surface area to produce enough power to meet our needs.

That includes bulbs that don't need to be lit, such as the tremendous amount of energy that is used in shopping malls at night when they are not open for business. Most cities are so lit up that it renders the head lights on cars useless, but we still waste fuel by using them.

This is another area that could support some research into the possible ways of making photo voltaic technology more efficient, so we would not have to cover the Earth with solar panels. There are areas of the Earth that receive sunlight almost every day of the year. There is a factor to be considered here, if we were to somehow miraculously convert our dependence to solar energy, what would be the effect of converting the suns energy to electricity as opposed to the current situation where some of the energy from the sun is absorbed by the earth and in any one location adds its cumulative effect to the overall temperature of the world. This energy would be absorbed by the solar cells, thus removing it from the collective energy available to the rest of the planet, and could possibly have an overall cooling effect. Of course, there would have to be a significant coverage of the surface of the earth with solar panels to be considered a major contributor.

As the technology stands today it would require a considerable amount of surface area to even come close to meeting our present needs. and I am sure in the near future, our consumption of energy is going to increase, unless we wake up and realize that there are many areas where we could economize, I believe, on a grand scale. Most of the electricity we use comes out of the wall socket, and it is easy to ignore what it takes to produce it, and so it is taken for granted. I don't think to many people think beyond the wall socket, down the transmission lines to the power plant that is spewing out tons of poisonous smoke in order to generate the electricity that comes out of that wall socket. This lack of awareness leads us to wasted energy. There should be a mandatory course in high school on the different forms of power generation and what it takes to produce them.

One solution would be to install solar panels on the roof of every house, thus making it independent to supply its own energy needs. In places where the sun shines almost every day, there would be an excess of energy produced, which could be sold back to the utility companies. Some power plants would still be needed to take up the slack in low light days, but the need for fossil fuel consumption would be greatly reduced. I am certain that there are factions of the power generating consortium that would be lobbying their hearts out to block any move that would lead to energy independence.

Walking and bicycling would add a modicum of health benefits to anyone willing to participate, and would also have a positive effect toward cutting down the obesity epidemic that is even affecting children in the U. S. Children don't walk to school anymore, even if its a short distance, and anyone wanting to run an errand, just jumps in the car and uses fuel that could be saved if we walked. We should change that term from running an errand to wheeling an errand. Cities need to implement better bicycle routes that don't have to compete with cars.

I don't know if an insidious plot is afoot, but 20 years ago in my own neighborhood, there were many small stores and shops within easy walking distance. Those services are only available in mega malls or shopping centers, and of course, these institutions are responsible for the demise of small business's, that also adds to the burden of fuel consumption. Of course the insidious plot is that the mega chain stores have been running small business into the ground for many decades, cutting off the close availability of goods. The small business has to charge a little more for goods, but by the time we add in the fuel, maintenance and ware on our vehicle, we would find that we are not saving much by having to drive miles to purchase a few necessities.

There is another factor that boggles the mind while driving in traffic, and that is, the drivers who are hell bent to make the next red light, as if they were participating in some competitive race. This kind of behavior is probably prompted by ego or frustration or both. It has been revealed in studies, that many people feel a surge of personal power and isolation, as if suddenly placed in a world of their own, when they get into their vehicles. This kind of driver needs to come back down to Earth and realize that their car is just a form of transportation and should not be transformed into an extension of their ego. This kind of driving not only creates dangerous situations in traffic, and uselessly burns more fuel than necessary. The driving habits of the individual and how insightful we are behind the wheel of our cars, can make a tremendous difference in the amount of fuel consumed overall. How fast we accelerate from a stop light makes a big difference in how many miles we get out of a tank of gasoline. Everyone should be conscience of the fact that their attitude behind the wheel of an automobile not only has a bearing on their own personal safety and the safety of others, but also would save them money and save on the overall consumption of fuel. With the present price of gasoline, I try to squeeze as much gas mileage out of my cars as I possibly can. Apparently, a lot of people don't seem to care what they have to pay at the pump, they still drive as if they were being chased by demons. Of course, those demons are our own ego demons and they could care less what the effect of excessive fuel use is doing to a diminishing resource or, the impact on the environment.

For the gullible, there are the car commercials that shows a speeding demon behind the wheel of the car that is being advertised. Car commercials make very poor role models. Of course, they are aimed straight at the ego, and the ego says *yessss, with that car I can show everyone how bad I am.* Neo Stone Age thinking.

There are many makes and models of vehicles that are produced around the world, and they are all in serious competition with each other. This competition is directly passed down to the buyers in the form of insidious advertisements that try to convince us that one brand is better than another, when in reality they are all the same, but the public believes these ordinary lies and proceeds to take them to the road to try and prove the validity of what we have swallowed in commercials, that aim their missiles right at the false pride of one ups-man-ship. We need to wake up and see the subtle manipulation we are being subjected to in almost all forms of advertisement, addressed in the chapter on, A Public Seduced.

We would be much better off if the car manufacturers would spend those billions of dollars on research to improve miles per gallon, safety, in their cars, and then they might have something to boast about, and we would have a better product to choose from. There are forces in the world that would keep things just the way they are at present for the sole purpose of immediate profit gratification, thwart evolution, and continue to uphold practices that could eventually lead to catastrophic collapse of our present way of life.

Maybe you have noticed that in every economic collapse, there are those who walk away very well healed and unscathed, and are ready to set up the conditions for the next glut scenario, but who can blame them for taking advantage of the masses that support this kind of behavior by swallowing every hook that is presented to them. Remember, only you can take care of your best interests, and those of our brothers and sisters who in mutual *love* and *understanding*, can bring this flight of fancy back from the brink, for a safe landing.

I mentioned that automobiles are no different from one manufacturer to the next, and the reason for this statement is that if we compare the basic performance of all autos, we would discover that they all use the same design parameters in the production of the drive train, which is the most important area where efficiency and overall performance are procured. The internal combustion engine is not that much different from the original design, with only minor modifications to allow for higher speed, by shortening the stroke, better oiling systems, stronger and lighter metals, more reliable fuel delivery systems [fuel injection], and computer control of the ignition system.

What manufacturers call emissions control, does nothing to improve the performance or the efficiency of an engine, and only creates a means of burning unused fuel in the catalytic converter in order to reduce the amount of pollutants that exit the tail pipe; fuel that should have been converted to energy in the engine and not wasted. All modern cars boast this equipment and if we were to dismantle different makes and models we would soon realize that they are all pretty much the same.

Most cars today are over powered, with high horsepower that just translates to more gas consumption and lower gas mileage. More horsepower is appealing to the ego and we seem to be more than willing to hand over our pocket books to possess it under our hoods. More wasted energy. The only real difference in cars of different manufacture, are in the appointments and visual appeal, but as far as longevity goes, what matters most is how well a car is maintained, serviced, and how it is driven.

If somehow we could get around the big oil lobbyist in congress, then perhaps government could put pressure on automobile manufacturers to begin to research and design more efficient fuel use by the internal combustion engine.

If gasoline could be turned from a liquid state to a gaseous state before it enters the cylinders, it would create a more efficient burn with less waste, if any. In the present design, which is fuel injected as standard, the fuel is still in a liquid state, and is squirted directly into the cylinders, or in the case of throttle body units, the fuel is squirted into the intake manifold. In either case the fuel is still in a liquid state. A gaseous state injection would require a closed system to keep the gas from escaping and causing external fires, and might require more oxygen for proper combustion, which could be implemented with a small super charger if necessary. Any system that would produce a more efficient burn, might require more oxygen. The present systems are designed to function on the oxygen that is present in the air, although, if the fuel were in a gaseous state, the normal amount of oxygen might suffice, because the volume of the fuel would be less to produce the same amount of horsepower.

There are other methods that could be employed to improve the overall efficiency of engines. One change would be to replace all the sleeve bearing with ball bearings, thus reducing the friction of all the moving parts and at the same time, increasing the life of the engine. Yes, this would be a little more costly, but well worth it in the benefit that would ensue. If an engine is serviced at the recommended intervals and is not abused, it has been shown that most of the engine ware occurs at start up, when all the oil has had time to drain out of the moving parts, and before the oil pump has brought the oil pressure up to the prescribed level. To alleviate this condition, an auxiliary electric oil pump would feed oil to all moving parts for 10 seconds before the starter is allowed to engage, and the auxiliary pump would cut out as soon as the engine started allowing the mechanical pump to take over, which is more reliable than an electric pump over long periods of time. The only problem with this scenario is; does the driver have ten seconds worth of patience to spare at every start up, and bank robbers trying to make a quick get away might not like this feature.

I grew up in the era of muscle cars, which in most cases were rather boxy and not too aero dynamic, although beautiful to look at, the wind resistance was a major factor in the amount of fuel consumed, and these cars were much heavier than current models, that have a much better air flow design. Newer cars are much lighter than cars from the muscle car era, and in most cases the hood and wind shield is designed to push the car down to the road as speed increases, making it perform as if it was a heavier car, and giving it the ability to handle the road better at higher speeds. Still there are some areas that could be improved to allow a smoother flow of air over and around the car, or trucks, which even in this day and age are still boxy and not very aero dynamic.

There is not enough research being done on the alternative sources of energy that could be made available for public consumption, mainly because of the resistance to change that is prompted by the motivation for profit. It would require the rebuilding of the infrastructure of the power producing industries. This change is going to come whether we want it or not. There is only so much oil, coal and natural gas in the ground. So the sensible course would be to develop these alternative sources before they run out. If we wait till the last drop of oil is used up, then, we are in for a rude awakening that would shake our social system to its very foundation.

The population of the world has a tendency to take all the conveniences that the modern world produces; for granted, and they don't think much about what goes into making them. From observing people, I would say, that if our industrial production were to slow down or stop; the first reaction of the populace would be anger [why can't I have my *Twinkies* anymore]: which would then turn to fear; and then would come panic. It is the latter reaction that is dangerous. When in the panic mode, we seldom make intelligent decisions and is tantamount to going berserk. If we can avoid panic, and keep our heads when faced with a major social dilemma, we could then come together and at least have a chance of finding solutions that might just enable our survival. Panic would only insure certain collapse, that could lead to barbaric behavior.

There is too much emphasis on profit and not enough contemplation on what is going to take place in the future if we allow this train to run at full speed until it runs out of track. We are already experiencing the effects of scrapping the bottom of the oil barrel by means of fracking and tar sand mining, with the effect of poisoning the air we breath and the water we drink.

There are some modes of transportation that can only operate on fossil fuels, unless some one comes up with a way of powering a jumbo jet on photo voltaic energy, or perhaps some form of power cell that could replace the massive amounts of fossil fuel that airliners consume, both commercial and military. Bio fuels are being experimented with at this time. But, if we had to grow crops to produce enough fuel to feed our whole system, we would probably be left with nothing to eat. Hydrogen could be used as an alternative fuel, but again there is a finite amount of this gas available. There is plenty of hydrogen on Jupiter. Maybe we could construct a pipeline to this gas giant. Not likely, and any transport of resources from other planets in our solar system would require a tremendous amount of energy just getting there and back, and would be prohibitively expensive as a commodity to the public. Better start getting back in shape now folks, we may have to go back to the original form of transportation: bi-pedal.

There are thousands of flights that cross our skies every day, consuming millions of gallons of fuel, both in commercial and military flights, and are as responsible for polluting the atmosphere, as much or more than ground traffic is, although, no mention is ever heard of this contributor as a major player of atmospheric pollution, and the blame is mostly laid at the feet of ground based transportation.

If we could find our way to peaceful solutions involving world conflicts, then much of this military consumption of fuel could be eliminated, and employed for more productive uses. We are still stuck in the inertia of the massive military mobilization that took place during World War II. That effort was of such a tremendous magnitude that I believe the wave of that war is still carrying the whole world along with it, and so much was left over, not in only arms and technology, but in the paranoia that remained even after the conflict was over. That made it impossible to dismantle the war machine, mostly because the two remaining super powers were unwilling to find a peaceful solution to their problems, leaving the world in a state of permanent cold war.

Third world countries have become militarized even when they could not afford such a move, leaving their citizens in dire straits. These smaller nations are only in the process of mimicking the super powers who at the end of World War II did not realize that they were now the role models for the rest of the world, especially those countries that were just rising and impressionable. The sad fact is that the two super powers continued to promote war, and almost coming into nuclear confrontation on several occasions. That was not the kind of role model the world needed then, and its not what is needed now, but at present, the Bear and the Eagle are rattling their sabers at each other again. The present paradigm of conflict is going to be very difficult to turn around, since it has had sixty-six years to take root, and is so appealing to the more oppressed regions of the world, giving them a false sense of pride in their effort, when in reality, all they are doing is destroying themselves and what few resources they have at their level of production. Of course, there is always some industrialized nation that is willing to sell arms to those who don't have the means to manufacture them. Lives for money.

If the two super powers, at the end of the war to end all wars had said and agreed that; alright, we have removed the threat of the entity seeking world domination: the Axis Powers, and it it now time to turn our swords into plowshares, the world would have settled into a much more peaceful state than the one it finds itself in now, with violence erupting everywhere, and the separation between people and countries growing larger every day. Instead, the super powers fell for the very myth they were fighting against in the first place. It does keep the war machine complex of manufacturing happy, but what a price.

This is where autonomy is going to play a major part in the future of our evolution, and only an individual who has stepped outside the box and begun to make up his or her own mind about what the truth is, and what the effort of keeping us fighting each other over ideas, is really about. It is really about profits, reinforced by those few who have something to gain from war. The masses are controlled, some by fear, some by ego, some by money, it all works if bought into.

It has been said many times, but adhered to so very little; that the out of the box thinkers won't believe everything they hear and only half of what they see. Only a gullible person believes everything that is presented to their eyes and ears. If in doubt, run it passed your heart and soul, or do your homework and research, and it will give you the filter you need to come to some grounded conclusion.

There is no need to use energy just because it is there and available, and again it is the individual thinker who is going to decide what they really need to spend their portion of energy on, and to what economy of use, we can manage.

There are many areas of the world where every home could be equipped with solar panels, making them not only self sustaining, but independent of the power grid, leading to the reduced use of fossil fuels, and therefore reducing the pollution that is pumped into the atmosphere. The cost is daunting, but just sit down and figure how much we pay over 60 years of electric bills. These conversions should be subsidized by the government if they were really serious about preserving the environment. I don't think they are, and the subject only seems to be broached during election campaigning, and then government goes on with business as usual, protect the rich, which really need no protection, continue with the same energy sources that are already beginning to dwindle, and keep a sharp eye on the bottom line. Sometimes it feels like trying to swim against a tsunami, and it is, a tsunami that is on the verge of drowning us all.

Well, this tide is not going to be turned back unless we begin the arduous task of trimming the tree and planting governments feet back on the ground where it belongs. [See the chapter on Government] The federal government takes on tasks that should be addressed by the individual states and are only pertinent to specific local needs. The economy of the USA was much stronger when regulations were imposed. Deregulation only opened the lid on Pandora's box, and effectively declared open season on the consumers, allowing the greedy, license to kill. The president that allowed this to commence, was not thinking of the hard working tax paying middle class people who elected him in the first place. On top of that a subsequent president reduced the tax burden for the rich and super rich, employing the false hope that the trickle down theory would commence, but there is no trickle down, greed does not allow it.

The tax system is deliberately fraught with loop holes and complexities in order to make it work for those who are wealthy enough to take advantage of loop holes. A simple system should be established where everyone, regardless of their monetary status, pays a fixed percentage of income tax. It should be obvious to everyone that this is the only equitable way of administering taxes. Tax loop holes are just license to cheat. Who said that cheaters never win? Of course they do, if allowed to do so.

There are so many loop holes in our tax system, that there are billion dollar corporations that don't pay any taxes, and on top of that they are subsidized by the tax payers. Talk about pork barrel mentality, or is it just plain insanity. I prefer the latter, as it describes a sickness that seems to be deeply rooted in the psyche of the human conscious mind. The only reason I would describe it as a sickness, is that it seems to be out of balance with all the other conscious elements that make up the human psyche, such as love, compassion, moderation, understanding, etc.

There is the possibility that we are experiencing a form of collective insanity where by we are not taught to balance our desires and drives, that can lead to an almost neurotic quest for riches, and the protection of those riches with no awareness of the consequences to the whole of humanity. It is a fact that the more affluent an individual becomes, the more remote the rest of humanity becomes, adding to the separation.

This separation is quite evident in the way that governments eventually come to dispatch their duties, by being exclusive to who they come to represent. Eventually it seems, that special interest takes over and begin to exert a dramatic influence on the representatives of the people, creating an imbalance in the benefits of participation in such a organization. It is a crude way to run a government. The separation allows some to think that they are above reproach or in a higher standing than the people they are supposed to be serving, completely forgetting that they were put there by those they look down on, not because of elevated intelligence or abilities, but supposedly as trustees for the electorate.

Its time to shake the tree folks! Government is only going to work as well as the people that administer it, no matter how well written the foundations are.The only thing that will work well in government is integrity and self determination. If our government officials can not act on their own and of their own volition and make decisions without coercion, deception, fear, and the hook of silver crossing palms, then the boat is sinking right before our eyes. Nothing can save us but our higher self, in government, or in our personal lives. We are going to have to open the windows to our soul and let the light shine through, or suffer the sentence of an exile. An exile that could have had it all but instead chooses to wallow in apathy instead of using all the gifts that have been bestowed upon him by the cosmic intelligence.

A tree sometimes overburdens itself, producing too much fruit that eventually falls to the ground and just rots if there is no one interested enough to harvest said fruit, and take on the task of caring for the tree by keeping it well trimmed and healthy.

There are too many of our citizens, young and old that do not much think about what is taking place in government, a direct result of the inadequate educational system and limited news media, that does not offer enough exposure to the realities of governmental processes to turn out a well informed public. Schools should be teaching students how to be active in their government by employing lesson plans that would create actual interaction with the legislative process on a real time basis, and this process should begin at the elementary level. At present the curriculum of schools is designed to turn out fuel for the machine, not self actualized citizens.

Our sun is the major source of energy, supplying and supporting every form of life on the globe. It seems that this energy source would be of utmost importance in the minds of researchers who are seeking alternatives to fossil fuel consumption. Every home could be outfitted with a solar collection system for heating water and making electricity. A six foot magnifying glass concentrating the suns rays on inverted fins in a water collector would be adequate to produce enough water for utility purposes as well as radiant heating for the home, and an array of solar cells to supply the electric power. This is where our government should be putting our money to work instead of trying to play big brother to the world and squandering our resources on fighting punitive wars around the world. So much could be done to improve our environment with the money that is spent on supporting our burgeoning armed forces. The facilities that do military research could turn their attention to research out alternative infrastructures, ending the dependence on oil as our major source of energy. This needs to take place in short order, with an ever increasing population and a dwindling supply of oil, will, in the future add up to a disastrous situation.

The whole world should be uniting in this effort to convert us to cleaner energy. Pooling technologies from different countries would accelerate the effort, instead of the present mind set of trying to keep everything a nation does in its research classified, and under lock and key. It would be a much better and more amicable world if we could share information with each other, which in my opinion has always been a source of hostilities between nations. If we shared our secrets with each other, there would be nothing left to fight about and everyone would be on an even footing. Is this not worth considering; you policy makers? Or is the fight and the competition the real underlying motive. Is this what turns people on? Well, I think we need to make another leap in our evolution. The fight, fight scenario is beginning to wear a little thin, and is also thinning our chances of ever achieving the higher destiny that we are capable of attaining. Unjustified war is a total waste of energy in every form, human and material. *When will they ever learn.* Apparently not yet, *and on the morning after, one tin soldier still rides away.* We are caught in a loop or a whirlpool that we don't seem to be able to swim away from. We as individuals are going to have to draw the line, because governments can't. Too much posturing to get past, and too much resistance to change, so its up to us. All we need to do is demonstrate our Love for everything and everyone in our daily living, and hope that the heat of our efforts, eventually rises to the top of the barrel.

Lets use our own personal energy, along with the gift from our star sharing some of its energy with Mother Earth, who in turn shares it with us in the form of everything that sustains us; in order find ways of creating a vibrant, livable, and enduring environment for us and for future generations.

Chapter 8

My Path

My path has become the path of the warrior. This does not refer to the traditional warrior or soldier that is part of a military establishment, but instead refers to a person that is waring to change his domestication or initial programming in order to seek out independence from antiquated thinking, for the purpose of helping myself, those near and dear to me, all of mankind, the flora, the fauna, and the environment of this beautiful world that we have inherited; from the eminent possibility of devastation and annihilation.

We are showing no compassion or respect for this wonderful gift that has been bestowed on us by creation, and as such, creation is not going to show us any compassion or respect in kind. Mindfulness has not become one of our innate characteristics, or has not been in our priorities for a long time, if indeed it ever was, as is evidenced by much of recorded history. But, how can we show respect for our world when we can't even show respect for each other, using any minute difference in physiology or ideology to create untenable situations and pressures on ourselves and others, that can eventually lead to war. Much of this is created by our domestication; what we are taught to believe in, during our upbringing at that most critical and impressionable age.

Domestication entails breaking our spirit [in varying degrees] and totally deviating us of the path that our true nature would demonstrate. We are powerful in our natural state, but early on in life we are instilled with the anchor of fear, and because we are torn between what we are and what we become, we learn to hate. This hate that seems to be turned outward, is really a form of self hate. What most of us don't realize, is that we are connected to everything in the universe through the quantum field, and what we do to others we also do to our selves, and it encompasses the material world as well. We are also of the material world. Physically, our bodies are composed of the same building blocks that everything else in the universe is, which is more than our physical senses can see or feel, and can only be felt at the spiritual level.

The warrior is trying to get back to what he was before the domestication took place, the plane of all possibilities, and not the limitations of a fixed program. I do believe that our children need our protection and guidance as they are growing and developing, which is what all creation does with their young. But, I also believe that every individual should be allowed to seek out their own path in life. In clarification,

I will state, that my intention is not to cast an evil light on domestication, which can be a strong contributor to our survival. The only problem I see in domestication, is that a whole lot of outdated strictures are passed on to the next generation. Our social evolution has lagged behind our technical evolution, creating an imbalance that allows us to use powerful technology in very destructive ways. It seems to be harder to change our minds about ideology and religion than it is to accept new concept in technology.

Some of this is due to our religious beliefs that are based in fear, such as the salvation of our souls, if we deviate in any way from prescribed dogma. The seductive power of heaven and especially hell, where we can burn forever, are very powerful tools in keeping the believers in control. Sin, such as murder won't condemn us to hell after we die, but will condemn us to hell while we are alive, since I stated before, what we do to others we do to our selves.

I belive that the only one who can save my soul is me, due to my perception that the powerful belief structures of religions, governments, learning institutions, and cast in stone individuals, do not allow for any deviation in thinking or belief, thus no evolution. Much of this structure has nothing to do with the belief in God or a creator, but is a power structure that is designed to hold its constituents in sway, since power does not like any competition that might alter its hold. This is not just a religious problem, but a governmental problem as well. Government also represent power structures that don't like to be challenged, and in actuality present a dogma of their own, again making evolution difficult. So, as far as domestication is concerned, every sentient being has a responsibility to examine their belief system and think about what it is that motivates them to walk a particular path in life.

I started my religious experience as a Presbyterian Christian, going to Sunday school and then attending the sermon after, with my mother, sister, and sometimes my grandmother on my moms side. My father did not get into religion until he started to feel his mortality, and also as a means of replacing the social intercourse that is lost after retirement. In that first encounter with religion, I enjoyed the singing of hymns and as far as I was concerned, as a child, that was the way of spirit for us and all the congregation we belonged to. With the intensity and the ardor of the innocent, I was deeply impressed and much of that is still with me. The initial intent of most religions is altruistic, the problem is that the ego has a way of worming its way into all aspects of life, and can and does rule us; for it loves power and control if allowed free rein.

My mother being a firm believer in discipline, enrolled me in Catholic school when I started kindergarten, and I attended there until the completion of the third grade. It was a little strange being the only protestant in an all Catholic environment, But it really didn't bother me much. I have always had a propensity to explore different aspects of life with an open mind, even as a child, and for me it fell into the category of exploration. It was not that unpleasant, except for an occasional comment by the sister teachers about their prejudice with respect to protestants, and how we were not of the true faith, and probably hell bound. I don't think I believed in hell even then, so it was just idle comment to me.

The next three years of school, fourth, fifth, and sixth grades, along with my sister, I attended a rural one room school at the Red River Fish Hatchery in northern New Mexico, since my father worked for the New Mexico Fish and Game Department. This one room school employed one teacher, and housed around twenty students; from grade one to grade eight. To me this was the best school I ever attended. Everyone knew everyone else and it felt more like a family than an institution, which reinforces my belief that every human endeavor works best on a small scale, be it school or government, man seems to function better at a small scale. I think its because everyone knows how everybody feels about what is going down at any given time.

Those three years stand out as some of the richest years of my life, and is where I first experienced heart felt love for someone of the opposite sex, but destiny had other notions, and I had not yet discovered that destiny is a malleable thing, and can be changed to suit the individual, so I flowed with the river of time until I discovered at a much later time, that I could actually swim against the current.

Not only was everyone in the school my friend, but we lived in an almost totally natural environment. Our small house was situated in a box canyon with a large meadow to the side, and the Red River flowing a few yards from the house. At night the song of the river would lull me to sleep. I would spend most of my free time exploring the canyon, and it was an endless fascination for a young mind and able body.

The sky at night, especially when there was no moon, was so brilliant, it seemed that I could almost touch the stars. I was quite upset when I was informed that we were moving to Santa Fe, where my father was to be stationed and work from. That is where I went to school until I graduated from Santa Fe High School. I met my future wife in the tenth grade and we married a year after graduation. My parents joined the Church of Christ in Santa Fe, so naturally my sister and I had to join. This church was very similar to the Presbyterian Church in its beliefs and practices, so it did not create any radical change for me.

My wife and I dated through two and a half years of high school, and though she was Catholic, it never seemed to make much of a difference to either one of us, until the actual planning of the wedding, where it was discovered that I was not a Catholic, which started to create a little tension between the two families. At that point I took a crash course in Catholicism and was once again baptized [for the third time] as a Catholic. It did not bother me as much as it did some other people. I just took it as a new exploration and challenge, as I often viewed many of the major changes that occurred in my life, and still do to this day. After our marriage we practiced that religion and baptized our three children in the Catholic Church.

After a span of some ten years after marriage, we began to taper off in our religious practice and slowly over many years we went to church less often, which I believe was brought about by the fact that after ten years of participation in any one church, one hears every thing that is to be said, and after a time it seems to be a lot like being on an endless treadmill, covering the same old ground, over and over.

Some people don't seem to mind this constant reiteration, and seem to be quite content to stay on the treadmill for the rest of their lives. True domestication certainly opens up an avenue in which people want to stay in their comfort zone, and that inhibits any desire to explore any other possibilities or question any of the strictures and structures that propel them on their walk through life. There is also a false sense of security being a member of a world wide ideology where everyone is of like mind, removing the awareness that all around them there is an element of control being exercised on them.

If we believe in hell, where we can burn forever, there is probably not much we would not do to save our souls from that kind of agony, and heaven certainly sounds like a hell of a better alternative. Truth be told, heaven and hell are right here and now. It all depends on circumstance and choice.

Religions have a tendency to infer to their congregations that God put everything in creation for the sole benefit of man, and it's our prerogative to do with it as we please. Though I do believe that God intended us to benefit from the diversity and abundance this beautiful world has to offer for our survival, I don't think he meant for us to trash and push every resource to exhaustible limits. This kind of closed loop thinking, where the dogma does not evolve at the same pace as technology, can and will lead to disaster, and is probably the prominent reason for my moving away from organized religion.

Some theological ideologies have not changed much in a thousand years. Some spin-offs have occurred in recent times, but are not that much different from their parent religions, although some have dropped the confession to priests and the hell premise. The fact always remains, that the strict adherence to the basic tenants of a belief system has to be followed implicitly, and that makes it impossible for any evolution to germinate.

Our technology has completely run away from our social evolution and our conscious awareness of just what we are accomplishing, if anything. The glamour of technology gives us such a feeling of comfort and security, that we have a tendency to ignore every other aspect of our surroundings: just like kids in the candy shop. The lure of the hook is powerful indeed. There is nothing wrong with technology. The problem at this point, is the tipping of the scales in favor of technology, and aided by the gold it brings, creating a monumental imbalance between renewable consumption and extinction of flora, fauna, and resources: followed by our own demise. Sounds morose you say! Well just consider the number of species that have become extinct in the last three hundred years, and how many are on the verge of extinction now; due mostly to the exponential increase in the human population and the added demand for space to dwell, and resources for our consumption and sustenance. A little detour on my path, but quite relevant to my overall world view.

So, I have invented my own religion, although I would not call it religion per say; since religion indicates a fixed set of rules and guide lines [dogma] that cannot be broached by anyone but the hierarchy, who supposedly know best, what God intends for us.

What I have done is to pick out what I believe to be the purest intention of many religions and belief systems from around the world, creating an amalgam of ideologies and incorporating it into one cohesive system, along with a whole lot of common sense, that works for me and will work for anyone whose intent it is, to set their course in an autonomous direction.

My system consists of not only mysticism, but of logic as well, and is not as rigid as it is in dogmatic religions. It is fluid and can evolve at any time that enlightenment may strike, and it can strike at the most unexpected times. This entails the warrior to constantly explore his own inner self as well as information and ideas that he finds along the path of his quest for the truth. I don't think it serves well to practice anything by rote, and then sit back and believe that salvation is at hand. When I stumble on a revelation that feels like I just stuck my finger in a wall socket, I am free to scrutinize, evaluate and incorporate it into my belief system. Someone in a dogmatic situation would probably call it the work of Satan and dismiss it outright.

Our inquiring minds are like a tool that if discarded and never used, will cause it to rust and witter away, rendering it useless. Believe me, the hierarchy of any religion is not any more intuitive than anyone else participating in that religion, The problem is that we turn our own power over to them and let them make all the decisions for us. It's also easier that way. Most in the hierarchy of any religion are learned men who have devoted their lives to studying the doctrines of their respective religions, but the ego has a way of seducing us into thinking that we have now become the unquestionable authority, and thus the roots of stagnation begin to spread. At this juncture, very little ever changes, and if anything does, its for convenience or to fortify power, not to promote enlightenment. There is no outward look, as if to say, this which I and my religion believe in, is the only thing that exists or is valid in the world. All religions have this opinion of their beliefs, but it just creates a moribund situation.

What about the other religions and faiths? Do they not believe that theirs is the only valid belief? Something is amiss here. As far as creation and evolution are concerned, I don't think God is sectarian in His or Her overview of the cosmos. In studying other belief systems, I have come to the conclusion that all religions and beliefs, at their core, are aiming at the same target. Most believe that a God exists, and their purpose is to bring out the higher qualities in the human spirit: to give purpose to life and try and alleviate the suffering and turmoil in mans nature. A nature that by way of our intelligence can take us up to sublime and joyous existence or haul us down to the pits of hell, where we can wallow and drown. Make no mistake: heaven is here as well as hell, which is apparent in the over abundance that some experience; to the squalid conditions that others are forced to live in.

We make the choice: heaven or hell, and it has to be an informed choice, which can only occur if we explore our own reality and question ourselves as well, of what we are taught. It is my belief that we all know at the intuitive level of our being, what is right and what is wrong, and simply relates to how we would prefer to be treated by others. Love is the key factor in the equation of right and wrong. Love that has to begin with our selves, and then extend to other of our species. Then blossoming out to encompass our whole ecology and environment including all the other living creatures that share our world. The path of the warrior is not an easy one. Its like walking up stream against the current of a strong river, but its the only way that inspiration and insight can be garnered.

One of the tragedies of extreme domestication is; that insight and love we inherit as part of our birthright is inexorably supplanted by hard and fast rules, that has the effect of viewing our world and our existence as a struggle that never allows joy and happiness to germinate. It states that we must fight for our survival tooth and nail. Love has the opposite effect. It gives us joy in what comes to us and allows us to look beyond the trials and tribulations as challenges that; if faced and resolved, will strengthen us along our chosen path. Love also levels the playing field for everyone, instead of the exclusive way we relate to each other. Extreme domestication is a breaking of the spirit that is usually accomplished with extreme pressure or even physical brutality, and is meant to lead us to total submission to authority.

If we are on a valid path, the young will recognize it and will follow without coercion . The reason that there is so much rebellion in our children as they move toward maturity is; they can see and feel the false premise that our world view is based on. A child is as intelligent at birth as he or she will ever be and their spirit is unblemished by any sort of programming. So, it is hard to fool a child, they can see right through lies and false premises. This negative effect at first accumulates due to a feeling of helplessness. But as the child begins to mature, he or she begins to realize that they are not so helpless, and begin to rebel. Some will go as far as to die or seriously ruin their lives, but most finally give up and become domesticated, since the instinct for survival is so strong in humans, we are willing to compromise ourselves in order to survive.

I, like most people of my generation, played the game by the rules in a forty two year career in aerospace electronics, where I had to turn a blind eye to the fact that I was contributing to death and destruction by applying my efforts to hardware that was used in missiles and other weapons of mass destruction. A large percentage of what we produced was for military use and somewhere around forty percent was for commercial use in communication satellites and space exploration vehicles. The lure of good pay was very persuasive in surrendering to a career that supported war. If taken out of context, the work itself was very challenging and was very satisfying as long as I did not think about what the end product was to be used for, and for most of my career I was able to do just that. Our efforts were wrapped in the guise of national security and patriotism, and I for one was willing to concede that we had enemies in the world that were out to crush us. I was able to maintain this orientation for most of my career, but towards the end my enthusiasm began to crumble and my work ethic began a down hill slide.

Something happened to me in the mid nineteen seventies that was happening to a multitude of people around the world. I was introduced to the psychedelic world of drugs. Illicit drugs that is. People were already strung out on legal drugs and I have always considered alcohol as a drug, a very popular drug too.

I was swept up like a gale that blew me away to places in my mind that I never knew existed. I don't necessarily think that this a good way to proceed, but to me it just happened, and had the effect of cutting the rope to the anchor that had held me in my place since my domestication was complete: which happened somewhere around my junior year in high school. It was a late rebellion for sure, but it did serve the purpose of setting me free to explore other possibilities that previously I would not have dared to approach. One positive aspect of the drug scene for me was; I mingled and befriended people that I don't think I would have met if I would have stayed on the straight and narrow.

I was finally set free to explore avenues of life that were previously verboten, although somewhat disconnected because of the nature and inherent instability of drugs and the fact that they were often used in the party mode. Fun yes, but not much insight at times like that, although communication and discourse did seem to be facilitated. I do have to add that music, which I always loved, came to my noesis like a jumbo jet at full throttle.

It took me a long time to extricate myself from the drug scene, but when I finally managed to do it, I discovered the sense of freedom was still with me and I was able to explore life in a more spiritual and cohesive manner. There is no going back to the farm once you have experienced the proverbial Paris.

It was during the mid nineteen seventies that I first read the first seven books by Carlos Castaneda about his apprenticeship with a Yaqui Indian sorcerer [Don Juan Mattues], and at the first reading, the impression I got was one of just having read a series of books about fictitious characters in fantasy setting. At first I did not take them seriously. I did enjoy the writing and went on to reread them several times, at which point they made more sense to me every time I went through them. I discovered practical tools and practices to deal with everyday problems and also past programming. I learned rituals and practices for getting rid of psychological pain that had been with me since childhood and subsequent years. There is so much baggage we carry throughout our lives that only serve to weigh us down and create obstacle on our path through life, and can also affect our health.

It was my good fortune to meet several apprentices of another Toltec Master; Don Miguel Ruiz, and studied with three of his apprentices one at a time over a four year period. Again I learned practical methods of removing the trash that had accumulated in my mind over a lifetime. Any time we are maligned, physically abused or mentally abused, there is a permanent scar that takes root in our psyche and can be a strong force in the way we react to situations and the way we order our lives. There were many reaction and decisions that I made in my life, which after reviewing later, did not make sense. And I would ask myself, why did I do that, or why did I take this course of action. It just did not feel like the course my true self would have taken.

In the course of studying the methods of a shaman, I realized that many of the decisions that we make are strongly influenced by traumatic events that took place in the past. Events that we have forgotten in our conscious minds, but are permanently embedded in the sub-conscious, where they can spring up at any time and dictate a course that is usually counter productive, or just rears its ugly head to cause us more pain, and pain for others as well.

One of the most useful tools that I acquired, was the art of stalking. Here the individual stalks his of her most painful or demeaning experiences, and brings them to the forefront and relives them. In a prescribed ritual they are offered up to the cosmos. The procedure removes the energy stored in the sub-conscious and disperses them among the energies of the universe. The memories of the events still remain, but they no longer contain any energy and become as benign as a cured cancer.

When I initially went through stalking, some of the events I wanted to be rid of, were of a very painful nature, and re-living them was as painful as the original event. However, once the ordeal was over and the pain and crying had subsided, it was replace by a feeling of buoyancy, well being and joy. I always felt like a weight had been removed off my shoulders, and that bag of rocks felt a little lighter. Every time I stalked a traumatic event in my life, I was effectively removing one of those burdensome rocks from my bag. It was recommended to me, to do a stalking every day or at least as often as possible, since we always encounter negativity in our daily living. Once we are relieved of our major issues, then stalking becomes more simplified, unless we experience some other major occurrence, such as the passing of a loved one, or anything that deeply affects us.

One modality that has been of great benefit to me, my wife and family, or anyone in our sphere of influence, who is willing to suspend their hard core beliefs in the exclusiveness of the medical establishment: is the hands on healing practice of Reiki. The word means universal. This is a form of energy healing that is channeled by the practitioner and applied to the client through the hands to various parts of the body. It can bring about the healing of injuries or chronic health issues to anyone who is willing to suspend any prejudices and just lend themselves to the moment. The practitioner should also be imbued with a strong and loving intent, which will make the procedure more effective. The recipient must also suspend all resistance and at least give the procedure the chance to work in the way it was intended. Humans have the ability of allowing or blocking the healing by resisting the flow of energy. The positive side of this modality is; if it does not work, it won't hurt you, but usually does work if the client has some faith in alternative healing and the abilities of the practitioner.

Although Reiki is an ancient practice that has its roots in Tibetan Buddhism, it had been lost through the ages, and was rediscovered by Mikao Usui, a Japanese doctor, circa late eighteen hundreds and is now a very popular and effective mode of healing. In an epiphany and spiritual inspiration he rediscovered the symbols used by Buddha for healing. The practice was so effective that before long it had drawn many disciples to the practice, and now has become a world wide form of healing. It is used extensively in alternative medicine and rejected by the established medical profession. It just does not fit their dogma.

To become a practitioner of Reiki, one must study with a Reiki Master Teacher. There are four levels in the modality. First, second and third degree, as well as Master Teacher, and only a qualified Master Teacher can effect the training of an apprentice, which can be done in six months to a year, depending on how fast the apprentice is willing to proceed. There are many Master Teachers if anyone is interest in learning this powerful modality, that perhaps is already in some other alternative healing practice, such as massage therapy. Those two healing practices go well together. After the apprentice has completed one of the degrees, the teacher will attune the apprentice to that level and a certificate of compliance will be issued, stating the successful completion of that level of training.

One of the benefits of Reiki is that the practitioner can affect healing to himself or herself, by the same methods that are used on the client. There have always been people that displayed the natural ability to do hands on healing.

Historically, there are many documented cases of people with the innate ability called healing hands or the laying on of hands. With the Reiki system, healing is readily available to anyone who is interested in becoming a practitioner, or seeking a way to self healing.

At present there is an unbridgeable moat between alternative healing and the established medical profession . The former is spiritual in nature and the latter is scientific and physical. In my opinion, the marriage of the two is altogether essential to affect a complete healing of the physical and spiritual body. I would in no way discredit either form of healing, be it physical or spiritual, since I have benefited from both. When I was six years old, my life was saved with the removal of an appendix that was just hours from rupturing, and in later life I was healed by spiritual means. I know they are both vital to my overall health and sanity.

I believe that many of the reasons we become ill, are directly related to the way we live; psychic trauma, stressed out, and what we consume in our daily meals. Also, much of this is brought about by the way we are poisoning our environment. There is a direct affect on our health by the stress of daily living in a society that does not seem to find time to unwind because there is always something to do or someplace to go and the struggle to make ends meet in an over inflated economy, There is something always trying to keep us out of balance, and this is where we as individuals have to make room in the rat race for our own salvation.

I know how difficult it is to let go of those stress factors that rule our lives, factors that only contribute to debilitation and don't bring any joy to our lives.

Somehow society is going to have to make a decision about what is important; is it going to be striving to keep up or is it going to be attaining some measure of well being and joy in our lives. There are so many subtle and not so subtle forces that are trying to steer the course of humanity in the direction of the never ending treadmill that only wind up in a dead end, by those whose intent is feeding the glut, that never seem to get or have enough.

If I knew then what I know now, I would more than likely have become an artist, craftsman, or musician, working in wood or other media, for that is where my heart has always been and that is what I do now. But like many people, I was steered toward an industrial career. One of the major problems is the emphasis the economic structure places, of the value on the different paths and aspirations of the individual. Music, arts, and crafts are viewed as non essential and not much economic benefit ever trickles down to the aspirants who have the talent and would chose that way of life, if the scales were not so out of balance. This causes many people who would be more fulfilled as artisans to chose careers in science and industry, while still pursuing their real path as a hobby in their spare time. I did just that, until I finally realized; that is where I always wanted to be. Once I fully realized this, my last few years in the electronics industry were somewhat meaningless. I retired early and went into woodworking full time, which I pursue to this day. What I now realize is, that at my age I will never be able to accomplish what I could have done in my prime. Energy and drive definitely diminish with age.

Music, arts, and craftsmanship are one of the most essential parts of our nature and really, its what separates us from being automatons. All forms of creativity, be it scientific or artistic are valid, but there is a tendency to put all our eggs in one basket and say this is more valid than that, mostly related to funding and profits, creating a gross imbalance in the way we fund our artistic endeavors.

One of the disciplines I have explored is Buddhism. I especially relate to the middle way concept. I have come to firmly believe that the middle of the road is the only way to view all possibilities, and from that point, it is conceivable to relate to all issues and all ideologies. One of the problems of present day society, is that we tend to take extreme positions, right or left of the middle way, we then cannot conceptualize the motives of the other side, who are also at an extreme. The end result is that we wind up shooting at each other because we have become so entrenched in our extreme beliefs that we can no longer see the similarities in each other.

All wars are a product of extremism, and all it produces is walls that can no longer be scaled by negotiation or any other method of civilized resolve. War is the breakdown of civilization, although there are those who propose that there are more humane ways of conducting a war, or go as far as to romanticize war, when in reality, there is nothing humane or romantic about death and dismemberment over nothing more than ideas. Doctrines of different nations, such as freedom and socialism, although held as high ideals by the proponents, are often used as excuses to wage war. These suppositions always fail, since history shows that the use of brutal force to change another culture will only create a stronger polarization of that cultures stance. They will go underground if necessary, which leads to more conflict and slaughter.

Freedom and socialism or any other ideology will only come about when the people affected by a particular regime are fed up with it and decide to change it for themselves. It is my contention that all forms of ideology should be tossed into a big vat and thoroughly amalgamated into one common world view, which would then dissolve everything into a middle of the road perspective. The middle of the road view automatically suspends judgments, since all possibilities come into focus, and from the middle of the road we can see ourselves in all situations. Its a question of balance.

Our world is becoming smaller everyday, through communication and advanced modes of travel. Its time to strive to adopt a common world view and cease our waste of resources, human and material, on war. We can then begin to use these resources toward a common good. Again, only Love will see us through, and only through Love instead of hate ruling us, will we ever be able to restore the possibility of a paradise, where love and beauty become our prime objectives.

Another theocracy that I have drawn from in an attempt to normalize my esoteric views; is Hinduism. Primarily the practice of meditation and mantras. Meditation helps me stop the internal dialogue that keeps the mind running in circles with ideas that in most cases don't serve any useful purpose, but to miss lead me. Stopping the internal dialogue in meditation can eventually lead to a still mindfulness even when not in meditation, and will allow one to *"See"* his or her world through eyes that are not being influenced by prejudiced thoughts or ideas. *"Seeing"* is a concept used in shamanism to denote the ability to get to the very heart of the matter, and putting the mind in neutral is the only way to accomplish true *"Seeing". I have discovered that the thought process is many times faster if it is not verbalized.* It took me awhile to discern my thoughts without putting them into words. When my mind is still and free of dialogue, my thoughts come at lightning speeds. I think because we use language so extensively in communicating with others, we also have a tendency to put our thoughts into words, but it definitely slows down the thinking process. When my mind is still, the meaning of my thoughts are intuitive and consequently I can react much faster if the need arises.

Another useful practice while meditating is to view the internal dialogue from the perspective of the observer, where an objective position is taken, and the observer tries not to participate in any of the thoughts that he is witnessing. This allows the meditating party to discern the validity and quality of the thoughts that are being witnessed. A feeling usually accompanies the viewing of thoughts, and can draw out emotion as if a movie were being watched. These emotions may be joyful, sad, alarming, or offensive. If we can view our thoughts and manage not to latch on to any of them, eventually they will just dissipate. If we do latch on to any of those thoughts, we will just reinforce them by building a story around them. It is very important to remain the observer.

Mantras are the repetitive vocalization of essential prayers. Though most of the Hindu mantras are in Sanskrit, they can be translated into other languages if the practitioner wishes to know the meaning of the prayer. I have learned some Sanskrit and can usually tell what the prayer is about. I was told by an instructor that the power of the mantra is in the sound, and we always did them as a chant.

I prefer to know what the words mean. There are many books on mantras and some have the English translation along with the Sanskrit text. Some ancient practitioner discovered, that there is a powerful effect if the mantra is repeated one hundred and eight times during a recitation; thus the one hundred and eight beads on the mala that is used by most people that recite mantras. Again, it is useful to have a clear mind when reciting mantras, and not be ruminating about some thing that will only distract and detract from the purpose of the recitation. And what is the purpose? Well, tradition says that by repeating the mantra one hundred and eight times, the premise of the prayer will be effective.

I have my own theory of what takes place when I execute a mantra in the prescribed manner. I believe that part of our collective world view is embedded in our DNA, and thus is very hard to change. Some of our views have been part of the collective conscious reality for tens of thousands of years and have become part of our physical makeup, and supported by the mental aspect. I would go as far as to say that the subconscience is more physical than mental. So, my proposition is that repeating a mantra one hundred and eight times a day for forty days, begins to change an aspect of our DNA, since it is repetition that created DNA originally. Whatever the effect may be, they have been instrumental in changing the way I think and relate to the world around me.

There are mantras for specific situations and purposes, for instance: healing others, healing oneself, pushing back chaos, and many others. Some of the mantras I use are supported by an elemental; earth, fire, water, wind and sky. I have composed some mantras of my own and use them in my own personal sense. Anyone can make up their own mantras, depending on what they are trying to effect in their lives, for what we think and what we believe is what will eventually manifest in our lives. We are all magicians by birthright, and we have it within our power not only to change the course of our lives, but to effect changes in the world view as well. A few billion intents aligned to one purpose could change the collective world view into something that might elevate our consciousness to be stewards instead of destroyers of the *Blue Planet*. We are born blank and unbiased and we acquire a world view as we are programmed in our upbringing; by those who are close to us and can exercise their influence on us: parents, teachers, close relatives, friends and enemies alike.

World views can be changed and should at least be examined by everyone, and everyone has one. The power of the world view can be very influential and a powerful force in our daily lives, since it states what we believe in and how we are to structure our lives. Some of my world view before I was conscious enough to question its validity, was composed largely, although not completely, of ideas that were handed down by my parents, relatives, teachers, and were an amalgamated soup of other peoples beliefs, and some were just plain ordinary lies.

I define ordinary lies as programming whose roots are founded in past conflicts, hate, prejudice, or just complete fabrications, that are no longer valid. In most cultures, it seems that we are duty bound to re-fight the conflicts of our ancestors that may have occurred many lifetimes ago, and often make no sense in the present. If we are entrained with issues from the past during our up-bringing, then we have no choice but to make that part of our world view, until we consciously decide to change it. If parents and teachers were aware and consciously awake, they would understand how damaging it is to a child if they are imprinted with concepts based on prejudice, hate, and lies.

There comes a time in every ones life when they are free of coercion and are free to examine their fundamental beliefs. However, there seems to be a trend in the present world view that states: once we reach maturity, we should stop growing and embrace what we have gathered so far and go with that for the rest of our lives. Higher education is acceptable as long as it does not change our world view. Some world views continue for the purpose of keeping us in the feudal mode, such as remember the Alamo, which works well for keeping the separation of the human race alive.

I have personally known people who have no inclination to question their belief system after they have passed the impressionable age, which most of the time coincides with maturity or the accepted world view of where maturity should be. At what age are we mature? It is my contention that we never reach maturity until the final curtain falls, and we should continue to modify our world view when necessary, throughout our lives, supported by our own experiences and what we glean from everything around us. Any thing less and we are selling ourselves short of what we are capable of.

This concept is in my experience highly augmented by seeking out our spiritual nature. This is something that organized religion falls short of imparting to us, because of the inflexibility of the dogma and rules that they adhere to, making it impossible to preach the modification of a world view. This would be considered rocking the boat, and religions do not rock the boat or their government might decide to change their tax exempt status, or they would offend part of their congregation and loose them.

The seeker is on his own in this arena. This is an arena of search and research, evaluating and rejecting or accepting ideas only when the heart key turns and says, well that fits, and I will follow this path until I have a reason to modify it again. Evolution should be a constant in our lives, not only of our world view, our spiritual views, but our cosmic view as well.

Kabbalah, a branch of Hebrew mysticism, is another form that I have brought into my conscious sphere, although to me it seems more practical than mystic. I suppose the concept of God is mystical, and Kabbalah to me is a guide of how life works or can work if these principals are applied, including the depiction of the choices we can make as we travel the path up toward the higher self.

There are five principals that apply to Kabbalah. [1] There is an upper force, that represent God or the Creator, whatever one chooses to call it. With our egos we oppose this upper force. Our egos have evolved over thousands of years, and we must now find a way to change, in order to once again unify with the upper force. [2] The upper force is always benevolent, presenting us with the light of truth, and it is up to us to evolve to the point that we realize that our egos are destructive and have only led us to suffering and pain. We must break out of the ego mode and in the process become more like the upper force. [3] We were originally created as one soul to enjoy and aid each other, but ego shattered us into billions of souls. And since we have become separated, we actually hate each other. The result has led to war, pain and suffering which we augment with power of our intelligence. Kabbalah is trying to lead us back into soul unity where we can once again emulate the upper force and reclaim our divine nature. [4] When we contemplate the immense ego that exist at this time, we can see how destructive it can be. There are two ways we can go. [a] we can continue on our present course and try to evolve by beating ourselves up in wars and chaos, running from suffering, while its getting harder to find safe haven in a shrinking world. [b] Or we can say, I have had my fill of suffering, and try and seek out the light, and find a path to spiritual development that is no longer drawn to pain and suffering, thus opening up a wider avenue of thought and perception that would eventually lead us to a more meaningful life with love and joy. [5] Much of the unrest in the world today is due to people not being able to find any meaning on the treadmill that most of us find ourselves on, and only in coming back together heart and soul and take control of our egos, can we effect change.

Going to work everyday to eek out a living that is getting harder to maintain because the working class is being squeezed harder everyday by those who amass wealth and can't ever seem to get enough. We need to take control of our egos in order to again walk in balance.

There are three types of people in the world. [a] Those who have awakened and are no longer able to fool themselves that everything is copacetic, and that big brother or some government is going to take care of us or has our best interest at heart. [b] Those that deep inside know the truth, but are unwilling to make the break from the familiar to the unknown. Because change is so alarming to some, the familiar hold sway on us, even if it is a place of suffering. [c] Those with no morality or scruples, and a burning desire to amass material wealth, who would go as far as it takes to accomplish their goal. Those entities would sacrifice others as well as the whole planet to get what they want. What they want is an illusion, but the ego is fully entrenched in these situation and it would take a proverbial miracle for an entity like that to do an about-face. But miracles do happen. I believe that the Kabbalistic Tree of Life offers a visual map of the possibilities for enlightenment and spiritual growth. See illustration one below the description of the Sephirots.

The squares on the tree of life are numbered one through ten. They are called sephirots or emanations. The emanations come from the upper force; Creator or God, and to me represent the various facets of the human spirit and of all creation. The emanation from the higher force are in the form of white light, but the rest of the sephirots are treated as if white light were to pass through a prism and the result is the individual components that appear as different colors. Making the creation multi-faceted. The colors represent the energy levels at different stages on the tree of life. Red is the lowest frequency and violet the highest as seen in the visible spectrum. White light is the combination of all colors and represent Kether, the crown, and the omnipotence and beneficial aspect of the source.

I will offer a brief description of the ten sephirots and what they mean to me. Any desire to go into more depth will have to be undertaken by the seeker through qualified instruction. This is not intended to be a crash course in Kabbalah, but a brief description of what the ten sephirots represents.

The Kabbalistic view of the tree of life states that: The light of the creator worked its way down from Kether [1] through the various paths connecting all Sephirots to the base which is Malkuth [10]. I prefer to work my way up through the tree, from the base to the top, because I feel that is where we are born onto this existence.

Malkuth [10] Kingdom____ is the place of action, our

bodies and the material world, our origin when we come into this plane of this existence. At this point we are very malleable and receptive to every form of information that comes our way. This is the basic level of survival with the sun to nurture us. Through our desires and flesh we experience the material world, joy and tribulations in daily living. Here we procreate, and is represented by the two red triangles just above the square. This is the same as the base in the Hindu Chakra system.

Yesod [9] Foundation____is the place of community or country that we begin to identify with as we become more aware of our surroundings and our communities world view. Here we begin to form our personalities based on our domestication and education. This is represented by the orange and red triangles and resides in the center pillar.

Hod [8] Empathy and Splendor____is the place of intellect and human reason and can demonstrate how connected we are with our surroundings. Here we have developed nurturing and communal attitudes where we can see ourselves in some one else's place, or do we strive for our own benefit only, letting the ego dictate our course. It is difficult for the young to have empathy, since ego is an instrument of basic survival; it is very strong in the young. Ego is also strong in older people, but it has been tempered by knowledge and wisdom. Hod is in the region of yellow and orange.

Netzach [7] Victory____is the place where we begin to show signs of independence and interface with the material world. Victory is not of battle, but victory over ego and the beginnings of the autonomous being who values his own counsel as well as the counsel of others. This is also the place of developing emotions and instincts to be and to have. It also resides in the region of yellow and orange.

Tiphereth [6] Beauty____resides in the center pillar and is an amalgamation of all the other Sephirots that surround it, with a strong influence from the Crown. Beauty can only be achieved when all the other emanations are in balance. If we have no empathy for others our judgments are bound to be cruel. If there is no loving kindness, and no light from the Crown, then how could Beauty possibly exist? The higher we go on the tree, the more selfless we become and the clearer our perception of self, others and the universe. We are on the path of return, and is represented by the area in green, and is also the place of the heart in the Hindu Chakra system.

Geburah [5] Strength____is power and more importantly, self discipline. This is about doing what needs to be done and the courage to follow through. As we mature and are more able to "*see*" to the truth, about ourselves, and others. These insights lead to power that can be misused for personal gain in an over materialistic world. Here we require focus and integrity to achieve anything of lasting value. This emanation is nested at green and blue; the third eye in the Hindu Chakra system.

Chesed [4] Loving Kindness and Mercy____is compassion and purity of heart. Being compassionate, merciful and kind in this emanation, is only valid if these acts are done with no ulterior motive, with no strings attached, and done only for the results. This requires us to be in this world but not of it, and to be moral and ethical. This is the level of soul and unselfish actions, the level of free will, and where we display our true individuality. Mercy connects Heaven and Earth and is a measure of our higher self. This emanation is also nested between green and blue.

Binah[3] Understanding and Judgment___is the ability to know and to judge with true understanding, to act and have the courage to do so. It represents focus, stability and power. Judgment like power is another force that can easily be abused for personal or prejudicial reasons, which would only lead to abomination. This a place where we become our own priests. This emanation straddles violet and white and corresponds to the Crown in the Hindu Chakra system.

Hokmah [2] Wisdom___is thinking: a clear concept of what is, and the proper relationship between all the aspects involved. It is a culmination of all we know, tempered by the influence of all the other Sephirots on the tree, plus the light from the crown and beyond. Also represented by violet and white.

Kether [1] Crown___is unity. Kether contains all the potential of all that will be and all that has been. It is the head of creation, the God Head, and the seed of all possibilities. Represented by white, it is the presence of all color, omnipotence that infuses all other aspects of life. Common sense alone should tell us that all the emanations need to be in balance, in order to live a valid life.

Daath [0] Knowledge___is sometimes centered between Binah, Hokmah, Geburah, and Chesed. Knowledge is a vital input for the balancing of understanding, wisdom, strength, and loving kindness.

The tree of life can be laid over the human body to demonstrate the similarity to the Hindu Chakra system.

There are twenty two paths that connect the ten Sephirot and are the conduits that allow all the Sephirot to interact with each other. The tree is also divided into three pillars ; the left, middle, and right. The left pillar is known as the pillar of severity, with attributes of understanding, judgment, strength, empathy, and splendor; is the place where war is made from. If severely unbalanced, could also be the personification of hell.

The right side pillar with its attributes of wisdom, loving kindness and victory can balance both sides of the equation, through the center pillar that is called the pillar of justice, and acts as a fulcrum for both sides.

I believe that the whole point of this discipline is the on going balancing act that is life itself. If we can manage to balance the tree of life and allow the light from the Crown to shine through, we will have a chance at achieving some measure of enlightenment and the possibility of; *coming to the aid of our planet.*

To clarify my position of self actualization, by exploring esoteric literature on my own and with only the influence of a few teachers to guide me; that and my own perceptions: I am regularly presented with opportunities to modify my own behavior and way of thinking. These possibilities occur because I have already set myself on the path of discovery. Once the mind and heart are open, everything comes into view, and synchronicity takes over, opening up the field of possibilities.

Paths On The Tree Of Life

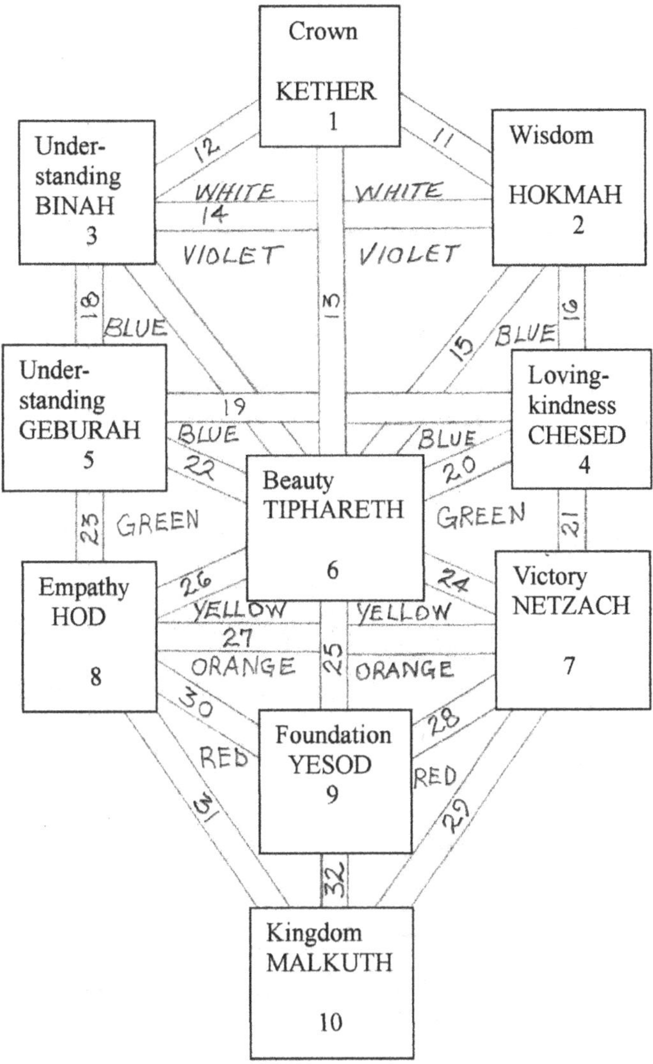

I can't say that I don't stumble. Once in a while I still do something stupid, and my ego jumps out before I can grab it. Until the day that I can make the ego my friend, I will have to be in a constant state of awareness to keep it from getting out of my grasp. This tells me that I am still in the warrior state; still fighting to control my ego and modifying the programming and domestication.

Most orthodox disciplines would say that it is impossible to achieve salvation on my own. Of course, they have tradition and dogma that to them is sacrosanct only because it has been used in the familiar form and eventually becomes a statute or law that cannot be broached without the blessing of the Elders, Cardinals, or anyone high enough on the chain of command that hold the keys to the kingdom.

One of the reasons I am writing this book, is to try and instill the idea that at some point we are going to have to start to trust our selves in making up our minds on the pressing issues that face us and our world, both as individuals and in the collective, since the collective will always be with us.

Since our emergence as mammals, we have been dependent on care and love for our survival and well being, and does not mean that we can't make up our own minds about what we believe as truth. If we ever arrive at the truth, then it will be the same for everyone, for the truth is the truth and can't be falsified. However, we will never arrive at the truth of anything unless we are willing to question what we are taught to belive in, and what is the motivation behind those beliefs.

I think the questing soul will come to the conclusion that much of what we believe to be cast in stone, come from a time when everything was cast in stone. There is a dire need for us to apply our unbiased scrutiny and try to bring our thinking and beliefs up to speed with our technical achievements. Humanity seems to have boundless energy when it comes to external accomplishments, such as building or making any of the wonderful contraptions that may serve us or rule our lives: it depends on how attached we get to our material toys. When it comes to spirituality we seen to bog down and are content to leave it up to someone else. They prescribe and we attend, and nothing ever evolves, since evolution happens at the individual level, not at the group level. There is too much mass in a large group, and its like moving the proverbial mountain.

But wait! How do we explore and hold our own perceptions as sacred and binding without starting a war with the person standing next to us, whose opinion about salvation and deity is in direct opposition to our own? The answer is: *Respect.* Respect for different ideologies. After all, they are only ideas until the time when we all agree that something is the truth. This requires interaction that till now has been impossible without taking up arms or seriously offending someone.

Interaction that allows one to listen to another with an open mind, and say, I will consider your opinion and weigh it with tolerance and respect that I myself would expect. Not an easy thing for ego based humans to do. Lets rein in those egos and quit acting like we are still in that jungle of long, long ago, where a quick reaction could save our bacon. Now its just a mind trip; a battle of words, and we can easily hold our own without conflict. Our weapon toys are getting to dangerous to hand them over to the ego.

Fear and paranoia are running rampant in our world

today and everything that is considered entertainment these days is riddled with bombs and bullets, and it's very difficult to shield the young people from the devastating influence this kind of presentation has on everyone; for it affects most everyone. Maybe if it was balanced by presentations that portrayed humane aspects of life, the scales might even out, but fear anger and rage sell more tickets at the box office, and most movie producers try to give the audience what they think will sell, not what they need. I have watched many movies that have socially redeeming value, but most of those are not big box office smash hits, and are only available at rental stores. My point is; its another of our imbalances, and somehow we need to make a decision; do we want to keep feeding the mega ego, or do we want a better more balanced world.

All the disciplines that I have described can lead to health, both mental and physical, if the seeker is willing to explore the spiritual terrain. There is a personalized niche and comfort zone for everyone if we allow it to bloom, for ourselves and for others.

There is a poem written by Rudyard Kipling that always resonates with me when I happen to come across, and read it. It reinforces my belief in the individual seeking his or her truth, through their own resourceful efforts. The poem is as follows:

> IF
> If you can keep your head when all about you
> are losing theirs and blaming it on you,

If you can trust yourself when all men doubt you
But make allowances for their doubting to,
If you can wait and not be tired of waiting
Or being lied about, don't deal in lies,
Or being hated, don't give way to hating,
And yet don't look too good, nor talk too wise:

If you can dream—and not make dreams you master,
If you can think—and not make thoughts your aim,
If you can meet with Triumph and Disaster
An treat those two impostors just the same;
If you can bear to hear the truth you have spoken
Twisted by knaves to make a trap for fools,
Or watch the things you gave your life to, broken
And stoop and build 'em up with worn out tools:

If you can make one heap of all your winnings
And risk it all on one turn of pitch-and-toss,
And lose, and start again at your beginnings
And never breathe a word about your loss,
If you can force your heart and nerve and sinew
To serve your turn long after they are gone,
And so hold on when there is nothing in you;
Except the will which says to them: "Hold On"!

If you can talk with crowds and keep your virtue,
Or walk with kings—nor lose the common touch,
If neither foe nor loving friend can hurt you,
If all men count with you, but not too much,

If you can fill the unforgiving minute
With sixty seconds' worth of distance run,
Yours is the earth and everything that's in it,
And—which is more—you'll be a man my son!

If anything describes a middle of the road and balanced outlook to me: well, this is it, in a beautifully crafted nut shell. If we can begin to believe in ourselves and our own power, the power to rule our lives, and not the power that destroys: If we can gain insight and not keep it to ourselves; If we can share with no strings attached, we have a chance of ascending the Tree of Life, and finally coming home.

Come home! Where did that come from? I thought we were home. There is another input I wish to interject here, that has had an influence on my amalgamated development. It is the study of: *The Course In Miracles.* The main premise here is that we humans have created and continue to create the grand illusion that is represented by the world and universe all around us. That we initiated and continue to feed the separation that states that we are individuals with no connection to each other or any other aspect of creation, This of course is the ego. The Course states that we are all one and the same, and that someday the inevitable will happen; we will all come together and find our way back to our beginnings, where there is no cast system and the understanding that the only difference between us is external, and not much at that. At the soul level we are all the same. Studying the Course In Miracles is an enlightening experience.

Another healing aspect that can greatly benefit the body and the soul, since our well being is directly tied to our physical health; is exercise. No need to run a marathon, or press three hundred pounds, or swim a hundred laps in the pool.

However, a sane and moderate cardiovascular program would work wonders toward a healthy life. I am sometimes amazed at how well I feel after riding my bicycle just ten miles, and once in shape it becomes pleasurable.

Its too easy to just hop in the car and drive a couple of blocks to the grocery or drug store; thus denying ourselves the benefit of working out some of the toxins in our bodies and toning our muscles.

In our modern world there has arisen, a monster of the treadmill life style. There is easy availability to fast food for everyone, which research has connected to the epidemic of obesity, heart conditions, high blood pressure, that is affecting a major portion of the population, even the young. The good food venue in schools is becoming a thing of the past, or are being supplanted by catered food. Many fast food concerns are built next to schools in order to attract the students to eat their lunches there.

I don't mean to blast the fast food concerns, although there is much they could do to improve the quality of their products. The responsibility ultimately rests on the shoulders of the individual, and the real problem is that there are very few outlets for anyone to burn off excessive calories, so they just keep accumulating in the body.

Back to the treadmill! Who has the time to pack healthy

lunches for their school children or for themselves, when both parents have to work to make a living. There is also the problem of pier pressure to do the socially accepted thing and go down to the hamburger shack for lunch. Where both parents work, it's sometimes difficult to cook supper, so its pizza time and the calory meter pegs out.

There is a strange anomaly at work in our society. There are those who have the means to eat themselves to death, and there are those who are starving to death. Its just another symptom of the imbalance that exists in the world today, and the same imbalance is present in our economical system, which is directly related to whether we can eat or starve. There is enough for everyone if we could balance the scales of liberty and justice for allowances in the position we happen to occupy on the ladder of what we call success.

There is a basic problem in the foods we buy that are commercially produced. Most are infused with pesticides and herbicides and the meats are shot full of growth hormones and anti-biotics. The anti-biotics are needed because of the constrained conditions under which poultry and pork are raised, and growth hormones are used to get a high yield faster. Organically raised foods are a little more expensive, but if we care at all about our health, we should be willing to pay a little more.

It would be ideal if we could all own a two or three acre plot of fertile land to grow fruits and vegetables and raise a few heads of beef or pigs. In some parts of the country, where there is sufficient rain to support a crop this would work without much added expense. In my native state of New

Mexico, rain is not predictable, and though there are many crops grown here, they are watered by irrigation and wells. Plots of land in my state would require a well to water the crops. I would imagine that some people would consider this to be controversial, but is it not controversy that stimulates the mind and sets us on the path of evolution?

So for me and my path, only the broader base, firmly planted in the middle way where the view extends to the infinite in all directions, will enable me to make the informed decisions that are required of a sentient life form, and to manage those strong and powerful instincts, and not be ruled by them, for they can be savage if turned lose. I view my life, as if behind the reins of a very spirited team of horses that are galoping at full speed toward a precipice, and I with my hands firmly on the reins, have the power and conviction to slow and turn them before we go over the edge. So..................

I hold this torch high
As I walk throughout
This beautiful and magnificent
Cave of wonder and delight,
Without this light to guide me,
All the sublime architecture,
Natural and created would be
Lost to my senses forever,
And I would just stumble around
In a profound and chilling darkness
For the rest of my life,

So, I am thankful and grateful
For the gift of illumination,
I see all those who are here also,
Some with their torches lit,
Some dim, some never ignited,
I only aim, to serve as I can
To help ignite all the torches,
And collectively, we can light the way.

Chapter 9

Who Are We

Who Are We, what are we, where are we, what is my purpose in life, are questions that have been begging an answer since man first became self aware. As far as I can tell we are still trying to find answers to those very questions, and only coming up with a wide spectrum of theories that only spawn more questions. The result is a chain reaction of ideas that is only limited by the imagination,which is unbounded.

Who are we: Early man was a lot more concrete in his evaluation of the universe and much more pragmatic in trying to answer those four questions we just asked. For one thing, early man had less time on his hands to think about philosophical themes, mostly because of the almost full time job of dealing with survival. Having to live in an almost totally natural environment led man to ascribe esoteric meaning to the elements that had such a tremendous impact and direction in the lives of the early homo sapient.

As a hunter-gatherer, man ascribed deity status to the elements that so impacted and dictated the course of their lives. Rain, wind, and fire, as well as the seasonal changes were named as Gods, and prayers and sacrifice's were often initiated to try and gain the favorable conditions that made life possible, which eventually turned into ritual.

Of course one of the most powerful deities was that of the Mother Earth and Father Sun concept. Even at that early stage, man was already aware that everything responsible for our survival relates directly to the endemic health of our earth, and they expressed that belief in ritual.

These basic rituals eventually became religious in nature, and eventually led to one or more members of a tribe to be assigned the keepers of the belief system as it developed. Early shamans sprang from such assignments, and they in turn developed methods of healing, both physical and mental, along with the observance of ritual that would placate the Gods, in order to insure the favorable abundance required, not only for the survival, but the evolution of the race.

Abundance was something early man did not have to worry about, and had not propagated to the point of being a significant impact on the resources of the planet. We however, are at the point of eating ourselves out of house and home just by the weight of our present population, which is my main motivation for writing; *Now Is The Time For All Good Men To Come To The Aid Of Their Planet.* A distinct need to back off from the addiction of energy and resources that are taking us closer to the brink of depletion of those raw materials, and a renewed effort in trying to find better and renewable sources, as well as limiting our population.

The variety of flora and fauna that ranged through most of the inhabited lands at the time that the last ice age was in retreat, was more than abundant, to say the least, compared to what it is at the present time. Since man started as a predator, with added intelligence in his corner, it was just a short hop to the development of tools to aid in the hunt, domestic use, and later for use in war. The use of roots and greens for food and medicinal purposes developed into an art form that survives to this day.

It is the inherent characteristic of the survival mode, be it human or animal, to take as much as possible and cache away for future use. With early man, particularly in the colder climes, it was an absolute necessity. Winters were harsh in the northern latitudes and plentiful stores in the larder were necessary to the survival of everyone. Most every form of food substance in those early times were stored in a dehydrated form, or buried in the ice. The freezer was provided by nature and the dehydration by the warm summer air. These methods of preserving foods are still in use today in the more nature oriented countries of the world.

At this point in human development, it took practically everyone's efforts in hunting or gathering and processing to accumulate the necessary staples for survival. Thus, there were not many slackers in any particular group of people. Those who did not hold up their end could not be tolerated and only those who could not work anymore, such as the very aged and disabled, were then cared for by family members or anyone who could share.

Members of a tribe who showed special abilities or the desire to learn would go into specialized areas such as hunting or tool making, hide tanning, clothes making, woodworking and carving; could then barter and trade their wares for what they needed to survive. Many of these specialists were inventive and resourceful and would often come up with new tools and ways of improving a process.

It is obvious that man with his natural intelligence and ability to invent, make, and use tools, as well as having the ability to work in cooperation with others of his species, rose to the position of dominance in every corner of the world. Having said that, it is also obvious that man flourished and their numbers began to expand, thus requiring more and more territory and sustenance in the the process.

A very important factor in our early evolution is that early man had very little impact on the environment in the form of pollution. Everything used in the process of making tools and implements were derived from natural materials such as wood, rock and leather. All of these materials were natural elements and were of a bio-degradable nature, and with time these materials were very easy for the environment to break down and reabsorb. That is why so little survives of early man, except those articles that were made from stone, or fired pottery, which in effect is turned to stone in the firing. Any chemicals used in, say, the process of tanning leather also came from a natural source and could easily be absorbed by the earth.

I believe that real pollution began when people began to experiment with metals for tools and implements, as well as weapons. Harsher chemicals were employed in the smelting and forging of metal, and thus gave birth to an industry that in our recent history has given rise to much of the pollution that plagues us now. A wide variety of poisonous chemicals, as well as millions of tons of carbon dioxide are pumped into the atmosphere every day, thus creating a shroud that allows heat to be trapped, and causing the mean temperature to rise. It does not take much to upset the balance of our ecological system. Our global temperature is rising, and the evidence is undeniable. The weather is becoming more erratic and stronger in its effects, while at the same time the polar ice caps are melting, causing the level of the oceans to rise.

The earth has been through hundreds of warming and cooling cycles, without any help from us, going from a totally molten world to a totally frozen world to the tropical world that gave an exponential rise to both plant and animal life; in its four and a half billion year life span. Whether we are responsible for this era of warming or not, the effect on us will be devastating. It is however, a scientific fact that an increase in carbon dioxide in the atmosphere will cause warming and heat retention. I have in the past, vacillated between the idea that we are responsible for global warming, or that it might be caused by some natural phenomena, such as the increased solar activity that we are experiencing at the present time. This activity follows a twenty two year cycle and should reverse in another eleven years.

I however, am becoming more and more convinced that

the problem we are facing now is directly related to our inordinate appetite for material goods and wealth, coupled with our exponential rise in population. The records show that since the beginning of the industrial revolution, the amount of toxic gases has been steadily rising in the atmosphere, and we show no signs of concern, especially in the industrial quarter.

There are many scientists that are speaking out about the potential hazards that we face if we don't do something about the pollution we are producing. We are ruled by industries that have no desire to invest in renewable sources of energy, and would prefer to continue down the same old rut, mostly due to the addiction that we developed for the amassing of wealth and profits.

Changing our attitudes about renewable sources of energy would entail large investments and research to design and build a new infrastructure of clean energy sources. There does not seem to be anyone in the industrial complex or in government willing to set such an endeavor into motion. There is just too much emphasis on profits at present, and our government has got us in so much debt, along with military spending that we are barely squeaking by, with nothing left for investing in America. Our dept keeps increasing every year, so we print more money, and the value of the dollar goes down.

The general public for the most part is aware of the problems that pollution is going to create in the future, but is apathetic to move against the status quo, due mainly to the fact that we have not felt the full impact of the road we are on. It seems that people are not willing to respond to threats of any kind until the hammer falls, and by that time the catastrophe will already be in progress.

Of course, as I have stated in another chapter [Population], and in my opinion and the opinion of others, population and the burden and pressure we are placing on the resources of our world is a main contributor to the amount of pollution that is being created. Consumption and apathy are only going to lead us to choking on our own waste, and the depletion of our natural resources, which are not unlimited or renewable, unless we consider mining our land fills for the materials we have unconsciously thrown away and failed to recycle.

Meanwhile: Back at early man. The evolution and prosperity as well as expansion of humans continued on a grand scale, mostly in the social order and the esoteric, and mostly due to the need for cooperation in a hunter gatherer society. As long as an earthquake, volcanic eruption, mud slide, or flood did not bury whole communities, man thrived.

War seems to have always been part of our operating system, from the one on one situation to the full blown conflict involving nations. However, war does not seen to diminish the human population by much. Actually, statistics show that the population takes and exponential upward swing following a major conflict, therefore the term *Baby Boomer,* which was coined and stuck after WWII. Of course, for early man, wars were still fought mainly on a one to one basis and were usually over after the balance of numbers tilted to one side or the other. Today, we not only face a natural disaster we are creating with pollution, population and avarice, but we now have the means to destroy whole countries, and if enough nukes are exploded we could wind up frying every living thing on this planet. Technology, that good old double edged sword that can cut both ways. Somehow we need to rekindle Love and Spirit and find our survival right here, and not on some imagined plane. This is it folks; this is where we prove or disprove our intelligence. I think the jury is still out on that one.

Some five thousand or so years ago, give or take a few hundred years, man went from hunter-gatherer to farming and husbandry. Now the land was tilled, and an abundance of crops produced by the natural fertility of the soil along with predictable rains and river water for irrigation, soon gave humans the ability to produce abundantly, with surplus that could then be turned into revenue. The same can be said about the animals that were selected for domestication. Their care, feeding and selective breeding, made it possible for an unprecedented yield.

The shamans, the healers, the herbalists, and the people who studied the movement of the celestial bodies, have been with us since we began to emerge into human societies. These people were given a special place among the clans and tribes because they were willing to take on the responsibility of healing the sick and injured, as well as serving as mid-wives and advisers. They became very adept in the use of the myriad roots and plants that could be used in the healing of many of the illnesses that visited early man. The star gazers became very competent at predicting the seasons. When to start to prepare for the long winters, when the herds of animals would start their migrations, and make their appearance for the hunters, and later when the time was right for the planting of the different crops.

The shamans also became the instrument and guardians of the soul. They dealt with the matters of the afterlife, burial practices, and the taboos or accepted practices regarding spirit. These women and men were the forerunners of priests and organized religion, and sometimes all three aspects of healer, astronomer, and priest were combined into the duty's of one very dedicated person. The only help came from apprentices that would eventually take over the practice.

As the lore and knowledge on the three disciplines grew, the role of the shaman as healer, astronomer, and priest, was eventually broken down into its three component parts and healers became doctors, star gazers became astrologers first and later astronomers, and the esoteric and matters of the soul would become the domain of the priesthood.

As I stated before, many natural phenomena were assigned God status by early man, due to the impact the elements held over the survival of the races of men, that lived essentially right in the middle of those elements. Many of the ritual and practices were for the sole purpose of placating and pleasing these elemental Gods. Some religions to this day still have a pantheon of deities with one central most powerful God to rule them all.

Monotheism [the belief in only one supreme God] is believed to have taken root somewhere around 1500 to 1000 BCE. In Egypt, Amenhotep IV introduced Atenism sometime in the years between 1348/1346 BCE and raising the Aten to the status of Supreme God, while still allowing the worship of the traditional gods. Amenhotep IV officially changed his name to Akhenaten [agreeable to Atem] and even built a new capital city he named Akhetatan [horizon of the Aten]. During the construction, he moved the capital from Thebes to Akhetatan with the possible intent of removing his court from the influence of the priesthood, and signaling a strong commitment to a transformation in religious and political power.

Another religious form that sprang up in ancient Persia and which probably had a larger influence on the roots of Christianity, Judaism, and Islam is, Zoroastrianism. Founded by the prophet Zarathustra who modern scholars believe lived somewhere between 1500 and 1000 BCE. Zarathustra preached that there was only one God whom he called Ahura Mazda. Ahura meaning Lord and Mazda meaning Wise. Zarathustra thus considered God to be a Wise Lord. Zarathustra considered his Wise Lord to be transcendent but sill in constant relationship with human beings and the world that he created. The basic scriptures of Zoroastrianism are contained in 5 poetic songs called Gathas, which were written by Zarathustra himself, and have been expanded into more complex scriptures over the years. They are administered by the Zoroastrian priests. The Gathas contain 7 attributes that form the basis of the belief. They are Vohu Manah—Good Thoughts—connected with animals; Asha Vahishta—Justice and Truth—Fire and Energy; Kshathra—Dominion—metals and minerals; Spenta Armmaiti—Devotion and Serenity—The earth and land; Haurvatat—Wholeness—Waters;

Ameretat—Immortality—Plants; and Spenta Mainyu—Creative Energy—Human beings. These attributes, in later traditions are personified and become, as in Christianity, similar to Angels. This religion also employed ethical dualism: The belief in good and evil, right and wrong. Prayers and ceremonies are performed before a sacred fire that is considered the light of God, who is light, warmth, and energy, but they do not worship the fire itself, and is just used as a focus for the symbolism of God.

Zoroastrians in Persia came under great pressure to convert to other religions due to Greek, Muslim, and mongol invasions of Persia. Many moved to India, but there are significant numbers of adherents to be found all over the world. The motto of this faith is Good Thoughts, Good Words, and Good Deeds, and is the center of the faith that does not hate the world or dwell on sin and guilt. Sounds like a religion I could embrace.

Judaism, ascribes its roots to the God of Abraham, Isaac, and Jacob, and is believed to be the cause of all existence. Historically, the ancient roots of monotheistic Judaism lie in the ancient Canaanite religion mixed with elements of Zoroastrianism where early Jews were divided between those who were comfortable with the worship of Yahweh, the one and only God, alongside other local deities, and those who were strictly monotheistic, worshiping only Yahweh.

Christianity has its roots squarely in Judaism, as is evident in the old testament of the bible. The new testament, especially the Gospels, deal with the life of Jesus Christ and his teachings and the core of what Christians are supposed to believe in and practice, and in my opinion, not just on Sunday, but 24/7 365.25 days a year. The reason it does not always work that way, is that we are truer to our selves, which includes the ego and desires, than we are to ideals and the higher self. Also, in my opinion, religions have a tendency to become cumbersome with over thought dogma. When you have 2,000 years to play around with an ideal, its easy to go of the deep end, as every generation in those 2,000 years had a chance to add their two bits to the plot.

To me, what Jesus taught is quite simple, elegant and straight to the point, and seems like a stark contrast to what the Christian adherents and churches profess and practice. Christian churches have always tried to be shrouded in mystery. The cathedral grandeur and the postulation that here is the house of god, certainly inspired some very awesome architecture. They were and still are marvels of skill, and they contrast with the modest modern churches, which began with Protestants that broke away from the Roman Catholic church.

And, speaking of reformations, the ideologies of all the spin offs of Christianity can't agree as to what the one true doctrine should be. At this point enters man on the scene with all the different ideas about how to run the system, and what and who is teaching the right dogma, when the ten commandments which are basic common sense, and the teachings of Jesus Christ are straight forward and in my opinion are not so complicated that there is anything left to interpret. Two thousand years is a long time to pass any kind of knowledge down and expect it not to be somewhat corrupted. In the chapter, My Path, I try to show the importance of the autonomous individual making up their own mind as to what rings true and what is just dogmatic construct. This path requires more exposure to different concepts from around the world, such as the shamanic disciplines that were once part of every culture, but which are now only practiced by indigenous cultures, although a resurgence of shamanic practices has occurred in people who are on a path of knowledge and enlightenment and believe that the individuals salvation can not be placed in the hands of others; it has to come from within, by being in agreement and balance with your heart, soul and spirit. To me it signals a new and more realistic reformation.

The Islamic religion started around 622 AD because of a disagreement with both Jews and Christians. They did not agree with the divinity of Jesus Christ as being the son of God and believed that He was just a prophet as was Muhammad.

They also disagreed with the Jews because they did not believe in Jesus as a prophet, and believed that both Judaism and Christianity were corrupted. Islam has one of the largest followings on the planet with around 1.3 billion followers.

In Judaism and Islam there are two or three sects that disagree with the orthodox component, but Christianity has fragmented into hundreds of reformed and re-reformed churches, mostly due to the fact that in countries where Christianity took root, there is usually more freedom of expression and tolerance for the beliefs of others; at least from the fourteenth century on. Before that time, the Catholic church kept a very tight rein on anyone who tried to change the teachings of the church, which produced several inquisitions of punishment and torture and even death if people deviated in the slightest from the prescribed law of the church. Eventually, through revolution and evolution, enough freedom was gained to sustain major changes, and large groups of like minded people would go off and start their own church based on their shared beliefs, with a minimum of blood shed and discrimination.

There are many other major religions such as Hinduism in India, which dates to antiquity and has a following of around 900 million people. They believe there is one supreme Entity {Brahma} that manifest itself through many gods and goddesses.

Buddhism was founded by Siddhartha Gautama {the Buddha} in 520 BC in northeast India and has a following of around 360 million people around the world. I will not attempt to describe here, the twenty nine other religions I know of, as it would take a book in itself to do so.

Although brief by historical standard, I have spent some time describing religion from earliest beliefs to modern religions because of the major impact it has had on our social behavior. More than any other factor, religion has prompted everything from the most benevolent and altruistic acts to all out idealistic wars. Freedom to believe is a fairly modern concept and has taken root in some places in the world, but certainly not everywhere. I suppose the future will tell if we ever evolve to where everyone can take an autonomous stance and still be treated as a viable citizen with love and respect.

I believe that many of our social ills stem from non acceptance of the individual, and in trying to stuff people into molds that don't fit their basic makeups or desires and aspirations. Most people eventually succumb to the molds and accept living by rules that often chafe and bump at us as we go along. However, our drug and alcohol, mental and penal institutions are full of those people who can not accept the molds and in their rebellion some times go to extremes of crime or self annihilation, sometimes slowly, sometimes quickly, and even at a young age. The pressure toward conformity and success is so strong that in some cultures failure is usually followed by inferred suicide.

Some molds I believe are of a beneficial nature, but I believe that the problem comes from the way we administer the rules and regulations. It is hardly ever done in a loving way and most rules are administered by force and severe pressure to conform, and only causes people to take a defensive position. In my own experience, I was much more likely to adhere to rules from someone who was willing to give me a break and help me through, as opposed to someone who treated me like a criminal. I also encountered many teachers, be they parents, relatives, or casual observers who professed one thing and did just the opposite. I even heard many say; do as I say not as I do. If you can't take your own advise, it means you don't really believe in what you are saying, and most people, especially the young can see right through that kind of B. S.

An other bolt out of the blue came to me when our grand children were born. Two of our grandchildren spent a lot of time with us when they were growing up, and I realized how differently I related to them than I did to my own children, to whom I was often a task master and an enforcer and was not the loving or understanding dad that I should have been. Well, that is the way I was brought up and I went into parenting right out of high school and just proceeded to carry on with the same rules my parents adhered to, although I think not quite so harshly and with more displays of love than my father did, who hardly ever displayed his love, and not because he had none, it was just the way men were expected to behave at that time; unemotional and hard in their bearing. After having a close relationship with my grandsons, I actually changed my outlook toward my sons, realizing that it was not to late to become someone that they could come to love instead of fear or even hate, in the extreme. I have noticed that the sterner and more rigid a person is the more they tend to confuse fear with respect, when they are two totally different concepts. Fear is based on coercion and threat, and respect is based on love and acceptance.

What Are We: We are self aware beings of higher brain capacity than any other species on this planet with the capacity to chose our destiny and our accomplishments for good or ill. Some believe that we are born to live out our destiny and that nothing can change it. And yes, if we stay in the groove of our up bringing and domestication, that is the destiny we will live through out our lifetime, remaining true to the behavior dictated by what we have been imprinted with. I know destiny can be modified to be what ever we choose it to be. All it takes is climbing out of the groove and looking at the possibilities that are available, and there is no limit to that; that is what evolution is about.

We are paradoxical through our ability to make choices that affect our lives, those we interact with, and the world at large, materially and ideologically. If evolution is our legacy, we have come a long way from those ancestors who lived in trees millions of years ago. In our evolution through homo sapient and having developed the powerful tools of reading, writing, mathematics, and the various sciences, we have been builders of magnificent utilitarian structures; some of which have lasted thousands of years.

On the other hand, we have also been destroyers of each other, our works and it seems that we are now in the process of destroying the very thing that has sustained us through out our whole existence; the ecological system that gives rise to every thing we need to survive. Perhaps not intentionally, but certainly through our drive to grow and expand and create all the products that we can no longer do without, and with an increase in population, the demand for more raw materials. We are industrious by nature and our mega industries require unlimited raw resources. Those industries also require an immense amount of energy to transform those raw material into a usable form of materials for manufacturing. We have a limited number of resources that we can use, in the form of natural gas, coal and oil, as well as the minerals and metals.

All of these sources of energy are highly polluting, especially coal and oil, pumping millions of tons of C02 and other poisonous components into the atmosphere. The two other sources of energy are wind and solar, and have barely been tapped into because coal and oil industries and their powerful lobbying are intent on keeping things just as they are, since it would entail a reinvestment of profits to change over to renewable sources of energy.

What is going to happen when we exhaust the earths capacity to give us another drop of oil or the coal runs out. We are already grabbing at straws by trying to extract oil from shale and tar sands, and our willingness to poison the ground with harsh chemicals that will have an impact far into the future. We seem to be more than a little short sighted as we forge our way into the future, only thinking of our immediate gratification, with no thought as to the consequences of our actions.

More than plenty makes for waste, and we do waste our resources on amassing more than we need. One of the biggest waste of resources is war. The war machine requires tremendous amount of industrial products and resources that could be put to better uses. I am sure that there are industrial factions that view war as an economic booster, but it only shows how far out on the limb we have gone to procure and amass wealth. We are capable of so much more, but we seem to be caught on a treadmill that is going no where in any real evolutionary sense. We are not taking care of our planet, its diverse and beautiful flora and fauna, and certainly not its people.

Where Are We: Our home is on a beautiful and complicated world whose ecology hangs on a fulcrum of balance in its strategic path around our home star, exposed to just the right amount of energy to produce life in all its myriad forms. A balance that could be and has been upset many times in its four and a half billion year history. We share the sun with eight other planets, [I still consider Pluto a planet, whether it was produced by the solar nebula or a captured world from outside our system, it now revolves around our sun] some of which are gas giants. Some of the planets in our solar system may have been capable of supporting life at some time and may still harbor some simple forms of life, but Earth is the only one to have produced the higher and complex forms of life, at least as we understand life to be.

Our solar system is poised two thirds of the way out from the center of a spiral galaxy we have named the Milky Way; a galaxy that is one hundred thousand light years across, and resides in a cluster of galaxies called the local group, of which the Andromeda galaxy is one of our galaxies closest neighbors, and the only galaxy that can be seen with the naked eye.

There are billions of galaxies in the known universe with billions of stars in them, and all those stars have planets revolving around them. I would contend that with these conditions, the possibility for life in countless forms and on countless worlds, is a foregone conclusion. I say, in different forms because even on earth, there are different paths that evolution has taken, and life could be based on elements other than carbon.

Before the extinction of the dinosaurs sixty five million year ago, raptors were already showing signs of higher intelligence and were far more advanced than mammals, and would probably be the dominant species now if their extinction had not occurred. That extinction gave mammals the edge they needed to evolve and become the dominant form of life. So even in nature it is still a roll of the dice and the right conditions, but with so many possible places for these conditions to come to fruition, I have no doubts as to the existence of life throughout the universe.

Within our own galaxy and other galaxies that we can observe, there is still star formation taking place, and new worlds are being born where life can take hold in the distant future, and at the same time worlds are being destroyed when their suns super nova. Our own sun will super nova in five billion years. Will there be any humanity around to witness that event? If there are humans at that time, and that is a very long time, perhaps they will have devised a means of traveling to other star systems, to insure the survival of the race.

More than likely, there are older species, and younger species, of intelligent beings within our own galaxy and may have already devised the mean for intergalactic travel, but that could only happen if they have been able to survive themselves and pull together as a united world, or federations of worlds. For us on earth, space exploration has been motivated by competition with other nations and no real research is being done to improve the efficiency of the propulsion systems used in space exploration. We will never get to the stars using roman candle technology; its just too inefficient.

Science has proposed that our galaxy is composed of seventy percent dark matter and dark energy, which at present cannot be seen, and its presence can only be measured by its effect on visible matter. If we discover what this matter and energy is, and can learn how to manipulate it, it could possibly become a powerful means of propulsion.

Reaching for the stars is a lofty dream for sure, but I don't think we have a chance until we get our selves and our home world in order. So now is the time for all good men to come to aid of their planet, and ourselves. I have stated that we have a strong paradoxical characteristic about us through our ability to make decisions that can take us hurtling in a thousand different directions, and in my opinion the reason is, that we put so much emphasis on our brain power that we totally ignore all our other senses of consciousness such as what we feel in our hearts and souls, creating an imbalance in our motives and actions. In hurtling through life, we have no time to absorb what is happening around us, what it is we are actually accomplishing, if anything, or are we just being kept busy to the point of total distraction.

The axiom, stop and smell the roses, is not just a pretty phrase, it means stop and take stock of our lives, read our moral compass, put your ear to the ground and try to make sense of what you hear. We humans are so easily mesmerized by glitter, that we lose our selves in trinkets, bobbles and bangles, and the lure of money and gold. And, its not that there is any thing evil about these things that capture our imagination and occupy all our time, its just that we don't realize that they are only icing on the cake, and our real evolution does not depend on anything more than a clear mind, where our internal dialogue is not keeping our backs pinned to the wall one hundred percent of the time.

The human race is still in its infancy. Two or three million years is just a drop in the cosmic bucket, and like most infants, its survival hangs in the balance. If we as a species can make it to maturity, we may have a chance to realize our full potential. This is going to require us to expand our horizons by pulling ourselves out of the mundane existence we find ourselves in at present and just stop and evaluate our condition and where we want to go from here.

We are not only beings of material substance with material needs, but also spiritual being with strong connections with the energies of the universe. We are born that way and exhibit that connection by the fierce independence that we exercise in our youth. The young are always rebellious, due to their connectedness with everything, and can still see and sense, that adults have cut themselves off from spirit. This cut off point is called maturity, when a child becomes an adult by buying into the the prescribed formula that is our societies, and there are many social orders in the world, and they all have their can do and can't do. Just as a horse eventually gives up bucking and allows a man to ride on his back, so do humans give up their autonomy and start to pull on the rope with all the other domesticated subjects in their particular society. This domestication also demands the adherence to the can do and can't do. Within any social order, if someone breaks the rules, they will be punished, even if it did not hurt anyone else.

Domestication is a comfort zone where everyone is in agreement of the prescribed rules that govern society and usually makes no room for descent of any kind or evolutionary leaps. The main ingredient in domestication is fear of the unknown and ranges from cultural difference, to what might occur after death.

Staying in the groove may feel comfortable and safe solely because it is the temple of our familiar, but as far as evolution and improvement of our species and the salvation of our planet, we are going to have to climb out and look around at the choices we are making. Sacrifice is something that evolution requires of those who are willing to push on the envelope in order to move us forward.

What Is My Purpose In Life: My purpose in life has been redefined many times over in the process of development from the time I was born to my present age of seventy five, and since memory still serves me, I see the many life changing choices that I have made. Some are of small consequence and some have had major impact on me. Some choices I am in full agreement with and some I regret. The ones I regret, I have made an effort to make peace with and in most I have succeeded. The rest I am still actively working on, because regrets are like an anchor that hold us back from moving forward and evolving. I now realize that the past is gone, like water to the sea, and if I try to live in the past and regret, I am only going to torture myself with things I can not change. That would be just another form of staying in the groove and wallowing in my personal mud puddle.

Forgiving ourselves is not an easy thing to accomplish,

mostly because we are usually harder on ourselves than we are on anyone else. It is totally possible to drive our selves mad, from internal and external influence, and thus arises the need to clean out the attic of the clutter that only serves to bar our way forward. This cleaning needs to be done periodically, just as our home requires cleaning when they start to look and smell bad. A mind that is allowed to harbor regrets and mistakes, is like a house that never gets cleaned; not a comfortable place to live.

There have been many ups and down in my life, some of them taking me to great heights and some of them causing me great pain and suffering, some of them even life threatening. Some of my low points I now realize were actually of my own manifestation and could have been avoided if I had been more aware of what I was doing. Something I have learned to do now if something hits the fan, is to ask myself; what role did I play in this manifestation, and very often I will find that I had something to do with promoting the scene. Of course there are those incidents that come out of left field and we don't have any control or blame in the matter. My only recourse then, is to deal with the situation as best I can, and try to move on, and even some of these situations can be avoided by remaining conscious and visually aware at all times. It is amazing what we can perceive all around us when the mind is quiet, and not jabbering away, in effect blocking out all the other senses.

I have never been so dedicated to one thing that every other aspect of life was sacrificed. I feel fortunate that my interests have varied to the point that I have sampled much that life has to offer. I have heard from many that a Jack of all trades is a master of none, and that may be true, but I usually immerse myself in learning and applying to the point of being quite accomplished, and some of those endeavors are still active and will be with me for the rest of my life.

I spent forty two years working for a state of the art aero space company that manufactured highly sophisticated electronic products for the military and commercial markets. Here was an opportunity to climb high in the corporate ladder of success, which as you advance would require more and more dedication, more of your time and in a lot of ways more of your soul, which could eventually result in being the only focus in my life. Instead, I chose a middle of the road position and the result was a comfortable living with time to explore other aspects of living. Recreation was important to me and I would stop and smell the flowers every chance I got. Consciously or unconsciously I think I have always believed in the middle of the road concept, except of course, when driving a vehicle.

I believe my purpose in life is to explore, learn as much as I can and to act upon what I know for the benefit of this beautiful and diverse planet we call our home. I certainly do not adhere to the religious premise that we are on this earth to suffer, which from my perspective is a very unenlightened and narrow view of our reason for living, and is mostly for the purpose of keeping people in fear and nailed to the cross. Counter to that, I believe we should seek to be joyful and happy. The dark side will visit us from time to time, its unavoidable, so it does not make much sense to purposely seek it out.

When I think of the biological interaction that has to take place to produce life in any form, its hard to justify the waste of life that occurs every day, be it humans, animals, or trees and plant life. I realize that there is a symbiotic relationship related to survival between us and the flora and fauna of the planet, but we humans take all our gifts from nature for granted, in most cases, harvesting for the sake of profit, and killing for the so called sport of it. Hunting was once a necessity, but that time is long gone. Take a digital camera with a powerful telephoto lens and see how many ten point bucks you can capture. You will come to see that a live deer will give you much more pleasure than a dead one. There seems to be yet, in humans, a need to kill, or just a matter of uncontrolled ego. I am sure that ego was very useful when hunting was a necessity. I believe, that time is long gone and only adds to the pressure on the fauna from loss of habitat.

I feel the same way about war, where humans are actually hunting each other and those who promote war are content to sit back and watch the blood flow from a remote and safe place. And, why not, they have a lot of willing fodder for their game. War and armies, and the machines associated with war, are a tremendous burden on societies that are called upon to support such efforts. Of course there is the profit aspect of war for those who don't have to give up their lives to fight. The waste is not only monetary and resources, but in human life. Most often the young, just reaching maturity and cut of from life or maimed; pay the price. I reiterate here;

those who want to make war should be in the front ranks of the battle. I think, if we could institute an international law that stated that we are not compelled to fight a war unless the makers of said war are leading the charge, war would just fade away, and diplomacy would become more fashionable.

There is nothing romantic about killing, torture and maiming, although it has been portrayed that way in movies and books, mostly because of our strong attachment to the macho ego based attitudes. There are still those who think that seeking a peaceful solution is going to rob us of our manhood, and this attitude is now spreading to women who for so long had the better sense of not engaging in armed conflict. Even they are being infected by the macho worm.

War occurs throughout all of society for various reasons. Some are purely idealistic, while some are caused by poverty and social standing. We don't seem to have evolved to the point of seeing that we are all equal at birth and death, and should be treated as equals in between those two extremes. After all, we are all, regardless of our worldly circumstances at birth, come into existence with nothing and we leave with nothing. Every thing we claw for in life turns to dust in the wind in the end.

Wars are constantly being fought on the local level of almost every nation. Some may be justified and some I believe are prompted by the example and stance that the various governments of the world set, especially the more industrialized nations. These nations should be setting a better example for the rest of the world.

There are justifiable wars. When a maniacal and insane

person, who is beyond reason, sets their sights on world domination and genocide, there are no alternatives but to stop them for the benefit of humanity. These instances are rare and most wars could be avoided if the rest of the world would apply pressure to the offenders, with diplomacy and sanctions. When the whole world is frowning down on your country, and the leaders have not lost their sanity, it would make them think twice about how they are treating their citizens. This of course would require a world united, and an acceptance and active participation with respect for other cultures whose ideology might differ significantly, understanding that ideologies are just ideas made manifest, and does not alter the fact that at the core level, we are all the same, and should relate to one another as such.

Humans take their ideas much too seriously, and have a very strong tendency to get attached to those ideas to the extreme point of giving up their lives for them, especially when fighting to convert someone else to a particular way of thinking. Our values can never be taken away from us if we really believe in them, and it is not right to try and coerce others into changing their values, especially by force. If we work in a peaceful manner, eventually the playing field will level out, but this also requires a give and take on both side of the line. This works for individuals as well as nations. The ego however, is always telling us to stand fast and don't compromise, and so we have the birth of an enemy, instead of a friend.

This is not who we are at present, but I believe that we should work at becoming more open and accessible to every one around us, and eventually making it the *The Dream of the Planet*. For many it would be a dream come true, and a road to a much improved future. Success in settling our global differences would also relieve some of the pressure on our Mother Earth, and we could then move on to restoring the paradise that Adam and Eve lost.

Our intelligence is a powerful tool, but it can be used in positive or negative ways. The choice is ours to make at every turn. I don't think we can continue to take our world for granted, and I think conscious living is the next step in the many steps we have already climbed, toward survival and enlightenment.

Chapter 10

The Future

Trying to predict the future would require a fully functional crystal ball, and I haven't had much success in finding one. So, all I can do is expound on what I would envision the future of humanity to be. It has been said that one can judge the future by analyzing the past history of our existence, and our past is certainly full of accomplishments; some wonderful and some rather damaging. If our future is to be dictated by our past, then we will continue on the same helter skelter path we are on at this present moment, scrambling and clawing our way toward riches and material goals, while leaving the rest of the world behind to suffer the deprivation that comes from only a handful of citizens reaping all the benefits of the world economy.

The wealth and abundance of the world is in serious disequilibrium, created by a mind set that sets its goals on amassing as much as our personal power and leverage can procure. We seem to display a strong tendency toward addiction, which is just another way of saying that we become so attached to things like money, food, drugs alcohol, status, and the list goes on, narrowing our view and keeping us focused on just one aspect of living. Anything outside of our basic survival; food, shelter, clothing, and spirituality, is fertile ground for addiction and attachment, and even the basic needs can become addictive, such as over eating, etc. Of course this can only happen when we have over abundant means at our disposal.

One means of amassing wealth is to corner the market by eliminating the competition, and is a tactic that is alive and well in present day society. We see less and less mom and pop businesses. Small capitol businessman can not compete with the large corporations, and this deprives the small businessman and self actualized citizen from attaining any kind of independence and success. This also creates a void in the job market, that would otherwise be filled by lower wage earners. I personally would like to see more support for small business even if the prices are a little higher. For instances the convenience of a local market will offset the difference in price by savings on fuel and wear and tear on our vehicles, and the ones I knew as a child were more diversified and personal than, the mega markets, sometimes catering more to the local tastes. Of course, this will never happen unless small business is supported by the consumers.

I realize that the lower end of the middle class, and those at the poverty level, who are making minimum wage or lower in some cases, have no choice but to seek out the lowest price retailers that they can find, and in some instances, like Wal Mart employees, have to seek out additional help, such as food stamps, to be able to make ends meet. It seems to be the accepted trend these days, to keep the wage scales as low as possible, even if the companies profits are high.

In the future I would like to see a fair wage for everyone, and its not like mega corporation can't afford it. At present the addiction toward unbridled profits is so great, that even the most successful corporations are willing to squeeze their employees in order to maximize their profits. The only worker who can make a decent living wage today, are those who have an education or skill that is in demand, such as engineers and technicians, for example, in the burgeoning electronics field, or any other field that demands competent technical skills, thereby using those skills as leverage to obtain a bigger slice of the pie. In reality all jobs are necessary or they would not exist, no matter how mundane they may seem, and all employees are filling a void that is necessary for the successful operation of any business, from high tech to hamburgers.

There is no respect for the individual in the market today. Its top dog eat lowly dog, and perhaps its always been that way, but I believe its time to evolve to a more equitable system and distribution of the wealth and resources of the world, which can only happen if we can look upon each other as equals, regardless of our social standing. We have to realize that we are only in our status or position because of circumstance and opportunity and not because of any

God given endowment. The constitution of the United State and many other countries included, declare that all men and women are created equal and deserve fair and impartial consideration, but those are only words and are meaningless unless they become part of the internal belief system of everyone, especially those who are in positions of leverage; those closest to the purse strings.

There are those individuals who start with zero and by cunning and perseverance and a good business sense can rise to wealth and prosperity, and there is nothing wrong with having the capability to succeed; it is actually necessary for an economy to thrive. I also believe that wealth and prosperity come with a responsibility to the public welfare, by realizing that an individuals success in business could never happen if not supported by the public, by patronizing a particular product or business. No one rises in any business venture without a broad base of public support, and that dictates that business should be willing to give back some of their good fortune to those who made it possible in the first place, something like the way the credit unions work, by redistributing the left over profits at the end of the fiscal year.

This could be accomplished by giving their employees a good wage and good benefits. I realize that the goal of business is to make a profit, but in this day and age, profits seem to be the only thing that matters, and it feels like there is a consensus that its alright to squeeze the public as much as possible, which is directly responsible for the decline of the middle class, and the lack of jobs. Pinching at the top creates less opportunity at the bottom. More of the wealth of the world is going to the top few percent and none of it is coming back down to nurture the base that made it all possible. Giving people a wage that would pull them out of the poverty level, would enhance the middle class and bolster the entire economy.

I know redistribution is a fourteen letter word to many, but if you think about just how much leverage large amounts of capital can command, and how much damage or how much good it could do for the broader base of humanity, I think some restraint is called for. This could only work if done on a voluntary basis and could only come about by the light of inspiration touching the minds and hearts of those who hold the capital reins, an epiphany no less. Well, good luck on that one!

Many would say that this idea is a form of socialism. Well, I don't think there is anything wrong with being social. We live in a world society, and we have seen what happens when the broad base of society gets fed up with being taken advantage of. Of course, it does not have to come to that if the broader base of society realizes that they hold the power in their hands just by shear numbers and their buying power. Just as countries who think they are in the right to impose sanctions on other countries, so can the broader base of the population impose sanctions anywhere they feel necessary. The USA became the country that it is, not by people standing around watching the British take advantage of them, but by actively taking part in what ever it took to free themselves, and hopefully, in the future, the majority of the population will take a more active role in their government and issues that at present are moving humans toward an untenable state of affairs.

To capitalists, socialism is a bad word, and to socialists, capitalism is a bad word. In their pure form, both are extreme philosophies, and the only thing that is going to work is the middle of the road approach in the crucible of the mind, where the two philosophies can be crushed and blended together to form a more equitable system for all. All ideas fall under this umbrella, and the only thing that makes different points of view untenable, is our propensity of gravitating toward extremes at the mention of anything that is new or different in our noesis.

In the future I imagine a world society where everyone is on the same footing as far as opportunity for education and the right to at least a comfortable way of life. In the U.S., it is proposed that everyone has the same opportunities as everyone else. This is a false belief, in a society that so widely ranges in monetary standing, which makes all the difference when it come to higher education. Basic education as well as higher education could be available to everyone if we could put our taxes to better use than wasting them on war and destruction. As it stands now, if aspiring students that don't have the support of parents who can afford to pay for college tuition for their children, the only other means is to go into debt from government loan or credit cards or both. It is not uncommon for college students to amass debt in excess of a hundred thousand dollars, and makes it very difficult to have that kind of yoke around ones neck when trying to embark on a career. Not everyone has the inclination to attend a university, and for these individuals, the option of attending a trade school or state supported collage, where an associates degree could be acquired, would fill an essential need.

There is still a big demand for this level of education, where a high school education no longer suffices, as it did in the past. Everything that surrounds us is getting more technical by the day, and there is more demand for people who can repair and maintain complex systems. There are scholarships available to some of the lucky few, but they don't even come close to meeting the demand.

I would, and I am not alone, like to see a future where war is non existent and a world society that has matured enough to realize that war is one of the biggest waste bins that humans participate in. And, I am not speaking of the unavoidable wars that come our way from time to time, and even these wars could be avoided if the world united to put pressure on any particular country bent on world domination. But, the wars that could be avoided, are fought over such thing as oil, expansion and sometimes over ideologies that only demonstrate our level of addiction to our ego maniacal side, and the intolerance for social differences.

War has been with us so long that we have come to accept it as if it were one of the necessities of life. The waste in human life and resources is astounding, and it takes the best in human potential just at the age of maturation and sends them off to be killed because we believe ourselves to be the big brother of the world.

The different areas of the world are in different stages of evolution and they will take steps to change their situation only when they are ready for it, and no outside influence is going to help until this critical point is reached. The more technically advanced countries of the world do not realize that most of the so called third world countries are emulating them, and this should be reason enough for the more advance countries to set a good example; such as not using their technically advanced toys for death and destruction.

I don't think we should be left unprepared or defenseless, but I do believe that we are more in state of war than in a defensive position, by many times over. One of the biggest barriers in abolishing war is that war and money are in bed with each other, and until we come to value life, liberty and the pursuit of happiness above money, we will continue to bang our heads on the wall of senseless war.

We [the USA] spend an incredible amount of tax money on defense, and in a supposed time of peace. Of course there is never really any peace for us, since we are always fighting and meddling in some other countries internal affairs, or using our might to protect our special interest, spurred on by fear and sometimes just plain competition with some other world power, such as the Big Bear.

The World War II price tag was [in 2013 dollars] close to a trillion dollars and fell sharply to one hundred million dollars by 1948, and should have remained there to the present time. But instead, the Korean war came along and the defense budget rose to five hundred billion dollars. And following that the Vietnam war increased spending to six hundred billion dollars. Our most recent involvement in Iraq and Afghanistan has cost us over seven hundred billion dollars, and even with our commitment to pull out of the middle east, congress is asking for an even higher defense budget for 2014.

Our fixation with war and war produced profits is seriously impacting the quality of life for most American citizens, except for the one percent that reap the benefits of military spending. In the future, the scales need to be rebalanced or we will continue to deplete our resources and empty our coffers.

I have devoted a whole chapter to the topic of over population, and I believe that of all the challenges we face in the future, this one is going to be of utmost importance. The appetite that nature has instilled in the humans and for that matter in all biological organisms, is geared for over reproduction. Since most are still in the food chain, this over production is absorbed by the predator nature of all life forms. Humans have pulled themselves out of that loop in the natural process, and are no longer subject to that kind of attrition, except toward each other, or so it seems. Thus, a concerted effort to limit procreation should become paramount in the minds of all the world citizenry.

In my future dream, I see a world of citizens that does not bring children into the world that they have no means of taking care of. The world is full of children that are starving and living in abhorrent conditions, and will continue to rise unless some measure of awareness is attained. Sex and sexuality have risen to become one of our aberrational past times and is just another one of our addictive and attachment characteristics. The world needs to control the procreation process, if not by awareness and inspiration then at least by contraception. I reiterate, that the over burden we place on the earth is going to lead to a collapse of our ecological systems. Such a collapse would cause chaos and suffering on a scale equal to the nuclear winter of sixty five million years ago, that totally changed the face of existence forever. If we can not curb our appetites, then nature will do it for us, and nature is not going to mollycoddle us.

Another major source of contention is what we do to our environment with particular emphasis on the atmosphere, ground and water pollution, which are now becoming over burdened by carbon dioxide, methane, chemicals, waste products, and many other poisonous gases that threaten to cause a catastrophic heating of the atmosphere, while also unleashing poisons that are detrimental to all life forms. Yet, we continue to mine the earth and cut down the trees with reckless abandon. We burn coal in most of our power plants and not much of an effort is made to take the pollutants out before they reach the atmosphere, and there is no real push for the development of renewable sources of energy.

In my future vision, the industrial complex, which includes power generation, will finally become aware of the dangers of unbridled pollution. Or at least our legislative government will come to its senses, and realize that they need to act responsibly, with an eye on the future, instead of the current trend of profits as their only focal point.

In the future, it is going to be of paramount importance who we elect to be our representatives in government, with a limit of two terms maximum, and should not be allowed to vote themselves any benefits out side of the agreed salary. Any additional benefits should be voted on by the ones who pay their salaries; the tax payer.

In the future, lobbying will be eliminated and companies will not be allowed to be treated as if they were individuals, and candidates will be limited in how much they can spend on campaigning for office. Will light ever shine in our supposed democratic system? We can only be hopeful, since power and money seen to corrupt every thing it touches, and the only power that exists or ever existed, resides in the hands of the broad base of the constituency to control the elected.

When the mind becomes enthralled with gold, it seems to act as a shield for enlightenment of any kind, producing greed that narrows the vision into a tunnel, where peripheral vision and the whole view of life is non existent and acquiring more wealth is the only option left; it is one of the draw backs of being a paradoxical entity that has the choice of following the extremes to the highest plain or the lowest base.

We must come to realize, that checks and balances don't work with respect to governments. That falls in the hands of the constituency who at present put too much faith that their elected officials, thinking they will do the right thing on their behalf. It is obvious that it does not work that way, and the constituency is going to have to take a more active part in making sure their elected representatives have a clear and concrete notion of what is expected from them, and insure that none succumb to special interest, and we should have the option of firing a representative that does not comply. Its done in business to employees that do not comply with the standards of the company, and should apply to representatives as well, after all, they are in our employ. If special interests can spend millions of dollars for campaign donations and coercion, then they are probably doing well enough, and greed must be their motivation for further leverage.

In the future, the educational system will under go a radical change, where moral and spiritual concepts will be taught at the early and impressionable age, since most humans I know, do not realize that essentially we are still wild creatures, and that civilization is still a taught concept, not an automatic instinctive reaction like survival is. If we fail to teach the basic concepts that make us human and humane, spirituality, morality, the arts and music, then science and mathematics will only serve as loose cannons and bigger clubs, that could lead to our own self destruction. We have already come close to pushing the big red buttons and annihilating ourselves, and as long as those nuclear arsenals exist, or the the mega war arsenals, the threat will always remain.

I realize that its very difficult to put the monster back into Pandora's box, but we have to start somewhere and nothing ever happens unless we take that first step. There is also the possibility of individuals making small nukes, and if someone is insane enough to blow themselves and others up with dynamite, think of the pleasure they would derive from doing it with a small nuclear bomb! This is an issue that future societies will have to deal with. Of course, this is insane behavior, and another thing the future citizenry will have to solve, is; the creation of so many insane people. We unwittingly produce insanity in our cultures by passing our hate and fear on to our offspring's which produces insanity of varying degrees; something that touches almost all human beings, and should be a strong indication to everyone, just how far off the mark our evolution is taking us. Evolution can, and in my opinion has, taken a negative turn.

As a sentient race, the future requires us to question all our motives and actions before we run off half cocked on endeavors that do not benefit the whole. I know this is a concept that is very hard for most of humanity to accept. We are by and large steeped in the *Me* orbit, where every thing revolves around us and no one else matters. This might have been beneficial for our early survival, although, even in our beginnings, we had to show consideration for our immediate community or survival would be impossible with out the support of others. In that context, the world and all its citizens are becoming an immediate community by means of our modern transportation and communication technologies.

In the future the whole world will become one community and nations will be as states that exist within countries today. This is a concept that is open to consideration, since at present, people seem to be in a real struggle to control their smaller local governments, and the problems of a world government would be multiplied a thousand fold. Small localized governments have always been the most effective because of the embedded familiarity and the local needs, which vary in different parts of the world.

I think a world government is possible only if a major step in our evolution occurs; of how well we relate to each other; of how much of ourselves we can see in others. Right now the world is severely divided and for some reason can't see that we are all the same, by ninety nine, and nine tenths percent; our DNA proves that to be true.

The world has shrunk, and we are compelled to allow everyone the same rights that we enjoy, or would like to enjoy, understanding that what goes around eventually comes around. It may take centuries, but history supports the concept that nations rise to the top of the heap and nations fall to the bottom of the heap. Nations rise by the combination of ideals and might, and continue at the top until corruption cause them to fall by their own weight. After a rise to be a world power, nations think they have arrived and can now rest on their past accomplishments. Nations don't realize that what got them there was an evolutionary step and what will sustain them is to keep evolving and changing on demand. I believe that everyone would agree that change is the only thing we can count on.

Humans can get entrenched in their ideologies until a catastrophe comes along and sweeps them out of their complacency, and the ground lost, can never be recovered. Instead of considering the validity of our motives daily, we become mesmerized by our successes and succumb to doing everything in our power to keep anything from changing our status. However, just like the tortoise and the hare, when you snooze you lose. When humans stop, they get fat and think only of the gravy, and our thoughts no longer keep up with the changing times.

Can we really evolve to become a world community, or are we destined to struggle in hell forever; a forever that will only last until we severely damage our world? In my future the answer is, *yes.* We will continue to grow and evolve our ideologies to where they fit everyone, and we will seek methods of sustaining our dependence on energy without destroying our environment by also controlling our population.

In the future, the different world societies will heave a huge sigh of relief and finally and collectively dump that huge sack of rocks that our world culture has been carrying on its backs, and say; I am tired of living in hell, and we are ready to experience the paradise that this beautiful world was meant to be. Humans are powerful, but it does not mean that we have to change every thing we encounter, except our ways of thinking.

There are many challenges we face in the future. We are soon to find out that as our economic and technological base increases, the challenges will increase in the same proportion. But, take heart and understand; that evolution and well being does not have to depend exclusively on economic and technical excess. Once we take the blinders off and allow individuals to choose their heart felt path, we will not suffer from a lack of fulfillment. Science is not for everyone, and we keep trying to push the round peg in the square hole. That is never going to work, and only leads to neurosis and insanity. We have plenty of that everywhere in the world already.

In the future, the religions of the world will liquidate

their wealth and distribute it among the people they profess to serve, and people will consult their heart more and choose their belief system by what works for them, and with that will come the understanding that we no longer have the need to be herded around and told what to believe in. We must demonstrate that we have matured enough to be able to make up our own minds with respect to our beliefs, and take responsibility for all of our actions.

This will entail an investigation by the individual and an exploration of the different belief systems; something that is taking root in society at this very moment. Many people, myself included, are gravitating toward some of the more ancient modalities, along with modern beliefs, drawing from many, the keys that fit the individuals lock. Basically, all belief systems are aiming at the same thing; how to live a meaningful and fulfilling life, with a possibility of an after life.

The after life is very similar to trying to predict the future and no one has come back from the grave to tell us about it. The only link that we have is people that have had near death experiences, where it is claimed that they have seen the other side of the tunnel, where deceased loved ones await. Who knows what happens to the mind as it begins to shut down, and in that shut down we may experience our life flashing before us, and those who had the greatest influence on our existence. As far as I am concerned, what happens after death is still a mystery, simular to all the elements that were once a mystery to us. Perhaps one day we will discern what happens after this radical change occurs we call death, and find out what happens to our life force when we expire. I have watched people die, and one moment they are animated with life, though they may be sick and dying, and the next moment after death, I could sense that there is nothing there but basic element, as if something had left the body. Perhaps our life force goes somewhere or just joins the other energies in the universe; a mystery we may one day solve.

Believing in life after death comes down to a personal choice, and I for one want to believe that our soul and essence lives on after death, with the possibility of reincarnating and coming back with the wisdom I have accumulated in this life, and a chance to relive a more meaningful life. There have been many times when I felt that I instinctively knew how to proceed in some process and only need to explore the mechanical means to accomplish the task. This could have come about through a reincarnation process or perhaps through a DNA link. In either case, it's still a form of reincarnation. I think most people want to believe that there is more to come when this life is over, and I believe it is a form of hope for our survival and the possibility of applying the lessons we learned in this life; to the next life.

What ever happens after our death, our responsibility is to the life we are in now, and that life adjures us to actualized our conscious and perceptive abilities to the fullest extent, and not allowing our social and monetary status to blind us away from greatness and accomplishment that all individuals are capable of. I make this statement with my belief that we are all equal in our abilities to manifest the future we want.

The only blocks we encounter are those that are proffered by teachers who would keep us in the herd mentality, for the sole purpose of control, and which we buy into, mostly because of fear of damnation, non acceptance by our peers, or just plain lethargy, where its just easier to follow than to take a stand based on our own conclusions brought about by our curious and investigative natures.

In the future, those in positions of authority are going to have to make allowances for a broader point of view that is inevitable when the general population awakens and finally makes their voices heard. Authority is going to have to modify the police state mentality that seems to be growing in intensity under present conditions. Our right to freedom of speech and peaceful demonstration is going to have to be redefined and strengthened. Authority has a tendency to set itself up as unquestionable, and often employ's dictator tactics in dealing with the public. This can change if ego is taken out of the equation, and authority realizes whom they are serving.

Much of this control is taught at an early age by our parents or authority figures, so that by the time we mature, we are already ripe for control. Most parents I know, take the intelligence of their offspring's for granted and don't realize that they are as intelligent at birth as they will ever be. However, the mind, no matter how intelligent it may be, is still an empty vessel, and parents should realize that great care should be taken in what is put into that vessel, as it will form the basis of the child's future outlook on life. This is a clear cut case of "what we sow we will reap".

Unfortunately, ideologies flow down stream from parent to offspring, so there is a real need for would be parents as well as teachers, to explore their own minds and clear away unwanted garbage, before trying to impress their children and charges. If we plant hate and negative ideas, those are the tools the adult will have to work with. If we plant love and understanding, the future adult and all of society will benefit.

The bad news is: The future is fraught with uncertainty, and if history is to continue to repeat itself in the same old mind set of the fortunate preying on the unfortunate, then erosion of our higher ideals will continue to decline and lead us to the continued slavery of humanity.

The good news is: There is hope and there are the means, that the human race will awaken and take the evolutionary leap into a future where we will all feel the heart felt aspiration that: *Now Is The Time For All Good Men To Come To The Aid Of Their Planet*, which includes all the flora and fauna, that is so vital to our survival, fundamentally and whether we realize it or not, psychologically as well. We are linked to everything in the universe through the cosmic quantum level that created all the worlds and the creatures that live upon them, and if our perceptions are correct, touched by His loving hand.

My hope in this future is maintained by the trend that is already taking root in many people around the world, of not being fearful of standing alone and standing up for what we know is right and just. Perhaps in the near future, with critical mass of awareness and consciousness, people will tip the scale and a new era of evolution will begin, hopefully before we reach the point of no return.

All we need to do is: wake up and clean out the attic of our minds and allow the fresh air of our higher selves in. We need to blow all the musty mold away, and set a good example and a soft touch, since coercion only builds walls, and physical pressure just creates enemies. *Teach Peace.*

If we can clear away the cob webs of illusion, and keep ourselves from being snared by every sweet and sticky tidbit that comes along [and they come cloaked and sugar coated in so many devious ways that it takes some contemplation to discern the core intent] we may be able to free ourselves to make intelligent decisions and not decisions based on ego, pressure, fear, hate, bigotry, greed and misinformation; we may be able to stand on higher and firmer ground for the sake of manifesting a more meaningful and beautiful future, for ourselves and for our progeny.

Chapter 11

In Conclusion

From the *Big Bang* to the present moment, creation and evolution of the cosmos is hinged on the principal of opposites, from the atom with its positive nucleus and its negative electrons to the human persona of male and female, which would also apply to most of the creatures on the earth.

I could probably fill a small book if I tried to list all the opposites that occur in the physical universe, but my main concern here is to explore the opposites that humans experience physically, emotionally, and psychically.

In the universe at large, the opposites of all the elements follow the laws of physics and have no choice but to attract or repel, amalgamate or separate, and this would apply to the basic structure of our own physical bodies up to the cellular level.

It appears to me that the magic of *choice* begins with the multi-cellular organism where unique cells that perform different functions combine to execute tasks that can only be considered higher order responsibilities. Just to mention a few in the human body, there are multi-cell combinations that make bone, blood, muscle, nerves and in humans more brain cells than any other creature on the planet.

All of these attributes add up to create the pinnacle of evolution on this planet and I consider the paradoxical ability of *choice* to be one of our most powerful qualities. The only problem with choice is that it can be directed in any direction the individual wishes it to go, and that direction can be ruled by thought, anger, emotions, information, intuition or heart and soul triggers.

Thought alone is experiential and choices are made from what our program dictates and what we have learned. Thought choice can be misleading if we have not consciously made an effort to weed out the untruths that are embedded in everyone's programming.

Anger seldom makes a right choice, and the axiom; cooler heads should prevail, certainly would apply here. Other emotions can also mislead choice; like sorrow, if we are depressed, joyous, or hurt; choice can take a roller coaster ride. Information is usually slanted by whoever gathers it, and might be true or false or in between, unless it is information we have gleaned through our own experiences, but even that needs to be run through the filter of the heart to sift out the little goat heads that might have tainted us in the acquisition.

Intuition I believe comes from everywhere, including, inside us, and feels like the culmination of all the forces in nature and what we know, acting on the psyche to inform us about our situation. I believe intuition is reliable if we can manage to stay grounded and don't try to interject anything into the feeling. Intuition is like a muscle and needs to be exercised often, to make it familiar enough to be trusted.

One of our most powerful emotions is *Love;* like the love we might feel for a soul-mate and lover or love that we extend to others. There is no tutorial or manual on love and a parent might try to explain love to an offspring, but it would be in generalities only. I liken true love to two magnets of opposite poles coming into close proximity, and the rest just follows its own destiny. Love we extend toward our fellow man can only be made manifest if we can see ourselves in others; our commonality of species, and making allowances for differences, that are only products of social and regional beliefs.

Even if we all came from the same place on earth, we would probably find something to fight about, as is evident within nations today. Protestants against Catholics: Sunni's against Shiites, and the list goes on. When we relate to each other through the ego, we will always use the differences of one percent, that are minute, and ignore the ninety nine percent of our sameness. That is the real hell on earth, and no deity places us there, we, condemn ourselves to live in hell. One more reason to rein in the ego.

Love can be heaven or it can be hell: it can be beneficial or it can be fatal.

More often it is beneficial, since love is such a strong force, that it has the power to smooth out some very jagged edges. Love is only fatal when insanity is present.

Love strikes us like a force from the cosmos, but even here we are courting our old friend and sometimes nemesis, choice. Certainly choice can bolster our love for someone or it can cause it to wither and die.

I have been emphatic and reiterative about the concept of choice in most of the previous chapters, because, I feel, the course we take in the immediate and near future is going to set the standard that will effect the quality of life on our world for a long time, and will affect all of its inhabitants in the future.

By and large, most people make their choices through the conditioning and domestication we have been entrained with from childhood, and that usually becomes a form of automatic response to different situations. We already know how we will respond and its very predictable for anyone who has an agenda to push onto the public. All they have to do is format it with key elements and it becomes a shoe-in.

This kind of response causes people to be swept up and away with a feeling of belonging and contribution to a cause that they may not really know much about. If you are a Democrat you are expected to fall into line with the proposed platform, and the same is expected from Republicans. We wave our hats and push up our cliche signs and revel in the decisions that someone else has made, with our full support.

What I described above is devoid of any independent thinking or scrutinizing the material presented. Its the easy way, and when I have viewed on television a parties national convention; all I see is a flock of sheep on the floor, caught up in the moment of emotion. I've stated before that I don't believe in the multiple party system. In my opinion; all it does is split a strong majority into two, more manageable camps. These two parties can now expend their energy throwing spitballs at each other; while the elected craft their plans in the background. Horse manure you say! Well folks, I am just thinking like a politician here. The only difference is: I am disclosing it to you.

There is a real need for everyone to stop and become aware of how we are subtly manipulated, appealing to our emotions, by those who are adept in the craft. The chapter: A Public Seduced, describes some of the subtle and not so subtle ways in which consumers are influenced by advertising and almost every thing in the media is designed to pluck at our emotional strings.

Making decisions on the basis of our emotions is going to keep us tied to the yolk and the mill wheel, until that time when we can step out of the emotional rut, in order to make better informed decisions. Again, it comes down to choice. Next time you see one of these fantasy commercials, try and visualize the fish hook that the visuals and dialogue paint and if you want to get emotional, laugh, its a form of shield for me and it can work for anyone. Commercials on television have become soap opera's and to me have the flavor of Twinkies; yuk, although someone must like them, I still see them on the grocery shelves.

A major concern with me, and should be for every one,

since everybody is going to be affected, is; what is happening to the ecology of the planet. Not only are we poisoning our environment by the side effects of energy production and industrial fall-out, but now we are deliberately injecting toxic chemicals into the strata by means of *fracturing,* just to extract a little more natural gas. The water tables are becoming unusable for people living in close proximity to these operations, and these chemicals are not going to go away, they will just continue to spread as the ground water carries them further afield. This heinous process needs to be outlawed. Processes like fracking show a total lack of awareness or love for our world.

Since a large percentage of the population of the world uses natural gas to heat their homes and cook their food, we are facing the future dilemma of running out of this precious natural commodity, and I think fracking is a symptom of that loss. Natural gas is not the only natural energy source that is dwindling. Coal and oil are not renewable and once they are exhausted we are up the proverbial creek without a paddle.

How do we heat our homes in winter, when all the natural gas is gone? There are some systems of heating water by solar means and using radiant heating to heat our homes. This would involve a drastic change and without help would be cost prohibiting for most of us. We could all install some wood stoves around the house, but in a few years the world would be denuded of trees, and the air would be thick enough to cut with a knife. Trees are renewable, but our chainsaws are much faster than tree growth, which is quite evident by the tremendous loss of rain forest, that occurs on a daily basis.

We should already be going full tilt on developing alternative sources of energy, but no; the present day magnates of energy want to keep going as if these resources are going to last forever. They are effectively blocking further development of renewable technology by the act of hording profits and not investing in research, that and buying their way into the legislative process in order to render the government benign in pushing or supporting research in renewable technologies.

If we care to look, we can *see*, that our natural resources are heading toward extinction. With this in mind, we should be digging in our heals in research for alternatives, and if we choose, we can make our collective voices heard over the din of opposition; but its going to take all of us to hold back the tsunami of google bucks. If the ball on renewable energy does not start rolling soon, and we wait until all our resources are exhausted, we might as well kiss our way of life good-by.

Add to the above; the growing population of mankind and I *see* a major reset coming. Can't we see the curve of resources going down and the curve of population going up. We either begin to curtail that rising curve in our growth or natural processes will do it for us. There is a cliff of insurmountable obstacles facing us, in just making everyone aware that a problem exists and another hurtle to get people to adjust to limiting their progeny. Again, the media would be the best source of alerting people of the dangers of irresponsible procreation on the future, but the commercial media is so heavily supported by big money, that I doubt if they would even consider rocking the boat. Public television might be the only media that could alert the public of the danger of run-away population, since they are supported by grant money and public donations.

Most of the independent environmental organizations are dedicated to saving whats left of the wild places, flora and fauna included, and have been instrumental is securing and protecting large tracks of land. These organization are supported by a like minded membership and may be one of our last lines of defense. Certainly, the more people that supported these organizations the more power they could wield in the battle for conservation, from the hands of the exploiters of anything that glitters. Just like it takes big money to carve up the world, so does it take big money to protect it, and I will list a few of the more prominent ones here. The Sierra Club, The National Resource Defense Council, The Nature Conservancy, The National Wildlife Federation, and there are many others.

Most people are so closed off and ungrounded that I believe they never think about any future consequences with respect to the choices we make, and its all reinforced by ego, blind patriotism and lack of information. I consider myself patriotic and there is no other place I would rather live, except to visit, but I also reserve the right to agree or disagree and make my views known.

Religions play a major part in the attitude of people with respect to procreation. Go forth and multiply was proposed over two thousand years ago, when the population of the earth was much smaller, and I don't think the author of that statement meant for us to over-populate to the point of over-burdening our environment. The mind set of religions is two millennium in the past and I think they need to re-build their foundations, using modern circumstance as a model. This could address the needs of the present population. The churches of the world hold powerful sway over their congregations. If they could address some of the real problems that face humanity, from the pulpit, it would make a strong positive influence on a large portion of the population. The new and present Pope, Francis, seems to have a more realistic view of where our world is heading, and I think he sees that stagnation in the church has led to the loss of believers.

We are already at a straining point to feed the present population and there are millions that are starving, and those with meager subsistence. Of course, some of this is produced by over abundance in one hand and nothing in the other. As our numbers grow, so does demand, and over abundance can turn to deficiency. I live in an abundant world where everything is available. The future problem I face is; every time I visit the super market, the prices of everything in the store has jumped up, and not just by a few cents; its always a significant amount. I live on a fixed income and there is no way to keep up with runaway inflation. In my future, it will have to be, beans and bacon ever day.

Where do those price increases go? Certainly not for wage increases. Wages have remained stagnant for decades, so I have to think they go to higher profits, with nary a sign of trickle down. It is apparent to me, that greed is growing like weeds after the monsoon. I also speculate that people have a difficult time reining themselves in without some external intervention. Once upon a time, the government enacted regulatory mandates on many of our industries, and the result was a more stable economy.

This all came to a screeching halt when a puppet president succumbed to big money pressure and was instrumental in pulling out all the stops of regulation, allowing industry license to kill by putting the pedal to the metal and going for the gold. Another puppet president decided the rich don't have to pay their fair share of taxes and so the burden is shifted to the backs of the middle class.

Reformation is in order. We need to institute a realistic and fair tax structure, where by everyone pays the same percentage of tax, no matter how well healed they might be.

I for one am tired of seeing the wealth of the this country being squandered on wars that are driving us deeper and deeper in dept every year. I know the military complex keeps a lot of people employed, of course, at the risk of life and limb. If our armed forces were reduce to a peace time contingent, our tax money could be used to rebuild the outdated infrastructure of the nation, and would also create jobs for those who were released from military service.

Our intervention in world affairs usually creates more problems than it solves, for instance Iraq; that was stable because the leader knew what kind of leadership that country needed. That was before we invaded them. Now that country will be in confusion and chaos until out side influences leave them alone, which, after a few years, the pieces will fall back into place. Of course, intervention usually comes with an agenda and is seldom for humanitarian reasons, or security reasons. For instance, "weapons of mass destruction"; more of an excuse.

One of the pressing concerns for the immediate future is the preservation of the diminishing wild places on the planet. Most wild animal are in serious decline.

Some of it is due to illegal poaching of animals with valued parts, such as the elephant and rhinoceros, whose horns are sold on the world market, though there are international laws against this kind of commerce. There just are not enough concerned citizens to apply pressure on trafficking. There are rangers that try to keep the slaughter down, but there are not near enough of them to cover the vast expanses of a continent as large as Africa and all other countries face similar circumstances.

Another factor that is affecting wild creatures, is the loss of habitat. Again, expanding populations around the world are directly responsible for the shrinking world of wild animals, and is in turn being filled with domesticated live stock. The more population; the more live stock needed; the less wild land available. Earths human population is in an exponential rise, and can be equated to a chain reaction in a nuclear explosion. In unstable and highly radio active material when compressed, creates a condition called fission, where one electron causes one atom to split, which then produces two electrons, which causes two atoms to split and the reaction goes binary with atoms splitting at the rate of eight, sixteen, thirty two, sixty four, one hundred twenty eight, two hundred fifty six, and the reaction continues, creating explosions that only occurred in stars until the birth of the atomic age. Thus the term population explosion.

If a couple produce only two children, they would only be replicating themselves and the population would remain the same. If the same couple had four children, it would be akin to starting a chain reaction and population would bloom like an out of control fractal. One child per couple would begin to curb our increasing population.

Of course, this is only going to happen if everyone is aware of where run-away population is going to take us. The survival instinct in humans is so strong, that given the right conditions, most humans would revert to their feral state and anarchy would become the law of the land. Think Road Warrior was just an entertaining movie? Not just that! It was about what happens when civilization and law are no longer adhered to, and its everyman for himself. There is not much in the way of evolution under such conditions, and would be worse than living in the dark ages.

We need to allow our social evolution to catch up with our science. We have been putting all our eggs in one basket since the Renaissance; the science basket, that is. While all of this technical revolution and industrialization was being shifted into over-drive, we were still doing the barbaric dance of shooting and bombing each other, just for the sake of ideas, and any thing of a so called scientific break through, is used to build a bigger and better club. Even the space program was of a strategic nature.

I don't think we have any business shooting for the stars until we have made peace with ourselves and each other. Else; whats the use of spreading our stain to other worlds. When we can strike out as true explorers for the sake of our insatiable curiosity, we may have something positive to impart to the cosmos. Undoubtedly, we will encounter beings who find themselves in the throws of situations similar to the one we are in at present, of war and conflict, so, we will just have to steer clear of them. If there are space travelers that have come into our solar system, they are probably hesitant to make contact because of our hostile attitude. All they have to do is watch one of our science fiction movies to glean what our reaction would be toward space aliens. Our present cosmic view is one of shoot first and ask questions later, which also reflects our world view.

Evolution and growth in spiritual ways, happens on an individual level, and requires the seeker the ability of being fluid enough to adapt to different ideas.

In the chapter: My Path, I describe some of the regimens that I immersed myself in, in order to try and liberate my thinking and seek freedom from out dated programs and domestication.

Clearing the mind of all the garbage that we accumulate over a life time requires concentration and dedication and for me it was difficult because I didn't start exploring alternative spiritual practices until I was in my mid fifties, and the older we get, the more set in our ways we get. This is why

I strongly feel, that it would be beneficial to start children on a path of spirituality at an early age, and by that I don't mean the accepted religious practice, where every thing is learned by rote, and is only practiced a few hours a week. Immersion in spiritual practice has to be experiential, and becomes a way of living and thinking. For me, it changed my life, and although it was difficult, it became a matter of survival. I could see that if I continued in the rut I was in, the only place to go was down into an abyss from which there is no return: *Death*.

I now perceive that we can willingly live in hell and never make a concerted effort to extricate ourselves. I believe that reason is; the familiar is a powerful magnet that holds us in sway, and we continue to justify and defend our demise. Fear of change is strong in the humans, and the older we become the the less fluid and flexible we are.

Before I was exposed to shamanic practices, I was somewhat rigid in the way I conducted my daily affairs, mostly staying within my domestication and those rules that I considered to be truths. In childhood, people close to me infected my psyche with lies that I later found out to be based on some prejudicial or ingrained ideal, and having trusted those people, I accepted them as truths. Some of those lies caused me to make wrong decisions on major issues.

I also now realize, that their aim was not to hurt me and it is mostly a matter of being irresponsible with what we say and why we say it. Some came to me in the form of idle chatter we have labeled gossip, which is nothing less than a character assassination of someone we really don't know, and usually based on envy, fear, or from someone with a malicious personality. Most of the gossip I heard as a child seemed to be a way of people passing the time and having some conversation with each other, but for someone who is impressionable, no less damaging. When I was a child, adults would say just about anything that came to their mind, [only profanity was verboten] and I don't think they realized that a child is very open and always listening to what is going on around them. As a child, I always got the impression that adults didn't realize that a child's intelligence is bestowed on them at birth, and I think they confused knowledge with intelligence, and not understanding that they needed to use responsibility in what was said when children were around.

Of all the quirky things that humans engage in, gossip is one of the most damaging, to others, as well to our selves. Being a run of the mill human, I at one time engaged in gossip, and I now realize, I had to have been a little crazy. I am probably still crazy, but I am now aware of what constitutes crazy behavior, and through being able to be more fluid and flexible, I have better control of my thoughts, choices, actions and words. I used the term "run of the mill human", because it seem to me that societies try's to crank out people that think the same, act the same, and believe in the same things, and I think we would find that *we are* actually on the same page, if we were not programmed with erroneous information throughout our up-bringing.

Analyzing, in our own minds, what we believe to be truths, is very important in weeding out ideas and concepts that we decide no longer apply for us as autonomous individuals, helping us to clean out the attic and making room for the reality that: *Now Is The Time For All Good Men To Come To The Aid Of Their Planet*.

Aid will only come from those who have climbed out of the box and the rut, to a higher place, where we can get an over-all view of what is happening on this world of ours, and setting their intent toward being stewards of the Blue Planet. This attitude is in the hands and hearts of a minority at present, and I write these words in hopes of doing my part in tilting the scales toward a majority. I try to live in the moment, with one eye on the future; because the next moment is the future.

Reference List

[1] **GALAXY FORMATION AND EVOLUTION**
From Wikipedia, the free encyclopedia
http://en.wikipedia.org/wiki/galaxy_formation_and_evolution

[2] **GALAXY**
From Wikipedia, the free encyclopedia
http://en.wikipedia.org/wiki/galaxy

[3] **BIG BANG**
From Wikipedia, the free encyclopedia
http://en.wikipedia.org/wiki/big_bang

[4] **NEBULAR HYPOTHESIS**
From Wikipedia, the free encyclopedia
http://en.wikipedia.org/wiki/nebular_hypothesis

[5] **ORIGIN OF THE SOLAR SYSTEM**
From Abyss, University of Oregon
http://abyss.uoregon.edu-js/ast121/lecture/led24.html

[6] **FORMATION AND EVOLUTION OF THE SOLAR SYSTEM**
From Wikipedia, the free encyclopedia
http://en.wikipedia.org/formation_and_evolution_of_the_solar_system

[7] **GEOLOGICAL HISTORY OF EARTH**
From Wikipedia, the free encyclopedia
http://en.wikipedia.org/wiki/geological_history_of_earth

[8] **HISTORY OF THE EARTH**
From Wikipedia, the free encyclopedia
http://en.wikipedia.org/wiki/history_of_the_earth

[9] **GEOLOGIC TIME SCALE**
From Wikipedia, the free encyclopedia
http://en.wikipedia.org/wiki/geologic_time_scale

[10] **ANCIENT MESOPOTAMIA AND MEAR EAST**
From ALL EMPIRES Online History Community
http://www.allempires.com/article/index.php?q=21st_century

[11] **HUMAN**
From Wikipedia, the free encyclopedia
http://en.wikipedia.org/wiki/human

[12] **MIDDLE AGES**
From Wikipedia, the free encyclopedia
http://en.wikipedia.org/wiki/human

[13] **MONOTHEISM**
From Wikipedia, the free encyclopedia
http://en.wikipedia.org/w/index.php?title-monotheism&
printable=yes